Aldous Huxley:
a Study of the
Major Novels

Aldous Huxley: a Study of the Major Novels

BY

PETER BOWERING

UNIVERSITY OF LONDON

THE ATHLONE PRESS

1968

Published by
THE ATHLONE PRESS
UNIVERSITY OF LONDON
at 2 Gower Street London WC1
Distributed by Constable & Co Ltd
10 *Orange Street London* WC2

Canada
Oxford University Press
Toronto

U.S.A.
Oxford University Press Inc
New York

485 11099 7

16448

Printed in Great Britain by
WESTERN PRINTING SERVICES LTD
BRISTOL

To My Mother

ACKNOWLEDGEMENTS

This book had its origin in a thesis written for the Department of English, Birkbeck College, University of London. My greatest debt is to Professor Barbara Hardy, for whose generous support and encouragement during the subsequent stages of rewriting I am deeply grateful.

I should also like to express my gratitude to my wife and to T. Heiser who read and criticized parts of the book in manuscript; and to the officers of the Athlone Press, to whom I am indebted for many valuable comments and suggestions.

Finally, my special thanks to my wife for her extended patience and help in preparing the manuscript for the publisher.

P.B.

PUBLISHERS' NOTE

CONTENTS

Introduction

Essays analysing the decline of Aldous Huxley as a novelist have become a commonplace of literary criticism over the past two decades; and it is now something of a critical cliché to suggest that at some point during his varied career Huxley 'lost interest' in the novel as a serious art form. Certainly, no one would deny that, for a variety of reasons, the literary innovator in Huxley faded out prematurely: of his nine major novels only perhaps *Antic Hay, Point Counter Point* and *Eyeless in Gaza* can lay claim to our attention as works of exceptional literary merit. These three are probably sufficient to earn him the distinction of being one of the outstanding novelists of our time; but the fact remains that Huxley was never what he called 'a congenital novelist'. He never set out to be. His particular forte was that he introduced 'third programme' ideas into the modern novel; or, as one critic put it, he equipped the novel with a brain.[1] In so doing he largely ignored the body: for the traditional features of the novel, plot and delineation of character, he showed scant regard. The critics protested in vain: Huxley remained unregenerate to the end. Even so, it is tempting to conjecture that if Huxley's popularity waned towards the close of his career, it was the uncompromising nature of his ideas rather than any absence of literary merit that was finally responsible.

The truth is that Huxley was never read for those features which his work so clearly lacked. He belonged to that small group of authors—Peacock is the outstanding example—who have always been read primarily for the wealth of their ideas. Huxley, certainly, never disguised his intentions: this is an account of the 'preliminary research' for his last novel, *Island*:

[1] Anthony Burgess, *The Novel Today* (1963), p. 15.

I

Greek history, Polynesian anthropology, translations from Sanskrit and Chinese of Buddhist texts, scientific papers on pharmacology, neuro-physiology, psychology and education, together with novels, poems, critical essays, travel books, political commentaries and conversations with all kinds of people, from philosophers to actresses, from patients in mental hospitals to tycoons in Rolls-Royces—everything went into the hopper and became grist for my Utopian mill. In a word, *je prends mon bien ou je le trouve*, I take my property where I find it. . . (Foreword to Laura Archera Huxley's *You Are Not The Target*)

It was undoubtedly Huxley's ability to turn ideas into 'grist for the mill' that made him a master of the form of fictional essay which has been called 'the novel of ideas'. Walter Allen commenting on Peacock's dramatization of the intellectual notions of his age wrote: 'For anything comparable in our time we would need to imagine a novelist intellectually powerful enough to satirise in one book the exponents of, say, Marxism, psycho-analysis, the psychology of Jung, logical positivism, neo-catholicism, Existentialism, Christian Science, abstract painting.'[1] It is a measure of Huxley's achievement that in the nineteen-twenties he came close to realizing this ideal.

However, to regard Huxley as a mere twentieth-century imitator of Peacock is to invite over-simplification. Huxley did more than hold a mirror to the ideological conflicts of his day. Almost from the beginning he saw in the novel an exploratory vehicle for moral values; and his work soon became characterized by the search for a way of life which, in his own words, would 'fit all the facts of human experience' (Introduction to J. D. Unwin's *Hopousia*). The task which Huxley set himself was superhuman by any standards and stated in bald terms perhaps a trifle pretentious; but, today, no one would doubt the sincerity of his quest. He was not, of course, an original thinker, but his mind ranged freely over a wide range of topics—he was as familiar with the latest advances in nuclear physics as with the meditation practices of Cardinal Bérulle; and as the account of his 'preliminary research' suggests there was scarcely a field of human endeavour which did not, at

[1] *The English Novel* (1958), p. 135.

one time or other, attract his interest. From the middle nineteen-twenties his work began to assume the nature of a synthesis, and by a slow and painstaking process of evolution he was to arrive at the world-view which attains its final summation in *Island*. Whether the eclecticism of *Island* will have a lasting significance, it is still too early to say; but as the moralist of a scientific age Huxley remains virtually unchallenged. The novels themselves, thinly disguised accounts of his thought, record the stages of Huxley's growth from the detached sceptic of *Crome Yellow* to the contemplative mystic of the later works. It is this development, a dialectic of ideas in which the wisdom of the saints and mystics is poised in verbal battle against Darwin, Freud and the twentieth-century materialists, that makes Huxley's work a fascinating moral document in its own right, and provides the main substance of my essay.

In a study of this kind it is perhaps inevitable that some of the more literary aspects of the writer should tend to be neglected. However, in the first chapter, under the heading 'Novel of Ideas' I have considered Huxley's choice of form, while the final chapter discusses the relationship between the moralist and the artist. In the latter I have tried to point to some of the essentially literary features which give rise to Huxley's criticism of life, in particular his skill as an ironist, a skill which, I believe, places him on a footing with that other supreme ironist of English letters, Jonathan Swift.

Further, while it is clear that Huxley had a ready facility for handling difficult concepts, one of the chief obstacles to a mature appreciation of his work still lies in the obscure nature of his ideas. This is particularly true of the later novels: after *Brave New World* all the major novels require some knowledge of Huxley's source materials if they are to be adequately understood. *Time Must Have a Stop*, for example, can be almost meaningless without a prior reading of *The Tibetan Book of the Dead*. In fact, Huxley invariably seems to have assumed a far wider knowledge of science and mysticism than could reasonably be expected of the average reader. A further cause of misunderstanding has arisen from the failure to see the individual novels as part of a larger whole. As I have suggested, Huxley's work, fiction and non-fiction, is most satisfactory when viewed as a synthesis. None of the major novels, with the possible exception of *Island*, provides a comprehensive picture of Huxley's beliefs, and a great deal of adverse criticism has resulted from the study of his novels in isolation. In fairness to his critics it must be admitted that Huxley himself was chiefly to blame. He adopted and rejected ideas with an alarming rapidity; he was constantly modifying his position and his reviewers, especially, had a hard time keeping pace with his changing attitudes. In this book I have tried to set the novels in the widest area of reference, drawing freely on Huxley's non-fictional writings and source materials wherever possible. In so doing I hope to have clarified Huxley's ideas as they are presented in the novels and, perhaps, revealed some of the many factors which have contributed to his development as one of the leading moralists of the age.

I

The Novel of Ideas

While no one today would dispute Huxley's place as a moralist, there still remains considerable doubt as to whether he is a novelist in the true sense of the word. David Daiches in *The Novel and the Modern World* states quite emphatically that 'Huxley is no novelist; he has never mastered—is not really interested in—even the elements of form and structure in fiction. . . His novels are either a series of character sketches or simple fables or tracts'.[1] In the revised edition of his book, Daiches omits the earlier chapter on Huxley with the comment that Huxley is not a novelist 'in the strict sense'.[2] It is not the purpose of this essay to challenge these remarks or to define the nature of the novel but, in view of the general misunderstanding which has obscured the critical reception of most of Huxley's major work, some vindication of his choice of form would seem necessary.

Even the most casual reader of Huxley's early novels will be aware that he is reading something fundamentally different from, say, the novels of George Eliot or Lawrence. As Daiches points out there is little interest in the elements of form and structure, the characters do not develop and the plot is minimal. What we have in their place might be described as a highly charged dialectic of ideas shaped in the form of a moral fable. To define this form Huxley borrowed the term, 'novel of ideas'. The choice was perhaps unfortunate, for the term has been widely used in a different context to describe the kind of novel usually associated with such writers as George Eliot or E. M. Forster;[3] and the use of a term

[1] Chicago (1939), p. 209.   [2] Chicago (1960), p. viii.
[3] E. K. Brown, for example, describes George Eliot as 'our greatest novelist of ideas'. See 'The Revival of E. M. Forster', *Forms of Modern Fiction* (Indiana, 1959), p. 163.

which suggests that there is anything in common between, for example, *Howards End* and *Crome Yellow* is bound in the end to lead to confusion. However, as there is no suitable alternative, I restrict myself to defining the term as Huxley has used it. The relevant passage comes from one of Philip Quarles's notebook extracts in *Point Counter Point*:

Novel of ideas. The character of each personage must be implied, as far as possible, in the ideas of which he is the mouthpiece. In so far as theories are rationalizations of sentiments, instincts, dispositions of soul, this is feasible. The chief defect of the novel of ideas is that you must write about people who have ideas to express—which excludes all but about .01 per cent of the human race. Hence the real, the congenital novelists don't write such books. (ch. xxii)

The defect is an obvious one: there are no representatives of the working class in Huxley's novels—the carter and his wife in *Antic Hay* are a notable exception—and in practice the characters are all drawn from a small, closely-knit circle of the articulate intelligentsia of the day. They are seen largely as abstractions from which everything except the predominating idea has been stripped away; they possess no psychological depth and are not permitted to develop in any way. The interest is centred on their mental attitudes, the character-idea, rather than on social behaviour, and the dramatic qualities of the conventional novel are replaced by a series of verbal clashes, by what I have called a dialectic of ideas. Here is a typical extract from Huxley's first novel, *Crome Yellow*: Mr Wimbush, the owner of Crome, is showing his guests the sights of the Home Farm:

'This is a good sow', said Henry Wimbush. 'She had a litter of fourteen.'

'Fourteen?' Mary echoed incredulously. She turned astonished blue eyes towards Mr Wimbush, then let them fall on to the seething mass of *élan vital* that fermented in the sty.

An immense sow reposed on her side in the middle of the pen. Her round, black belly, fringed with a double line of dugs, presented itself to the assault of an army of small, brownish-black swine. . .

'There are fourteen', said Mary. 'You're quite right. I counted. It's extraordinary.'

'The sow next door', Mr Wimbush went on, 'has done very badly. She only had five in her litter. I shall give her another chance. If she does no better next time, I shall fat her up and kill her. There's the boar', he pointed towards a further sty. 'Fine old beast, isn't he? But he's getting past his prime. He'll have to go too.'

'How cruel!' Anne exclaimed.

'But how practical, how eminently realistic!' said Mr Scogan. 'In this farm we have a model of sound paternal government. Make them breed, make them work, and when they're past working or breeding or begetting, slaughter them.'

'Farming seems to be mostly indecency and cruelty', said Anne.

The party then pursue their way towards the stables where they stop this time in front of the pedigree bull; the conversation is repeated with slight variations:

'Splendid animal', said Henry Wimbush. 'Pedigree stock. But he's getting a little old like the boar.'

'Fat him up and slaughter him', Mr Scogan pronounced with a delicate old-maidish precision of utterance.

'Couldn't you give the animals a little holiday from producing children?' asked Anne. 'I'm so sorry for the poor things.'

Mr Wimbush shook his head. 'Personally', he said, 'I rather like seeing fourteen pigs grow where only one grew before. The spectacle of so much crude life is refreshing.'

'I'm glad to hear you say so', Gombauld broke in warmly. 'Lots of life: that's what we want. I like pullulation; everything ought to increase and multiply as hard as it can.'

Gombauld grew lyrical. Everybody ought to have children—Anne ought to have them, Mary ought to have them—dozens and dozens. . .

Gombauld ceased talking, and Mary, flushed and outraged, opened her mouth to refute him. But she was too slow. Before she could utter a word Mr Scogan's fluty voice had pronounced the opening phrases of a discourse. . .

'Even your eloquence, my dear Gombauld,' he was saying—'even your eloquence must prove inadequate to reconvert the world to a belief in the delights of mere multiplication. With the gramophone, the cinema, and the automatic pistol, the goddess of Applied Science has presented the world with another gift, more precious even than these—the means of dissociating love from propagation. Eros, for those who wish it, is now an entirely free god; his deplorable associations with Lucina may be broken at will. In the course of the next few centuries, who knows? the world may see a more complete severance. I look forward to it optimistically. Where the great Erasmus Darwin and Miss Ann Seward, Swan of Lichfield, experimented—and, for all their scientific ardour, failed—our descendants will experiment and succeed. An impersonal generation will take the place of Nature's hideous system. In vast state incubators, rows upon rows of gravid bottles will supply the world with the population it requires. The family system will disappear; society, sapped at its very base, will have to find new foundations; and Eros, beautifully and irresponsibly free, will flit like a gay butterfly from flower to flower through a sunlit world.'

'It sounds lovely', said Anne.

'The distant future always does.'

Mary's china blue eyes, more serious and more astonished than ever, were fixed on Mr Scogan. 'Bottles?' she said. 'Do you really think so? Bottles. . .' (ch. v)

Here we see the characters formulating the ideas they are to hold throughout the novel: Mary's anger and astonishment is that of the convinced birth-controller whose ideas on sex are indebted to Havelock Ellis; Gombauld's lyricism is born of a Byronic enthusiasm for life; Anne's endorsement of an 'impersonal generation' stems from an unqualified love of pleasure which she sees threatened by the responsibilities of marriage and child-bearing; while Scogan's realism, on the other hand, reflects the rationalist and the cynic who exemplifies scientific materialism. Once their ideas are formulated each character responds automatically with a predictable set of notions to any given situation. Scogan elaborately systematizes all the meaning out of life; Mary dutifully practises free love to rid herself of Freudian repressions; Anne flirts with Gombauld, but like Eros would be 'beautifully and irresponsibly free', and so on. Our interest is held in such a novel by the variety of the situations in which verbal clashes of this kind can be sustained and by the wit, liveliness and intellectual density of the dialogue.

The 'novel of ideas' is traditionally a vehicle for satire; and this occurs when the predominating idea becomes obsessional. The result is not unlike a morality play in which ideas and discussion take the place of passions and action. A further example will perhaps make the point clear. This is taken from *Point Counter Point* where Everard Webley approaches Lord Edward for funds to support the B.B.F., his fascist organization. Everard Webley is a potential Mussolini and Lord Edward a biologist so what takes place is more of a clash of ideologies than of personalities. Webley, who sees progress entirely in terms of the overthrow of parliamentary democracy, states his case first:

Organization, discipline, force were necessary. The battle could no longer be fought constitutionally. Parliamentary methods were quite adequate when the two parties agreed about fundamentals and disagreed only about trifling details. But where fundamental principles were at stake, you couldn't allow politics to go on being treated as a Parliamentary game. You had to resort to direct action or the threat of it.

Lord Edward, however, whose predominant idea is centred on the natural life cycle, sees progress entirely in terms of the conservation of phosphorus pentoxide:

Progress! You politicians are always talking about it. As though it were going to last. Indefinitely. . . You ought to take a few lessons in my subject. Physical biology. Progress, indeed! What do you propose to do about phosphorus, for example? . . . With your intensive agriculture . . . you're simply draining the soil of phosphorus. More than half of one per cent. a year. Going clean out of circulation. And then you throw away hundreds of thousands of tons of phosphorus pentoxide in your sewage! Pouring it into the sea. And you call that progress. (ch. v)

The satire here is more pointed than in the first example. Webley's obsession with force not only gives him away but immediately weakens whatever intrinsic value his idea might hold in the reader's mind. Lord Edward's idea, far from absurd in itself, is exaggerated to the point of absurdity so that it is the abstracting quality which is held up to ridicule, the narrow focus of the scientist which excludes everything not immediately relevant to his own purpose. To the novelist who sees human folly as the product of the abstracting intellect the 'novel of ideas' is an ideal form. The great vice of the intellect is its total indifference to everything outside its own area of reference and this has produced the professional one-sidedness which is the prime object of Huxley's satire. As A. N. Whitehead once put it, 'Wisdom is the fruit of a balanced development',[1] a phrase which might well have served as a motto for Huxley's critique of modern society.

The form, like the vice, was not new. Frye traces an unbroken tradition back to the Menippean satire, in which 'pedants, bigots, cranks, parvenus, virtuosi, enthusiasts, rapacious and incompetent professional men of all kinds, are handled in terms of their occupational approach to life as distinct from their social behaviour'. 'A modern development', Frye continues, 'produces the country-house week-ends in Peacock, Huxley, and their imitators in which the opinions and ideas and cultural interests expressed are as important as the love-making.'[2] Peacock was probably the first English novelist to write almost exclusively for and about intellectuals; later examples of the tradition include Mallock's *The New Republic* (1877), Lowes Dickenson's *A Modern Symposium* (1905), and to a lesser degree Douglas's *South Wind* (1917). The structural requirements of this kind of novel are relatively simple: in Peacock the country houses, which give the novels their titles, provide centres for endless discussion, innumerable digressions and the love-making which leads to a conventional marriage ending. The arrival and departure of the guests furnishes a frame for the house-party activities and a suitable point for breaking off when the author's store of ideas is exhausted. The house parties at Crome in *Crome Yellow* and the Cybo Malaspina of *Those Barren Leaves* follow closely in the Peacockian tradition, although marriage, of course, is no longer the conventional ending. In Huxley's

---

[1] *Science and the Modern World* (Cambridge, 1932), p. 246.
[2] Northrop Frye, *The Anatomy of Criticism* (Princeton, 1957), pp. 310–11.

other novels, what Hoffman calls 'favourite points of structural focus', such as the café, club or reception hall, serve as suitable centres 'where circumstances are favourable to a varied expression of intellectual diversity. . . To supplement them, there are the notebooks (as in *Point Counter Point*), correspondence (which serves as a substitute for conversation and varies the narrative procedure), the casual or accidental meeting of two or three persons, who continue their discussions in one form or another, and the prolonged exposition, in essay form, of any given or chance suggestion which the narrative may allow.'[1] The digressions, which are a characteristic feature of this genre, were originally introduced as interludes, breaks in the discussion, ostensibly to entertain the guests. Their main function was to provide a little light relief for the reader, and Peacock's novels abound with poems, songs, ballads and other entertainments shaped to this end. Other notable digressions in Peacock include Dr Cranium's lecture in *Headlong Hall* and the Aristophanic comedy in *Gryll Grange*. Mallock strikes a more serious note with Dr Jenkinson's Sunday sermons in *The New Republic*; and in Douglas's *South Wind* the extracts from Perelli's 'Antiquities of Nepenthe' offer a rich source of anti-clerical sentiment. Huxley uses all these devices, at the same time introducing a few of his own. His heroes are frequently poets and the verses of Denis Stone, Chelifer and Sebastian Barnack enliven the pages of three of the novels; Mr Bodiham preaches sermons in *Crome Yellow*, and there is 'a play within the play' in *Antic Hay*. The re-creation of fragments of eighteenth-century life, the chapters of Henry Wimbush's 'History of Crome' and the Hauberk Papers owe their conception to Perelli's 'Antiquities', while the excursion into the *bardo* world of *Time Must Have a Stop* and the mescalin vision of *Island* must count among Huxley's more original variations on this kind of interlude. To describe these insertions as digressions is perhaps misleading. In Peacock the songs and verses are essentially entertainments, but in Huxley the more striking interludes, although

[1] Frederick J. Hoffman, 'Aldous Huxley and the Novel of Ideas', *Forms of Modern Fiction*, p. 194.

digressive in so far as they put a temporary halt to the discussion, are invariably integral to the theme. Thus Henry Wimbush's historical researches are utopian sketches contrasting with the present-day futility of life at Crome; the fifth Earl of Gonister's experiments in rejuvenation an ironic counterpoint to Dr Obispo's pursuit of longevity, and so on. This gives Huxley's novels a thematic unity frequently lacking in the earlier novels of this type.

Huxley's method of characterization is likewise indebted to Peacock. The method varies from novel to novel: some characters are merely mouthpieces for ideas, others tend to embody the idea extending it to their behaviour and environment; some have a life of their own, others are mere caricature; but it is a difference of degree rather than of kind. The essential technique of reducing an obsessional idea to absurdity remains the same. Paul de Vries, for example, in *Time Must Have a Stop*, has what appears to be a perfectly sound scheme—it was, in fact, one of Huxley's own and the sketch contains a good deal of self-parody. He wishes to establish an international clearing house for ideas, where the work of varying specialists could be sifted and brought together in a general synthesis. His role was to be that of liaison officer and interpreter, 'the bridge-building engineer'. The reader is first put on guard by de Vries' excessive humility:

That was the full extent of his ambition: to be a humble bridge-builder, a *pontifex*. Not *maximus*, he added with another of his bright deliberate smiles. *Pontifex minimus*.

A little later he is talking of bridging the gap between the phenomena of spiritualism and the phenomena of psychology and physics; his exuberance introduces the expected note of absurdity:

For a synthesis there undoubtedly must be, a thought-bridge that would permit the mind to march discursively and logically from telepathy to the four-dimensional continuum, from poltergeists and departed spirits to the physiology of the nervous system. And beyond the happenings of the séance room there were the events of the oratory and the meditation hall. There was the ultimate all-embracing field—the

Brahma of Sankara, the One of Plotinus, the Ground of Eckhart and Boehme, the. . . (ch. viii)

As Walter Allen[1] says of Peacock, the comedy lies in taking the exaggeration beyond the point where we would normally expect it to stop. The young man's ego is finally deflated by Eustace's quip about 'the Young Man of Cape Cod, who applied the Quantum Theory to God'.

Peacock was fond of using environment as an extension of character: the owl-haunted towers of *Nightmare Abbey* provide the perfect setting for the melancholy broodings of Scythrop. Huxley, too, delights in similar amalgams of character and environment: it is not easy to dissociate Mercaptan from his *dix-huitième* parlour with the Crébillon sofa, or Mrs Aldwinkle from the decaying grandeurs of the Cybo Malaspina. They have no separate life outside their environment. Huxley's work is rich in devices of this kind, and perhaps no author has so lavishly employed the furnishings of the museum and the art gallery to reflect nuances of character and to provide an ironic commentary on the absurdities of human behaviour. No bedroom scene, in Huxley, is complete without its appropriate artistic accompaniment: there is the 'St Jerome' in Rosie's pink boudoir in *Antic Hay*; Mary Amberley's Pascin in *Eyeless in Gaza*, and the apotheosis of the Cardinal Malaspina in Irene's bed-chamber in *Those Barren Leaves*, to mention a few. Of the more bizarre effects Huxley achieves with this technique perhaps the most striking comes from *After Many a Summer* where the enraged Stoyte, momentarily imprisoned in the elevator, confronts the imaginary Vermeer. For a brief moment the real and the ideal meet in pointless confrontation—the world of Stoyte's apoplectic rage and the Dutchman's dream of consummated perfection. For half a page Huxley lingers over the mathematical harmonies of a perfected universe (while the elevator rises to the top floor) until Stoyte, bursting into a string of expletives, finally breaks free to pursue his murderous task.

It has been argued with a varying degree of validity that Huxley's novels are not strictly 'novels of ideas'. The argument usually

---

[1] *The English Novel*, p. 134.

states that beginning with *Eyeless in Gaza*, the essayist in Huxley takes precedence over the novelist, the narrative becomes 'a setting for the *exposition* rather than the *dramatization* of ideas', and consequently the novels degenerate into 'lengthy essays to which are added entertainments.'[1] There is undoubtedly some truth in this. Even a superficial comparison of, say, *Antic Hay* with *After Many a Summer* will reveal that the balance of dialectic has been disturbed: Mr Propter's monologues occupy a disproportionate length of the latter novel. However, it is a difference of degree rather than kind: *After Many a Summer* is cast in essentially the same mould as the earlier novels; an identical structural pattern can be discerned with Jo Stoyte's Hollywood-style fortress as the New World equivalent to Crome or the Cybo Malaspina, and Jeremy Pordage as the guest elect. However, many of Huxley's novels are more than mere 'novels of ideas' using the term in its narrowest sense. In *Point Counter Point* and *Eyeless in Gaza* Huxley certainly goes far beyond the scope of the original Peacockian formula, and both these novels would allow the formal critic of Huxley's work to quarrel with Daiches' assertion that Huxley was not interested in 'the elements of form and structure in fiction'. The method of characterization in these novels remains basically the same, but a discussion of their formal characteristics would not be out of place in any study of the modern novel; they are both novels which reveal a high degree of structural innovation. *Point Counter Point* with its counterpointed narratives might be described as a multiple 'novel of ideas'; while *Eyeless in Gaza* hardly belongs to the original genre at all. The conversion theme of this novel demanded a more complex analysis of character and a narrative which stretched over four decades, neither of which could be accommodated within the basically static structure of the 'novel of ideas'. The result was Huxley's most ambitious experiment in form; it contains some of his most highly developed characters, and, in spite of the copious notebook extracts, it can hardly be dismissed as a lengthy essay with added entertainments.

[1] Hoffman, op. cit., p. 199.

14

The utopian novels, *Brave New World* and *Island*, deserve special mention as they both carry a heavy burden of exposition. This, in itself, does not necessarily point to failure: the 'novel of ideas' by its very nature allows for a large measure of expository material. Perhaps the only criterion we can apply is that the exposition should be lively and that it should be tempered by a measure of dialectical opposition. *Brave New World*, which originated as a parody of the Wellsian utopias, is largely satirical and the expository material never loses its incisive quality. *Island*, on the other hand, as the portrait of an ideal society, offers little scope to the satirist—here the community itself is the norm and only such a peripheral character as the Rani of Pala, a Madame Blavatsky figure, allows for true Peacockian caricature. Further, the savage in *Brave New World* supplies a dialectical opposition which Will Farnaby totally fails to provide in *Island*. As a result the ideas lack the dramatic qualities they possess in the earlier novels. This is not to say that *Island* is completely without merit as a 'novel of ideas'; it is redeemed to a large extent by its sheer intellectual density and the wealth of ideas which it has to offer, but it is the one major novel to which the criticism of 'a lengthy essay with added entertainments' might fairly be applied. In conclusion, it must be said that it is not the least of Huxley's achievements that he has revived an outmoded form, to which only one major English novelist had previously aspired, and blessed it with the touch of his genius. Under Huxley, the 'novel of ideas' has approached the status of a major art form.

If the Huxley of the nineteen-twenties inherited a literary form, what of the ideas themselves? Peacock's chosen targets included perfectibilians, deteriorationists, status-quo-ites, phrenologists and transcendentalists. The names have disappeared; ideas change, and most of the intellectual fads that worried Peacock and his contemporaries are meaningless today: the phrenologist has given way to the psycho-analyst, the transcendentalist to the existentialist, and so on. However, it would still be true to say that the basic moral problem, for Huxley as for Peacock, has remained unchanged. Dr Opimian's prophetic utterance,

Science is one thing, and wisdom is another. Science is an edged tool, with which men play like children. . . If you look at the results which science has brought in its train, you will find them to consist almost wholly in elements of mischief. . . I almost think it is the ultimate destiny of science to exterminate the human race. (*Gryll Grange*, ch. xix),

must have had a particular significance for the author of *Ape and Essence*. In the early nineteenth century the word 'progress' was rapidly becoming a synonym for scientific advancement, and the problem of 'scientific and moral perfectibility' appears as the theme of Peacock's first novel. Dr Cranium's scientific determinism, which postulated that 'every man's actions are determined by his peculiar views, and those views are determined by the organisation of his skull' (*Headlong Hall*, ch. v), may have anticipated the theories of the behaviourists as David Garnett suggests,[1] but in 1815, Peacock could afford to treat the whole matter with the contempt it undoubtedly deserved. In Dr Cranium's description of his fall and rescue, however, there is the first suggestion of the scientific modulations of *Point Counter Point*,[2] the non-human as opposed to the human account of an event:

The whole process of the action was mechanical and necessary. The application of the poker necessitated the ignition of the powder: the ignition necessitated the explosion; the explosion necessitated my sudden fright, which necessitated my sudden jump, which from a necessity equally powerful, was in a curvilinear ascent; the descent, being in a corresponding curve, and commencing at a point perpendicular to the extreme line of the edge of the tower, I was, by the necessity of gravitation, attracted, first, through the ivy, and secondly through the hazel, and thirdly through the ash, into the water beneath. The motive or impulse thus adhibited in the person of a drowning man, was as powerful on his material compages as the force of gravitation on mine; and he could no more help jumping into the water than I could help falling into it. (*Headlong Hall*, ch. xiv)

[1] *The Novels of Thomas Love Peacock* (1948), p. 85n.
[2] Bernard Blackstone compares Huxley's technique with that of Erasmus Darwin. See *The Consecrated Urn* (1959), pp. 25-6.

Compare this with Huxley's account of Lord Edward listening to Bach:

Pongileoni's blowing and the scraping of the anonymous fiddlers had shaken the air in the great hall, had set the glass of the windows looking on to it vibrating; and this in turn had shaken the air in Lord Edward's apartment on the further side. The shaking air rattled Lord Edward's *membrana tympani*; the interlocked *malleus*, *incus* and stirrup bones were set in motion so as to agitate the membrane of the oval window and raise an infinitesimal storm in the fluid of the labyrinth. The hairy endings of the auditory nerve shuddered like weeds in a rough sea; a vast number of obscure miracles were performed in the brain, and Lord Edward ecstatically whispered "Bach!" (ch. iii)

In each case the causal pattern is traced in specific scientific terms, so as to exclude the possibility of human participation, each event being described as if it were the workings of a complex and intricate mechanism. Neither passage was, of course, intended to be more than parody but the wider implications of scientific determinism and their bearing on the moral problem were the immediate concern of both authors. In *Melincourt*, Peacock expressed the scientist's avowed disinterest in moral affairs in stronger terms. Mr Fax, whose character was based on Malthus, is described as one who

looks on the human world, the world of mind, the conflict of interests, the collision of feelings, the infinitely diversified developments of energy and intelligence, as a mathematician looks on his diagrams, or a mechanist on his wheels and pulleys, as if they were foreign to his own nature, and were nothing more than subjects of curious speculation. (ch. vii)

The scientific attitude was rapidly becoming accepted and when Mallock wrote *The New Republic*, six decades later, the *Origin of Species* was already seventeen years old; it seemed then as if the triumph of 'scientific perfectibility' was virtually complete. To the Victorian of the eighteen-seventies, the aim of life was progress, and 'progress is such improvements as can be verified by statistics'; as for morality, 'science, as science, does not deal with moral right and wrong . . . it has shown that right and wrong are terms of a bygone age, connoting altogether false ideas. Mere automata as science shows we are—clockwork machines, wound up by meat and drink' (ch. iii). To Mallock the mechanist nightmare was a reality and *The New Republic* with its utopian pretensions (the symposium was a traditional medium for the conception of ideal societies) was a vain attempt to restore the values of the past. At the turn of the century the scientist in Lowes Dickinson's *A Modern Symposium* speaks with the assured confidence of one who knows that the future is his:

. . . we, by means of science, have established progress. We look to a future, a future assured, and a future in this world. . . We believe neither in a good God directing the course of events; nor in a blind power that controls them independently and in spite of human will. . . We know that we have will; that will may be directed by reason; and that the end to which reason points is the progress of the race. . . And it is the acceptance of just this that cuts us off from the past, that makes its literature, its ethics, its politics, meaningless and unintelligible to us, that makes us, in a word, what we are, the first of the new generation.

By 1917 the reaction had set in. Douglas's *South Wind* sounds its own sad note of pessimism: 'What is the outstanding feature of modern life? The bankruptcy, the proven fatuity, of everything that is bound up under the name of Western civilisation' (ch. vii). It is no coincidence that the conflict between 'scientific and moral perfectibility' and a mounting sense of disillusionment should have overshadowed the writings of at least a few of the sensitive minds of the last hundred and fifty years. To the moralist concerned with ideas, the growth of the scientific, non-human attitude to the facts of human experience was always a potential threat to value. In the middle decades of the nineteenth century the conflict between science and religion reached a climax; by the nineteen-twenties a mood of dissatisfaction and futility seemed the only answer to a view of life which had apparently stripped away the last vestiges of moral value.

II

The Moral Dilemma

In one of his rare moments of self-revelation Huxley confessed, 'For myself, as, no doubt, for most of my contemporaries, the philosophy of meaninglessness was essentially an instrument of liberation' (*Ends and Means*, ch. xiv). There is no doubt that Huxley made his reputation as the philosopher of meaninglessness. The scintillating novels of the twenties with their surface levity and underlying pessimism 'epitomised the disillusions, desperate gaiety and moral confusion'[1] of the age; the critical epithets which greeted his work were invariably 'cynical' and 'irresponsible'. In retrospect it is clear that he was neither; he was always a moralist even when appearing the very opposite. The novels themselves were above all satires on 'modernism' and, while highlighting the sex and pleasure merry-go-round of the fashionable set, Huxley, like his own hero Calamy, was already seeking an alternative. As A. C. Ward pointed out, behind his cynicism, there was always a hint of resolution: '. . . his disgust and despair are not vented against human life as such, but only against the distortion of life he observes around him. . . Aldous Huxley can be claimed as a non-decadent and moral writer because there is always in the background to his books the implication that a more desirable way of life exists and must be found.'[2]

The search for 'a more desirable way of life', what Huxley has called a philosophy based on 'all the facts of human experience', is the underlying motif of all the major novels. The very meaninglessness of the life he saw about him was in itself a challenge; and it is not without significance that *Eyeless in Gaza*, Huxley's single complete expression of the conversion theme, his first novel to

[1] Geoffrey Bullough, 'Aspects of Aldous Huxley', *English Studies* (1949), p. 233.
[2] *The Nineteen-Twenties* (1930), pp. 118–19.

restore the meaning, stands central to his work as a whole. Everything he wrote earlier is in a sense preparatory, everything subsequent a tailing off, except for the final utopian vision of *Island*.
After *Crome Yellow* the theme of moral regeneration, leading to
Anthony Beavis's conversion, is latent in all the novels of the
nineteen-twenties: Gumbril's search for a better way of life is
premature and without a centre of reference but it augured well
for the future; Calamy is the first of Huxley's heroes to exchange
the society of the drawing room for the ardours of the contemplative life, and, although Calamy's efforts smacked a little of the
dilettante, it was hard to believe that another decade would pass
before they were finally brought to fulfilment; Philip Quarles
scarcely gets beyond the questioning stage, but the sincerity of his
introspection left little doubt that it was now only a matter of
time. What was lacking in these early novels were the redemptive
characters, the men of good will who were to point the way.
There were, of course, the false prophets, Scogan and Cardan,
those two eloquent exponents of the art of fine living whose lives
were exemplars of wrong behaviour; and Coleman who for a
time converted Gumbril to the apostasy of Rabelaisian complete
manhood; but these could scarcely be considered prototypes of
the kind of figure to follow. Rampion, the Laurentian portrait
of *Point Counter Point*, provided the first imitable model, but
Rampion, while indicating the necessity for change, proved to be
merely a passing phase. The first of the real prophets emerged in
Eyeless in Gaza; his name was Dr Miller, and under his guidance
Anthony Beavis became the first novitiate on the path to salvation. After *Eyeless in Gaza*, the exemplary characters, the 'virtuous, adultly non-attached personages', hold the centre of the
Huxleyan stage. Huxley had complained that there was a singu-
lar lack of non-attached human beings in literature: 'Literary
example is a powerful instrument for the moulding of character.
But most of our literary examples . . . are mere idealisations of the
average sensual man' (*Ends and Means*, ch. xii). Propter and Bruno
Rontini, the mystics of *After Many a Summer* and *Time Must Have
a Stop*, were to redress the balance. Meanwhile the Huxleyan hero

suffers a temporary eclipse: Jeremy Pordage, another morality figure like Scogan and Cardan, is too set in his ill-adjusted life of the senses to respond to the urgings of Propter; Sebastian Barnack achieves a state of responsibility, but only after Rontini's death in the last pages of the novel. It is not until *Island* that another Anthony Beavis appears in the figure of the world-weary journalist Will Farnaby, and the conversion theme comes to a final flowering in Huxley's last novel.

The search for salvation is, of necessity, a lonely affair: Calamy, we recall, felt the need to retire to the mountains, where he could meditate undisturbed; but as Huxley soon realized solitariness could never be a final solution. The search for a more desirable way of life, if it is not to be wholly monastic, is ultimately a quest for a new utopia. Even so, the rejection of the corrupt society was always the first step to personal regeneration. This note of rejection is sounded in almost all the major novels: one after another, the Huxleyan heroes turn away in disgust when faced with the problems of the sick society; and it is not until *Eyeless in Gaza* that a regenerated Anthony Beavis is able to return and play a positive role in the political turmoil of the day. At the same time Huxley's social aspirations were beginning to find an outlet in utopian fantasies. The meaninglessness, as in every other phase of Huxley's development, tends to emerge first: Scogan's blueprint for the Rational State, a travesty of Plato's *Republic*, later crystallizes into *Brave New World*. Here, in a society of mechanized slaves, personal salvation has been all but eradicated. *Ape and Essence* offers little more than a corollary to the earlier fantasy: the reverse side of the coin, where the more-than-human ideal of science and progress has given way to a less-than-human retrogression in the wake of thermonuclear war. The positive aspects of the utopian motif are depicted in a series of isolated communities in which the human spirit is free to seek liberation: there is Sir Hercules' eighteenth-century experiment in harmonious living in *Crome Yellow*; Wren's London of *Antic Hay* where a man could feel he belonged to the same race as Michelangelo; Propter's co-operative of transients set in the California of *After Many a Summer*; and finally, the answer to the critics of *Brave New World*,[1] the island paradise of Pala, where a philosophy based on all the facts of human experience is an integral part of everyday living, where the *Weltanschauung* is both the personal and social instrument of liberation.

The search for a more desirable way of life is clearly the most important single theme in Huxley's novels. What distinguishes Huxley's work from that of other moralists is the treatment of this theme within the framework of the 'novel of ideas'. The idea of conversion, for example, is central to both *Eyeless in Gaza* and Tolstoy's *Resurrection* but it is clear that apart from their parallel themes the two works have little in common. It is not just that Huxley's form and characterization owe nothing to the nineteenth-century novel, the whole moral climate has changed. In the eighteen-nineties, Tolstoy could appeal to what was still a traditional morality: to Nekhlyudov, at grips with the problems of a stricken conscience and the Tsarist penal code, Christianity was still a powerful moral force. For Anthony Beavis, no such traditional morality existed: science had made Christian dogmas intellectually unacceptable, and if the findings of science were true not even the basis of a humanistic morality remained. The challenge to moral values, then, as it appeared to Huxley in the nineteen-twenties, was substantially an ideological one, a matter of dialectic in which the appeal is to the intellect rather than the emotions. For this reason any examination of Huxley's development as a moralist must be, to a great extent, an examination of ideas: firstly of those which led up to the moral crisis; and later of those which under the pressure of meaninglessness motivated the desire to seek a new and better way of life.

The ideological breakdown expressed in its simplest terms lay in the antithesis between 'scientific and moral perfectibility'. The gulf that divided the values of scientific materialism on the one hand and those of the traditional custodians of morality on the

[1] In the foreword to the later editions of *Brave New World*, Huxley refers to the 'eminent academic critics' who said that he was 'a sad symptom of the failure of an intellectual class in time of crisis'.

other appeared by the early nineteen-twenties to be virtually un-assailable. It seemed as though the two strongest forces which influence mankind—'the force of our religious intuitions and the force of our impulse to accurate observation'—had come into such a position of frank disagreement that there could be no escape except by abandoning the clear teaching of either one or the other.[1] The moral dilemma, arising from the opposition of man's deepest instincts and his desire for a rational assessment of the world around him, appears on the opening page of *Antic Hay*:

God as a sense of warmth about the heart, God as exultation, God as tears in the eyes, God as a rush of power or thought—that was all right. But God as truth, God as 2 + 2 = 4—that wasn't so clearly all right. Was there any chance of their neing the same? Were there bridges to join the two worlds?

The scientist, seemingly satisfied with his own particular set of abstractions, could offer no answer, and to Huxley, as for many of his contemporaries, disillusionment gave way to the 'philosophy of meaninglessness', which appeared then the only rational answer to an apparently insoluble problem. The disillusionment with the laboratory is now part of the history of the twentieth century: scientific materialism had all but destroyed the founda-tions of religious thought, yet it had failed to put a constructive world view in its place. Russell, at the turn of the century, talks of the world which science presents as purposeless and devoid of meaning: man and all his works are but the product of a blind creation, 'the outcome of an accidental collocation of atoms', his universe but a freak of chance destined to a final end 'in the vast death of the solar system'.[2] This view, although perhaps extreme, was not exceptional for the time; by the end of the war, the full significance of the scientific discoveries of the previous half cen-tury were becoming evident. The 'delicious intoxication induced by the early successes of science' was over; what remained was the 'rather grisly morning after' (*Ends and Means*, ch. xiv).

[1] A. N. Whitehead, *Science and the Modern World*, p. 224.
[2] 'A Free Man's Worship', *Mysticism and Logic* (1917).

The situation was relatively new. As Huxley reminds us in *Point Counter Point*, the last two decades of the nineteenth century marked a high point in the belief in the ameliorative powers of science. The allegorical marble group of Science and Virtue subduing the Passions, which writhed with classical decorum in a niche on the stairs of Philip Quarles's club, embodied the hopes and aspirations of more than one eminent Victorian, and not the least distinguished among them, Huxley's own paternal grandfather, the most outspoken of all the advocates of scientific progress. To T. H. Huxley, science and religion were natural enemies; one produced progress and enlightenment, the other darkness and confusion—human progress was directly proportional to the victory of one over the other.[1] However it was during T. H. Huxley's lifetime that the first doubts as to the ultimate nature of this victory of progress and enlightenment were raised. The mechanistic view of the universe which had prevailed since Descartes and Newton was gradually being extended from the realm of non-living matter to man himself. Under the seventeenth-century world view, Cartesian dualism had allotted man and the higher animals a privileged position as self-determining organisms in an otherwise deterministic scheme of things; under the impact of Darwinism, man's privileged position was rapidly being undermined. It now appeared as a formidable challenge 'that man himself was biologically only a part of the system of creation and that his special place in nature on which his religion, his ethics and much in the creative arts had depended was a mere illusion'.[2] In his paper, 'On the Physical Basis of Life' (1869), T. H. Huxley asserted that the progress of science had always meant an extension of the province of what we call matter and causation, and the concomitant gradual banishment from all regions of human thought of what we call spirit and spontaneity. He concluded:

The consciousness of this great truth weighs like a nightmare, I believe, upon many of the best minds of these days. They watch what they conceive to be the progress of materialism, in such fear and powerless anger

[1] See William Irvine, *Apes, Angels and Victorians* (New York, 1959), p. 339.
[2] B. Ifor Evans, *Literature and Science* (1954), p. 73.

as a savage feels, when, during an eclipse, the great shadow creeps over the face of the sun. The advancing tide of matter threatens to drown their souls; the tightening grasp of law impedes their freedom; they are alarmed lest man's moral nature be debased by the increase of his wisdom.

The relevance of this passage to the work of Aldous Huxley scarcely needs comment; the debasement of man's moral nature by the increase of his knowledge (wisdom is hardly the correct term) is the key to the moral dilemma. It is said that T. H. Huxley never felt the sting of the problem; but the sins of the grandfather were in due course visited on the grandson. The extension of matter and causation and the subsequent banishment of the spirit play their part in the grotesque and nightmarish atmosphere which pervades the novels of the late twenties. There is, in these novels, what C. E. M. Joad described as 'a deliberate and constant purpose to represent the body as the determiner of the spirit'.[1] In *Point Counter Point* the repeated emphasis on determinism by the bodily functions almost completely overwhelms the moral basis of the work; and here is Cardan, the nineteenth-century materialist of *Those Barren Leaves*, meditating on the nature of encroaching age and death:

. . . the greatest tragedy of the spirit is that sooner or later it succumbs to the flesh. Sooner or later every soul is stifled by the sick body; sooner or later there are no more thoughts, but only pain and vomiting and stupor. The tragedies of the spirit are mere struttings and posturings on the margin of life, and the spirit itself is only an accidental exuberance, the products of spare vital energy, like the feathers on the head of a hoopoo or the innumerable populations of useless and foredoomed spermatozoa. The spirit has no significance; there is only the body. When it is young, the body is beautiful and strong. It grows old, its joints creak, it becomes dry and smelly; it breaks down, the life goes out of it and it rots away. However lovely the feathers on a bird's head, they perish with it; and the spirit, which is a lovelier ornament than any, perishes too. The farce is hideous. . . (Pt. iv, ch. ix)

As D. H. Lawrence once said, 'Our "understanding", our science

---

[1] *Guide to Modern Thought* (1958), p. 266.

and idealism have produced in people the same strange frenzy of self-repulsion as if they saw their own skulls each time they looked in the mirror. A man is a thing of scientific cause-and-effect and biological process, draped in an ideal, is he? No wonder he sees the skeleton grinning through the flesh.'[1]

Everywhere in Huxley we find science as the destroyer of value: Darwin, Freud, Pavlov, conspire in turn to present a world-view in which man is deprived of his birth-right as a free-thinking, free-acting individual. *Brave New World*, the society trained and educated on strict behaviourist principles, represents the climax of Huxley's nightmare-vision, the realization of that great truth which according to T. H. Huxley weighed upon the best minds of his day. Only the changes brought about by the discoveries of the nuclear physicists promised, for a brief time, to break the strangle-hold of scientific materialism. The mechanistic interpretation of the physical universe which had been current since the days of Galileo and Newton suddenly and unexpectedly collapsed at the beginning of the twentieth century. Einstein's theory of relativity destroyed the materialistic concept of matter. Physics after the advent of the quantum theory was, in Eddington's words, 'no longer pledged to a scheme of deterministic law'.[2] These arguments had a definite appeal to Huxley in the middle twenties, and there is always a sense of relief in the manner in which his charac-ters voice their approval of the Einsteinian revolution, as, for example, Paul de Vries in *Time Must Have a Stop*:

And what a revolution, he went on with mounting enthusiasm. In-comparably more important than anything that had happened in Russia or Italy. For this was the revolution that had changed the whole course of scientific thinking, brought back idealism, integrated mind into the fabric of Nature, put an end for ever to the Victorians' night-mare universe of infinitesimal billiard balls. (ch. viii)

For a time it seemed as though a reconciliation between science and traditional morality might be possible: scientific modernism was turning 'the staunchest mathematical physicists into mystics'

[1] *Fantasia of the Unconscious* (New York, 1960), p. 149.
[2] *The Nature of the Physical World* (Cambridge, 1929), p. 294.

(*Those Barren Leaves*, Pt. I, ch. iii); and in his premature approach to the perennial philosophy, Calamy, following the new thought, meditates on the absence of space and time inside the atom. The mood could hardly last and a little later Huxley reconsiders the same problem in a somewhat different light; he concludes pessimistically, 'We have learnt that nothing is simple and rational except what we ourselves have invented; that God thinks neither in terms of Euclid nor of Riemann; that science has "explained" nothing' (*Along the Road*, Pt. II).

That science had 'explained' nothing; this was the answer to the new idealistic philosophy of modern physics. The final disillusionment was not with the discoveries of science but with the scientific method itself. Ironically, at the very time when science was breaking its materialistic bonds, its basic premises became the object of doubt. The early pioneers of scientific discovery had failed to see the limits of a methodological procedure exclusively concerned with the abstract. Unwittingly, they had fostered an outlook in which the abstraction was taken for the reality; and the modern world inheriting this view had largely mistaken the physical world for the world as described by the physicists. In *Ends and Means*, Huxley sums up the part that science had played in the formulation of the 'philosophy of meaninglessness':

From the world we actually live in, the world that is given by our senses, our intuitions of beauty and goodness, our emotions and impulses, our moods and sentiments, the man of science abstracts a simplified private universe of things possessing only those qualities which used to be called 'primary'. Arbitrarily, because it happens to be convenient, because his methods do not allow him to deal with the immense complexity of reality, he selects from the whole of experience only those elements which can be weighed, measured, numbered, or which lend themselves in any other way to mathematical treatment. By using this technique of simplification and abstraction, the scientist has succeeded to an astonishing degree in understanding and dominating the physical environment. The success was intoxicating and, with an illogicality which, in the circumstances, was doubtless pardonable, many scientists and philosophers came to imagine that this useful abstraction from reality was reality itself. . . Our conviction that the world is meaningless is due . . . in part to a genuine intellectual error—the error of identifying the world of science, a world from which all meaning and value has been deliberately excluded, with ultimate reality. (ch. xiv)

So both the method and to a large extent the findings of science were rendered invalid; it marked the end of a conflict which had extended over two decades. The problem of the nature of ultimate reality remained, the reality in which were contained 'intuitions of value and significance . . . love, beauty, mystical ecstasy, intimations of godhead'. Once the breach had been made the way was clear for the perennial philosophy: mysticism was to prove 'the instrument of liberation'. The Victorian nightmare, the encroachment of matter over spirit, of the body over the mind, had proved in the end to be groundless; man was not wholly the creature that heredity and environment had made him, the product of his genes and glands. The 'divine Ground' constituted a third factor, immanent in all mankind, the true self and the principle of ultimate reality. It is a fitting final comment on the degree of Huxley's emancipation that in the island utopia of Pala the works and philosophies of science, except in their most practical and beneficial form, experimental agriculture and medicine, are totally banished, for the same reason that Plato excluded the poet from his republic—they were an impediment to human progress.

Why did Huxley seek a solution that, in the context of the middle thirties, was both unpopular and unorthodox? There is no simple answer. What is clear, however, is that the antithesis between 'scientific and moral perfectibility' recurs as a constant theme throughout the major novels, and that 'moral perfectibility' is almost always allied with spiritual values (except for the brief period when Huxley came under the influence of D. H. Lawrence).[1] The breakdown of the nineteenth-century concept of

[1] C. G. Jung, writing of the revolt against intellectualism, says that the movement at first 'committed the pardonable mistake of confusing intellect with spirit, and blaming the latter for the misdeeds of the former'. Commentary to *The Secret of the Golden Flower* (1962), pp. 84–5. Huxley 'committed the pardonable mistake' in *Point Counter Point*.

the mechanist universe opened up the way for a new metaphysic; while the realization that science was capable only of comprehending those aspects of reality that were amenable to mathematical treatment presented the whole question of religious experience in a different light. In this sense, Huxley's 'conversion' seems an inevitable reaction against the unbearable dominance of scientific intellectualism for which there was no longer any rational justification. In *Ends and Means* Huxley describes how the 'philosophy of meaninglessness' itself engendered the desire for a more harmonious way of life. The impossibility of living in a world which denied meaning raised the question whether truth and goodness could not somehow be correlated into the nature of things. Following on this, the approach to the perennial philosophy as a source of moral and spiritual value was essentially an empirical one: the fact that 'so many philosophers and mystics, belonging to so many different cultures, should have been convinced, by inference or by direct intuition, that the world possesses meaning and value' was sufficiently striking in itself to demand investigation. Huxley concludes that:

The ethical doctrines taught in the Tao Te Ching, by Gautama Buddha and his followers on the Lesser and above all the Greater Vehicle, in the Sermon on the Mount and by the best of the Christian saints, are not dissimilar. Among human beings who have reached a certain level of civilisation and of personal freedom from passion and social prejudice there exists a real *consensus gentium* in regard to ethical first principles. (ch. xix)

This was the first positive step towards an empirical theology, Huxley's highest common factor of all religions. There are, throughout Huxley's work, many formulations of what he has called 'the minimum working hypothesis'; here are the four fundamental doctrines of the perennial philosophy expressed in their simplest form:

First: the phenomenal world of matter and of individualized consciousness—the world of things and animals and men and even gods—is the manifestation of a Divine Ground within which all partial realities have their being, and apart from which they would be non-existent.

Second: human beings are capable not merely of knowing *about* the Divine Ground by inference; they can also realize its existence by a direct intuition, superior to discursive reasoning. This immediate knowledge unites the knower with that which is known.

Third: man possesses a double nature, a phenomenal ego and an eternal Self, which is the inner man, the spirit, the spark of divinity within the soul. It is possible for a man, if he so desires, to identify himself with the spirit and therefore with the Divine Ground, which is of the same or like nature with the spirit.

Fourth: man's life on earth has only one end and purpose: to identify himself with his eternal Self and so to come to unitive knowledge of the Divine Ground. (Introduction to the *Bhagavad-Gita*, New York, 1961.)

In Hinduism the divine Ground is the Brahman; in Mahayana Buddhism it is called Mind or the Pure Light of the Void; in Christianity, Eckhart and Ruysbroeck postulated an Abyss of God-head underlying the Trinity; and in the Mohammedan tradition, the authors of the Sufi Texts conceived of *al haqq*, the Real, as being the divine Ground or Unity of Allah, underlying the personal aspects of the Godhead. In regard to man's final end, Huxley suggests that all the higher religions are in complete agreement: 'The purpose of human life is the discovery of Truth, the unitive knowledge of the Godhead. . . . In India, in China, in ancient Greece, in Christian Europe, this was regarded as the most obvious and axiomatic piece of orthodoxy'. The advent of scientific progress had introduced a new factor: attention and allegiance came to be paid, not to eternity, but to a utopian future on earth. This, according to Huxley, constitutes the great heresy of our time.

The perennial philosophy in its minimal and basic form was intended to provide a series of beliefs for those who were not congenitally members of an organized church and to whom humanism was not enough. If, however, man's final end is a unitive knowledge of the Godhead, it follows that man's spiritual needs cannot be fulfilled unless his environment is conducive to this end. Once again science, or rather the application of pure science in technology, proves the block to spiritual progress. The means to this end depend, amongst other things, on personal responsibility within self-governing units. Without individual freedom there can be no spiritual progress; but as long as the results of pure science are applied for the purpose of making our industries more highly specialized, there can only be greater centralization of power leading to a progressive loss of civil liberty and personal independence. Further, the prestige of science and a general misunderstanding of scientific principles have led to a popular world-view which contains a large element of 'nothing-but' philosophy:

Human beings, it is more or less tacitly assumed, are nothing but bodies, animals, even machines; the only really real elements of reality are matter and energy in their measurable aspects; values are nothing but illusions that have somehow got themselves mixed up with our experience of the world; mental happenings are nothing but epipheno-mena, produced by and entirely dependent upon physiology; spiri-tuality is nothing but wish fulfilment and misdirected sex; and so on. (*Science, Peace and Liberty*, ch. i)

The political consequences of this kind of thinking are apparent in the widespread indifference to human values which is so charac-teristic of the present time: saturation bombing, atomic missiles, torture, human vivisection and the systematic starvation of entire populations are all manifestations of the 'scientific attitude' applied to national and international affairs. Allowed to continue, the effect of the 'nothing-but' philosophy, backed by all the powerful resources of applied science and technology, will not be a Well-sian utopia, but either the mechano-morphic nightmare of *Brave New World*, or the aftermath of the thermo-nuclear holocaust depicted in *Ape and Essence*. Either way unlimited scientific pro-gress means the defeat of mankind.

Since it is neither practical nor desirable for the masses to oppose rulers equipped with the latest in self-propelled flame-throwers and atomic weapons, the question arises whether there is any way out of the unfavourable political situation in which people now find themselves. Huxley asserts that only one hopeful issue has been discovered which is compatible with the ethics of the perennial philosophy. This is Gandhi's *satyagraha*, non-violent resistance, or what Thoreau called 'civil disobedience'; here lies the hope of future revolutions. Meanwhile what kind of society would be conducive to the final end principle? In the foreword to the 1950 edition of *Brave New World*, Huxley describes the basis of such a community: its economics would be decentralist and Henry Georgian; its politics Kropotkinesque and co-operative. 'Science and technology would be used as though, like the Sabbath, they had been made for man, not . . . as though man were to be adapted and enslaved to them.' Religion would be the consistent pursuit of man's final purpose, the unitive knowledge of the Godhead or Brahman and the prevailing philosophy 'a kind of Higher Utilitarianism in which the Greatest Happiness principle would be secondary to the Final End principle'. This was the first hint of Huxley's final utopia, the contemplative society where science and religion work hand in hand for the betterment of mankind.

III

Crome Yellow (1921)

Huxley is said to have congratulated himself on having avoided the traditional first novel of the twentieth-century writer, the novel of adolescence. Denis, the would-be hero of *Crome Yellow*, we recall, was writing such a novel, the story of little Percy who came down to London to live among the artists. This was the novel Huxley wished to avoid; the novel he would have liked to write was clearly something more akin to the work of the great Knockespotch, the imaginary genius, whose name was inscribed across the covers of the dummy books in the library at Crome. Like Knockespotch, he wished to free us from 'the dreary tyranny of the realistic novel'; he was tired of 'seeing the human mind bogged in a social plenum'. He felt the force of Scogan's advice to Denis: '. . . if you could only read Knockespotch you wouldn't be writing a novel about the wearisome development of a young man's character, you wouldn't be describing in endless, fastidious detail, cultured life in Chelsea and Bloomsbury and Hampstead'. Instead, he would be writing tales like the imaginary genius of Crome:

How shall I describe them? Fabulous characters shoot across his pages like gaily dressed performers on the trapeze. There are extraordinary adventures and still more extraordinary speculations. Intelligences and emotions, relieved of all the imbecile preoccupations of civilised life, move in intricate and subtle dances, crossing and recrossing. . . An immense erudition and an immense fancy go hand in hand. All the ideas of the present and of the past, on every possible subject, bob up among the Tales, smile gravely or grimace a caricature of themselves, then disappear to make place for something new. The verbal surface of his writing is rich and fantastically diversified. The wit is incessant. (ch. xiv)

33

It is too much to claim that *Crome Yellow* lives up to this; only a Sterne, or a Firbank, perhaps, could do justice to Scogan's enthusiasm, but it is reasonable to suppose that the intent was there. In Huxley's novels of the twenties, 'an immense erudition and an immense fancy' do go hand in hand and 'the ideas of the present and of the past on every possible subject' do come up with alarming frequency. There are 'extraordinary adventures and still more extraordinary speculations'; the episode of the dwarfish Sir Hercules; Gumbril's patent pneumatic trousers; or the tale of Cardan's betrothal to the lunatic heiress are all drawn straight from the pages of Knockespotch. The element of the fantastic and the grotesque never completely disappears from Huxley's work but, like the other qualities associated with Knockespotch, it is gradually subordinated to a moral purpose. It is not really surprising that the moralist dominates in the end for there was something decidedly irresponsible about Knockespotch in his desire 'to be relieved of all the imbecile preoccupations of civilized life'. It was this element of irresponsibility which Huxley's more politically minded critics were quick to seize upon. As a satirist, he lacked seriousness; his novels were entertaining but nothing more.[1] This kind of criticism need not be taken too seriously, but it has some relevance here. Of all Huxley's novels, *Crome Yellow* is the one where Knockespotch has his day. Nevertheless it would be wrong to deny serious purpose; it is all rather good fun, but an underlying gravity is never far beneath the surface. Here is Scogan contrasting present-day attitudes with those of the previous century:

Seventy and eighty years ago simple-minded people, reading of the exploits of the Bourbons in South Italy, cried out in amazement: To think that such things should be happening in the nineteenth century . . . Today we are no longer surprised at these things. The Black and Tans harry Ireland, the Poles maltreat the Silesians, the bold Fascisti slaughter their poorer countrymen: we take it all for granted. . .

At this very moment . . . the most frightful horrors are taking place in every corner of the world. People are being crushed, slashed, dis-

---

[1] See Philip Henderson, *The Novel Today* (1936), p. 119.

embowelled, mangled; their dead bodies rot and their eyes decay with the rest. Screams of pain and fear go pulsing through the air at the rate of eleven hundred feet per second. After travelling for three seconds they are perfectly inaudible. These are distressing facts; but do we enjoy life any the less because of them? Most certainly we do not. (ch. xvi)

Scogan strikes a characteristic pose of indifference. Once it would have been tempting to identify Scogan's attitude with that of the author; but today no one would doubt Huxley's concern. It was not only the horror but the indifference that he found so appalling: the 'yellow' of Crome is at times more than a little jaundiced.

Of the two house-party novels, *Crome Yellow* is generally preferred. In this novel a number of people are brought together at Crome, the country home of the Lapith family, where they entertain themselves in the traditional week-end party manner: they dance, versify, paint pictures, explore the extensive grounds, make love and assist in the annual garden fête. And finally, they talk almost incessantly, on an inexhaustible range of topics. Each character rides his favourite hobby horse: Scogan speculates on the future of man, while Mr Wimbush reveals the eccentricities of the past. 'The danger of such a method', as Jocelyn Brooke points out, 'is that the action of the novel—and the characters themselves—will be swamped by the stream of conversation; in *Crome Yellow*, however, the balance is almost perfectly maintained . . .'[1] The reader moves effortlessly from the moonlit gambols on the terrace to Mr Bodiham's sermon in the rectory study; from Mr Wimbush's researches to the antics of the insomniacs on the roof. Incident and exposition are skilfully blended throughout; while the author through the eloquence of the characters is able to air his erudition and, at the same time, ridicule the intellectual pretensions of his contemporaries.

The characters represent the various attitudes the author wishes to expose: the satire is light but always penetrating; and, one by one, the characters condemn themselves either by word or deed because their attitudes have no foundation in reality. There is no

[1] *Aldous Huxley* (1958), p. 12.

positive point of reference to which they can appeal, and Crome, like Eliot's *Waste Land*, is a world of empty posturing. Denis Stone, whose arrival and departure frame the novel, is a typical figure of futility. The product of an effete intellectualism, he is hypersensitive and, in his own words, weighed down with 'twenty tons of ratiocination'. His predicament owes something to that of his namesake in *South Wind*: like Denis Phipps, he is completely at home in the world of ideas, but when he is faced with a world beyond the college walls everything becomes obscure and embroiled. Even the simple act of retrieving a bicycle from the guard's van at Camlet station has its attendant humiliations:

'A bicycle, a bicycle!' he said breathlessly to the guard. He felt himself a man of action. The guard paid no attention, but continued methodically to hand out, one by one, the packages labelled to Camlet. 'A bicycle!' Denis repeated. 'A green machine, cross-framed, name of Stone. S-T-O-N-E.'

'All in good time, sir', said the guard soothingly. He was a large, stately man with a naval beard. One pictured him at home, drinking tea, surrounded by a numerous family. It was in that tone that he must have spoken to his children when they were tiresome. 'All in good time, sir.' Denis's man of action collapsed, punctured. (ch. i)

Denis's defeats pile up in the course of the novel. Scogan rides roughshod over his finer feelings; Anne resists all his attempts to win her affections, while his rival is attended with every success. There is a scene reminiscent of Peacock in which Denis sits helplessly watching Anne and Gombauld waltzing while he pretends to read; and another reminiscent of Douglas where the unfortunate Denis witnesses the happy pair apparently making love on the moonlit lawn.[1] Finally, convinced that his case is a hopeless one, he resolves to act. The result is not without irony: 'One is only happy in action', he reassures himself and sends the fatal

[1] In *Nightmare Abbey* while Marionetta, accompanied by the Honourable Mr Listless, plays the harp, Scythrop pretends to be deeply interested in the *Purgatorio*; for Denis, alas, it is *The Stock Breeder's Vade Mecum*. In *South Wind* the unhappy Denis Phipps discovers his rival with Angelina in the moonlit cave of Mercury.

telegram which is to recall him to London. It is only when he is
going that he realizes Anne is tiring of his rival and would wel-
come his attentions, but now it is too late. He abandons himself to
his fate, resolving never again to do anything decisive. Behind
Denis's inability to act lies a misconceived idealism of which he is
only too well aware. He confesses to Anne:

I can take nothing for granted, I can enjoy nothing as it comes along.
Beauty, pleasure, art, women—I have to invent an excuse, a justification for everything that is delightful. . . I have to say that art is the
process by which one reconstructs the divine reality out of chaos.
Pleasure is one of the mystical roads to union with the infinite—the
ecstasies of drinking, dancing, love-making. As for women, I am perpetually assuring myself that they're the broad highway to divinity.
(ch. iv)

   Denis like all of Huxley's intellectuals suffers from an excess of
cerebration; Anne, in whom we detect the forerunner of Mrs
Viveash and Lucy Tantamount, has no such impediments. There
is a smile of amused malice on her face when she retorts that she
would like to see herself believing that men were the highroad to
divinity. As the sexually sophisticated young woman of the
twenties, she knows exactly what she wants of life. It is all obvious:
'One enjoys the pleasant things, avoids the nasty ones. There's
nothing more to be said' (ch. iv). But beneath the veneer of complacency there is the faintest suggestion of the boredom which
characterises her way of life. As her flirtation with Gombauld
draws to its inevitable close, she betrays a certain weariness: 'If you
only knew how gross and awful and boring men are when they
try to make love and you don't want them to . . .' (ch. xxi). In
the end her indifference defeats itself. Looking for another source
of amusement, she turns to Denis, but too late; he has already
announced his departure.
   Mary Bracegirdle, like Denis, is of an idealistic frame of mind;
but whereas Denis's idealism is rooted in nineteenth-century
romanticism, Mary stands fair and square for everything that is
'modern'. An authority on all that is new in art, with a penchant

for 'the frightfully abstract and frightfully intellectual', she finds Gombauld's painting 'too *trompe l'oeil*' for her taste. On sexual matters she is equally advanced; a convinced birth-controller, she pleads the cause of the Malthusian League and is fully acquainted with the works of Havelock Ellis. Preoccupied with her repressions, she applies Freudian analysis to her dreams. As she explains to Anne:

I constantly dream that I'm falling down wells; and sometimes I even dream that I'm climbing up ladders. It's most disquieting. The symptoms are only too clear. . .

One may become a nymphomaniac if one's not careful. You've no idea how serious these repressions are if you don't get rid of them in time. (ch. vii)

Ivor Lombard, whom she thought had an 'interesting mind', appears a ready-made answer to her repressions. Unfortunately, Ivor does not take the workings of sexual selection as seriously as Mary would expect, and she finds herself suddenly deserted, freed from her repressions, but with a new and unexpected misery for which neither Freud nor Havelock Ellis had adequately prepared her.

The idealism of Denis and Mary Bracegirdle has a perfect foil in the realism of Scogan. Scogan is the rationalist and sceptic, whose ancestry can be traced to Keith, the erudite sensualist of *South Wind*.[1] He is something of a Knockespotch himself, a *raconteur* of encyclopaedic knowledge, who specialises in tales of eccentric aristocrats. But what is more important is that Scogan, as the exponent of rationalism, is the voice of scientific materialism. In this role he expounds the germ of the idea which was later to be developed in *Brave New World*: the 'vast state incubators with their rows and rows of gravid bottles' which will supply the world with its future population. Scogan's blueprint for the 'Rational State' also contains many hints of *Brave New World*. The 'Rational State' is a modern counterpart of Plato's *Republic*, in which the

[1] There is, however, an earlier version of Scogan. Cf. Jacobson in 'Happily Ever After', *Limbo*.

men of reason will be the 'Directing Intelligences'. The inhabitants will be classified into distinct species according to their qualities of mind and temperament: each child will be tested by examining psychologists and given an education appropriate to the task it is expected to perform in adult life. There will be three main species: the Directing Intelligences, the Men of Faith, and the Herd. The first will be the absolute rulers, while the Men of Faith will be used exclusively for directing the Herd, unaware that they are being used as the tools of a superior intelligence. For the Herd, the countless millions who lack intelligence and enthusiasm, there will be special treatment: they will be scientifically conditioned to believe that they are happy, that they are tremendously important and that everything they do is noble and significant. For them 'the earth will be restored to the centre of the universe and man to pre-eminence on earth'. Scogan's 'Rational State' illustrates the fundamental dichotomy between reason and faith; on an allegorical level it represents the nineteenth-century scientist's dream of progress, the triumph of science over religion, of the material over the spiritual. But it is a hollow victory. The only happiness for the majority will be achieved by a systematic conditioning in the very beliefs which science has worked so consistently to destroy. Science can only undo the damage it has done by restoring man to a state of pre-scientific innocence. This idea is later parodied in a scene of subtle irony. At the annual fête, Scogan, the voice of reason, now disguised, 'like the Bohemian hag of Frith's Derby Day', as Sesostris, the sorceress of Ecbatana, is seen confirming the villagers of Crome in all their worst fears and superstitions. Reason is, indeed, the false prophetess. The inadequacy of Scogan's 'scientific' attitude becomes increasingly manifest; he is condemned to a life devoid of imagination and speculation. Art has no appeal to him, except for the abstractions of the Cubists from which nature has been completely banished; nature, itself, offers even less—the London tube is the apotheosis of reasoning man, a world of 'iron riveted into geometrical forms', while religion is nothing but the most deplorable nonsense. The aridity of this kind of existence appalls even Scogan: 'How often', he exclaims, 'have I tried to take holidays, to get away from myself, my own boring nature, my insufferable mental surroundings' (ch. xxv).

A figure with some affinities to Scogan is Henry Wimbush, the antiquarian of Crome. Henry Wimbush has divorced himself completely from present-day realities; living almost entirely in the past, he is more familiar with Sir Ferdinando's sixteenth-century account books than his own, a fact which has enabled his wife to gamble away a considerable part of his fortune. After twenty-five years of patient research, he can claim that his 'History of Crome' throws some genuinely new light on the introduction of the three-pronged fork, a discovery only surpassed by his great antiquarian find of fifty yards of oaken drain-pipes. Like Scogan he dreams of a scientific future, one where all human contact has been rendered superfluous. There he imagines himself living 'in a dignified seclusion, surrounded by the delicate attention of silent and graceful machines, and entirely secure from any human intrusion' (ch. xxviii). A daydream inspired no doubt by Forster's *The Machine Stops*.

If the limitations of the 'Directing Intelligences' of Crome are all too obvious, the 'men of Faith' have little to offer in compensation. Priscilla Wimbush is what Huxley has called in another context, 'a spiritual adventuress'. In the past she would have entertained the curé, but in the context of present-day Crome she has only the Sunday newspapers and the Barbecue-Smiths. Because of her gambling losses she has been confined to the country, but has found a source of consolation in the 'New Thought and the Occult'. She now invests her money 'scientifically' as the stars dictate, practises auto-suggestion, and when she is bored there is 'the Infinite to keep in tune with', the Christian Mysteries and Mrs Besant. She has never seen a vision or succeeded in establishing any contact with the spirit world herself, so she has to be contented with the reported experiences of others, the function of Ivor Lombard and Barbecue-Smith. Barbecue-Smith is one of the prophets of the 'New Thought,' the author of 'Humble Heroisms' and 'Pipe-Lines to the Infinite', little books of comfort and spiritual teaching whose sale had topped the hundred and twenty thousand mark.

In spiritual matters, Mr Bodiham, the rector of Crome, is the voice of religious orthodoxy. Compared with the success story of Barbecue-Smith, his life is one long chapter of frustration. He preaches to the recalcitrant congregation of Crome in vain; he tries to make them understand the nature of God and what a fearful thing it was to fall into his hands, but all to no purpose:

When Savonarola preached, men sobbed and groaned aloud. Nothing broke the polite silence with which Crome listened to Mr. Bodiham— only an occasional cough and sometimes the sound of heavy breathing. . . There were times when Mr. Bodiham wanted to jump down from the pulpit . . . times when he would have liked to beat and kill his whole congregation. (ch. ix)

Blessed with a Calvinist streak, he had seen himself as one of the elect; he had interpreted the will of God and had prophesied an Armageddon. Time had proved him wrong. Now, a village Savonarola to whom no one pays heed he is reduced to raising funds for a war memorial from his reluctant parishioners, whom he regards with growing distaste and horror: 'In the village of Crome, it seemed, Sodom and Gomorrah had come to a second birth.'

One by one the characters are exposed as they try to evade reality. Denis's outdated romanticism lays him bare to every kind of humiliation and misery; Mary's 'modernism' leaves her equally unfitted to come to terms with the world, while Anne's sophistication merely expends itself in inevitable boredom. Scogan's rationalism cuts him off from every human aspect of life: nature, art, religion are all rendered meaningless. Henry Wimbush can only find fulfilment in the re-creation of a dead past while his wife consoles herself with Sunday newspaper prophets. Mr Bodiham is condemned to frustration; deserted by his vengeful deity, and ignored by his passive villagers. The only character completely at home in the world of Crome is Ivor Lombard; nothing mars his succession of social and amorous engagements; and this is the supreme comment on a society which accepts superficiality as the hallmark of achievement.

The various attitudes satirised combine to present a generalized picture of the post-war malaise—the spiritual aridity, the moral and intellectual bankruptcy. This is the dominant theme of the novel, but underlying it can be detected the causes of disillusionment; the war and the subsequent collapse of the nineteenth-century belief in science and progress. Huxley's immediate reaction to the war had been registered in *Limbo*, the volume of short stories published twelve months before *Crome Yellow*. Richard Greenow, the conscientious objector hero of the main story, contemplates war in the following terms:

He thought of the millions who had been and were still being slaughtered . . . he thought of their pain, all the countless separate pains of them; pain incommunicable, individual, beyond the reach of sympathy . . . pain without sense or object, bringing with it no hope and no redemption, futile, unnecessary, stupid. In one supreme apocalyptic moment he saw, he felt the universe in all its horror. (*Farcical History of Richard Greenow*)

The second story, *Happily Ever After*, is notable for the Rev. Roger Pemberton, whose platitudes on the hero killed at the front, 'He has died a hero's death, a martyr's death, witnessing to Heaven against the powers of evil', foreshadow the sentiments of Mr Bodiham. By 1921 the shadow of the war was beginning to recede: it is a relatively minor theme in *Crome Yellow*, but the author's feelings are nonetheless unchanged. Gombauld rebukes Scogan with heavy irony: '. . . I found the war quite as thorough a holiday from all the ordinary decencies and sanities, all the common emotions and preoccupations, as I ever want to have' (ch. xxv). And Mr Bodiham is introduced, primarily, one feels, to allow Huxley to reprint the substance of the Rev. E. H. Horne's 1916 address.[1] This interpretation of the war as the closing stages of Armageddon is offered without comment, but it must have been particularly distasteful to Huxley in its attempt to

[1] See footnote to Chapter IX, p. 62.

justify the most terrible conflict in human history as the will of a righteous and omnipotent deity.

The failure of science to justify its nineteenth-century role as the universal panacea is clearly underlined in *Crome Yellow*. Whenever science is touched on a mood of disenchantment prevails: man's deepest feelings and impulses have become the objects of scientific enquiry; the taboos of the previous century have been swept away and serious young women like Mary can discuss the most embarrassing questions with a philosophic calm; scientific openness has created a climate where 'love has ceased to be the rather fearful, mysterious thing it was, and become a perfectly normal, almost commonplace, activity' (*Do What You Will*). But, it is implied, this kind of knowledge does not lead to happiness. Even Scogan would like to see 'mingled with this scientific ardour, a little more of the jovial spirit of Rabelais and Chaucer' (ch. xv). On another level the 'goddess of Applied Science' has presented the world with one gift after another; love has been dissociated from propagation and one day an 'impersonal generation' may replace 'Nature's hideous system'. The scientific utopia, which foreshadows *Brave New World* is the exclusive product of the rational mind, but it is a world stripped of all human values. This is what Joseph Wood Krutch was later to call 'the paradox of humanism': that the further man progresses from the primitive state of nature, the more 'human' he becomes in the rationalist sense of the word, the more he alienates himself from all the values which have made him unique as man. The perfect analogy to the scientific utopia is the ant-hill: 'The perfected society is, that is to say, utterly devoid of human values, and its perfection is made possible by that very fact. It owes both its stability and its efficient harmony to the absence of any tendency on the part of individuals either to question the value of existence or to demand anything for themselves.'[1] The irony of the situation is evident: Scogan's men of reason, the 'Directing Intelligences', can restore human happiness, but only by reconditioning man to a belief in his old ideals, by restoring the earth 'to the centre of the universe and man to

[1] *The Modern Temper* (New York, 1956), p. 33.

pre-eminence on the earth' (ch. xxii). The implications are clear: man is essentially an irrational being; take away his irrationality and you destroy his essential being as man. Huxley, however, was still a long way from positing a non-rationalist solution. The 'men of Faith' are totally discredited as Mr Bodiham reminds us, and there is, as yet, no hint of a mystical or Laurentian approach to the problem (although Denis, we recall, was laboriously trying to make himself a pagan). The non-rationalist element of Crome is equally jaded: Barbecue-Smith is the prophet of the new age and it is not without significance that it is the 'Sorceress of Ecbatana', the Madame Sosostris of Huxley's waste land, who points 'the way to Paradise' for Mr Bodiham's parishioners, while the rector, seeing the village bathing belles, raises his eyes to heaven and exclaims, 'How long?'

In contrast, the past of Crome offers a tentative but positive point of reference. Henry Wimbush's studies of the Lapith family reveal a pattern of order and stability absent in present-day Crome. The prediction of the diminutive Sir Hercules:

> A time will come, wherein the soul shall be
> From all superfluous matter wholly free   (ch. xiii)

is ironic in the context of the novel, but prophetic in the light of Huxley's future development. However, within the walls of Crome, Sir Hercules, whom Burgum considers the hero of the novel,[1] does create a society where beauty and intelligence, reason and artistic sensitivity go hand in hand. That this society is destroyed by brute force suggests an analogy with the present: that sensibility and fine feelings have no place in a world given over to the power of force and brutality.[2] The contrast between a past that offered opportunities for expression and fulfilment and a present that is continually marred by futility and frustration is suggested in many ways. The three lovely Lapiths, the 'modernists' and *femmes supérieures* of their time, were confirmed transcendentalists, who read George Sand's *Indiana*; today they would

[1] See Edwin Berry Burgum, *The Novel and the World's Dilemma* (New York, 1947), p. 143.
[2] There is a parallel situation in *Island*.

have read Freud and Ellis and admired the abstractions of Tschuplitski. The courtship of George Wimbush and Georgina is one of the most delightful episodes of the novel; it is followed immediately by Mary's act of 'sexual selection' on the roof-top. In Sir Ferdinando's time, the young men of Crome spent their Sundays engaged in rustic sports; today, there is only Mr Bodiham's forbidding boys' club. Manningham's Diary for 1600 tells of men and women dancing naked in summer bacchanals on the moonlit hills, but that too had gone; if the young men of Crome wished to dance now, they had to cycle six miles to the nearest town. 'The pious magistrates had snuffed out for ever a little happy flame'; today, Henry Wimbush concludes, meditating on all the murdered past, the 'country was desolate, without life of its own' (ch. xviii).

It has been customary to describe *Crome Yellow* as Huxley's 'happiest' novel. Angus Wilson has called it 'idyllic, pastoral, bucolic',[1] and the prevailing mood of the novel is certainly closer to Douglas's *South Wind* than to any of Huxley's later work. Knockespotch rides lightly over a world of ideas ranging from Freudian repressions to Cubist painting, and such excerpts as Sir Ferdinando's sanitary arrangements suggest the opposite of serious intent. But allowing for the occasional incursions of Knockespotch, *Crome Yellow* is essentially a portrait of post-war malaise; a portrait which Huxley was to enlarge in the succeeding novels of the twenties. The reader is confronted with an intellectual climate in which neither reason nor faith offer any basis for life; the characters evade reality, unable to come to terms with a world which offers no tangible set of values which they can grasp. At the end of the novel, the fair is over, the dancers have dispersed and the last lights are being put out; the day of 'festivity' draws to its close, and Scogan is left alone, He speaks for them all:

'Life is always gay all the same, under whatever circumstances. . . Under any circumstances', he repeated to himself. It was ungrammatical to begin with; was it true? And is life really its own reward? He wondered. (ch. xxix)

[1] 'The House Party Novels', *The London Magazine*, II (August 1955), p. 56.

IV

Antic Hay (1923)

ntic Hay, Huxley's second novel, although shaped from the same material as *Crome Yellow*, is altogether a more ambitious and serious piece of work. The range and power of the satire has been extended, and even D. S. Savage, not the kindliest of Huxley's critics, has to admit that 'there is a pronounced thread of morality running through the tale's desperate gaiety'.[1] The scene has been moved to London and the 'meaninglessness' which was latent in *Crome Yellow* is now fully explored. Henderson, while ignoring the moral implications, aptly sums up the mood of the novel when he writes: 'Of certain sides of life in London during those years it gives an unsurpassed picture. The feeling of the pointlessness of everything, the intentionally senseless diversions, ridiculous games like "Beaver", the headlong rush to jazz and drink—anything to forget the war—the whole uneasy movement of the time symbolized so perfectly in the "Last Ride" . . .of Mrs. Viveash and Gumbril. . .'[2] *Antic Hay*, although freed from the country-house party formula of *Crome Yellow*, remains essentially a 'novel of ideas'; the characters are still mainly of interest for the viewpoint they express and the clash of ideas provides structural focal points throughout the novel. Thus, in Chapter Four, the Soho café scene introduces the main characters assembled for the first time and the themes of the novel are unfolded in a series of witty verbal exchanges.

In *Crome Yellow* the characters talk, but there is little that could be described as genuine debate; in *Antic Hay*, however, the characters attack each other's intellectual pretensions with a savagery which characterizes the mood of the later novel. The scene

---

[1] *The Withered Branch* (1950), p. 133.
[2] Alexander Henderson, *Aldous Huxley* (1935), pp. 135–6.

opens with Lypiatt declaiming aloud his verses to Gumbril and Mercaptan; his use of the word 'dream' sparks off Gumbril, who protests that, after the war, and the Russian famine, the word merely connotes Freud. Mercaptan joins in the attack, and Lypiatt is stung into a spirited reply:

'You're afraid of ideals, that's what it is. You daren't admit to having dreams. . . Ideals—they're not sufficiently genteel for you civilised young men. You've quite outgrown that sort of thing. No dreams, no religion, no morality.'

'I glory in the name of earwig', said Gumbril. He was pleased with that little invention. It was felicitous; it was well chosen. 'One's an earwig in sheer self-protection', he explained.

But Mr. Mercaptan refused to accept the name of earwig at any price. '*What* is there to be ashamed of in being civilised, I *really* don't know. . . No, if I glory in anything, it's in my little rococo boudoir, and the conversations across the polished mahogany, and the delicate, lascivious, *witty* little flirtations on the ample sophas inhabited by the soul of Crébillon Fils.'

Once again we have the dialectic of conflicting ideas in which the characters strike the intellectual attitudes they are to maintain throughout the novel. Lypiatt, like Denis in *Crome Yellow*, is easily recognized as the ineffectual idealist; in this novel he reappears as the self-appointed Messiah, the prophet whose function is to scourge the cynicism of the age. Gumbril, on the other hand, is the sceptic, whose sensitivity is hidden behind a mask of superficial wit. 'One's an earwig in sheer self-protection'; this takes us back to the beginning of the novel, where Gumbril first stumbled on his felicitous phrase, while meditating on the decline of values in the school chapel. It underlines his abnegation of responsibility which is one of the main themes of the novel. Finally, there is Mercaptan, whose concept of 'being civilized' is manifested in a sham dilettantism, symbolised by the aesthetic niceties of Crébillon's *Sopha*. The group is joined by Coleman, who is accompanied by his current mistress, Zoe. Coleman, whose blond, fan-shaped beard has been grown in imitation of the Saviour, is the anti-Christ of the party, the iconoclast, whose great zest for life is

expended in degrading everything remotely suggestive of value.
With Coleman's arrival a new motif is introduced; he relates an
anecdote of the days when he used to frequent the school labora-
tories eviscerating frogs. The detail has an unmistakable Coleman-
like ring about it: the frogs were 'crucified with pins . . . belly
upwards, like little green Christs'. He goes on to tell how the
laboratory boy came in and asked the usher for the key to the
Absolute:

And, would you believe it, that usher calmly put his hand in his
trouser pocket and fished out a small Yale key and gave it him without
a word. What a gesture! The key of the Absolute. But it was only the
absolute alcohol the urchin wanted—to pickle some loathsome foetus
in. . .

The introduction of the laboratory brings in the sixth member of
the group, Shearwater, the physiologist, who proceeds to enlarge
on the miraculous nature of the kidneys, while Coleman irrever-
ently sits down to devour a plate of them—sautéd!

'Shearwater's no better than a mystic', fluted Mr. Mercaptan. 'A mystical scientist; really, one hadn't reckoned on that.' . . .
    'It's only the deliberately blind, who couldn't reckon on that com-
bination', Lypiatt put in indignantly. 'What are science and art, what
are religion and philosophy but so many expressions in human terms
of some reality more than human? Newton and Boehme and Michelangelo—what are they doing but expressing, in different ways, different aspects of the same thing?' . . .
    'One reality', he cried, 'there is only one reality.'
    'One reality', Coleman reached out a hand across the table and
caressed Zoe's bare white arm, 'and that is callipygous.' Zoe jabbed at
his hand with her fork.

The scene concludes with Coleman expounding ecstatically his
interpretation of the 'one reality':

Reproduction, reproduction. . . Delightful and horrifying to think
they all come to that, even the most virginal; that they were all made
for that, little she-dogs, in spite of their china-blue eyes. What sort of
mandrake shall we produce, Zoe and I? . . . How I should like to have

a child. . . Ah, how delightful it would be! I long for posterity. I live in hopes. I stope against Stopes. I—

He is cut short by a well-aimed piece of bread from Zoe, which catches him just below the eye.

This chapter illustrates Huxley's dialogue at its most effective: the liveliness of characterization, the dialectic of ideas, and the gradual unfolding of the dominant themes of the novel. It lays bare with precision and conciseness an intellectual ethos where surface wit and cynicism have replaced a genuine search for value. With Lypiatt as their spokesman, the ideals of the past have no currency, while 'civilization' is presented as a sham re-creation of *dix-huitième* decadence. In a world of debased values science has usurped religion: the symbol of Christ is a crucified frog on a dissecting bench; the Absolute a pickled foetus, and the 'one reality' —callipygous. Freud and Stopes are the prophets of the new age.

This is largely a restatement of the theme of *Crome Yellow*, but in the following chapter the portrait is enlarged. A wider view of humanity is introduced by Coleman's apocalyptic vision of 'the seven million distinct and separate individuals' who make up the great city. This is a prelude to the next scene. As the party approach Hyde Park Corner, they see a fraction of the city's seven million gathered around the yellow light of a coffee stall. Among the peaked caps and workmen's jackets, they detect the Spanish comb of carved tortoiseshell belonging to Myra Viveash and the top hat of her escort, Bruin Opps. Myra and Bruin have been dining out at Hampton Court, but the food had proved uneatable and the champagne had tasted of Thames water. Now, at the first outpost of civilization, they are quelling the pangs of hunger. The scene is carefully constructed. Myra's unaffected horror of the food they had been expected to eat is followed by Bruin's disgust at having to satisfy his appetite 'in the street, in the middle of a lot of filthy workmen'. He voices his distaste for the lower classes in a diatribe against domestics. Meanwhile Myra Viveash, whose speciality is affairs of the heart, has cornered Shearwater and is

busily engaged in exploring the physiologist's interest in her pet
subject. Shearwater, whose life is one of sterile dedication, protests that his interest in human affairs is limited to the circulation
of the blood. Their conversation on the relative merits of the parts
of the human anatomy provides a counterpoint to the story of
two members of Bruin's despised lower class, the carter and his
pregnant wife who have walked to Portsmouth and back in search
of employment. The carter is explaining his plight to a sympathetic audience around the coffee stall. The carefully placed
juxtaposition produces an episode of brilliantly sustained irony:

'I used to do cartin' jobs', the man with the teacup was saying. ' 'Ad a
van and a nold pony of me own. And didn't do so badly neither. The
only trouble was me lifting furniture and 'eavy weights about the
place. Because I 'ad malaria out in India, in the war. . .'

'Nor even—you compel me to violate the laws of modesty—nor
even', Mrs. Viveash went on, smiling painfully, speaking huskily, ex-
piringly, 'of legs?' . . .

'It comes back on you when you get tired like, malaria does.' The
man's face was sallow and there was an air of peculiar listlessness and
hopelessness about his misery. 'It comes back on you, and then you go
down with fever and you're as weak as a child.'

Shearwater shook his head.

'Nor even of the heart?' Mrs. Viveash lifted her eyebrows. 'Ah, now
the inevitable word has been pronounced, the real subject of every conversation has appeared on the scene. Love, Mr. Shearwater!'

'But as I says', recapitulated the man with the teacup, 'we didn't do
so badly after all. We 'ad nothing to complain about. 'Ad we, Florrie?'

The black bundle made an affirmative movement with its upper
extremity.

'That's one of the subjects', said Shearwater, 'like the Great Wall of
China. . . I don't allow myself to be interested in.'

Mrs. Viveash laughed, and breathed out a little 'Good God!' of
incredulity and astonishment, and asked, 'Why not?'

The scene closes when the carter relates how when he got to
Portsmouth there were two hundred applicants for three vacan-
cies. This is all too much for Gumbril who has been listening
attentively. He appeals to the generosity of the others. Coleman

responds with delight at this manifestation of the 'one reality': '"Gravid," he kept repeating, "gravid, gravid. The laws of gravidy, first formulated by Newton, now recodified by the immortal Einstein. . . ." He roared with laughter.'

On the way home. Gumbril, his scepticism sorely shaken, is still preoccupied with what he has heard. 'It's appalling, it's horrible,' he exclaims to Shearwater. 'Those people at the coffee stall. . . . It's appalling that human beings should have to live like that. Worse than dogs.' But Shearwater is lost in his own private world of vivisection: 'Dogs have nothing to complain of. . . Nor guinea-pigs, nor rats. It's these blasted anti-vivisection maniacs who make all the fuss.' The indifference of the scientist touches a remote chord in Gumbril's consciousness. He recalls his war-time experience at the hands of the army medical board. There he had been treated like all the other poor wretches. It had been a real eye-opener. 'And to think that the majority of one's fellow-beings pass their whole lives being shoved about like maltreated animals.' Suddenly he is aware of poverty and wretchedness at every street corner, and he wonders by what right he is entitled to be contented and well-fed, the possessor of a good education with time and leisure for conversation and the complexities of love.

In this chapter the irresponsibility of the Soho café milieu is further exposed by reference to a wider social context: the pleasure-seeking Myra and Bruin, who ironically belong to the ranks of the unfed, are contrasted with two of the thousands to whom poverty and hunger are an everyday reality; while Mercaptan's little flirtations, Myra's affairs of the heart and Shearwater's complacent domesticity are all thrown into relief against the six-month pregnancy of the carter's wife, to which Coleman's sole response is a vacuous display of wit. This is a world without feeling or compassion: the physiologist's attitude to vivisection exemplifies the indifference of the majority of mankind; Gumbril's final poignant comment sums up the utter injustice of the human lot.

At the centre of the novel lies Gumbril's search for a positive source of value. In the wider context of Huxley's development it is premature and largely abortive, but it does mark the beginning of the moral theme, enlarged somewhat tentatively by Calamy in *Those Barren Leaves* and finally brought to fruition by Anthony Beavis, some thirteen years later, in *Eyeless in Gaza*. The dominant note is struck on the first page, where we find Gumbril speculating in his rambling way about the nature and existence of God:

No, but seriously . . . the problem was very troublesome indeed. God as a sense of warmth about the heart, God as exultation, God as tears in the eyes, God as a rush of power or thought—that was all right. But God as truth, God as $2+2=4$—that wasn't so clearly all right. Was there any chance of their being the same? Were there bridges to join the two worlds?

There was no ready answer. Goodness had existed and perhaps still did exist. He knew that; his mother had been good, 'diligently good', but it was a word people only used now 'with a kind of deprecating humorousness'. It was easier to be the sceptic, to be beyond good and evil, or rather below them 'like earwigs'. This is Gumbril's situation: to wear the mask of the sceptic, to play the wit and the cynic with the Colemans and the Mercaptans, and at the same time to be sensitive to human suffering; to feel indignation and pity for the couple at the coffee stall and have a conscience that plagued him.

In Gumbril the serious and the grotesque meet; the patent small-clothes for sedentary people are Gumbril's answer to a system of education symbolised by 'sixty-three answers to ten questions about the Italian Risorgimento', but they are also a symbol of his cheerful and ready acceptance of the way of irresponsibility. Having abandoned his pedagogue's career, the Rabelaisian 'complete man' is the next logical step; with his newly acquired fan-shaped beard, his padded American coat, Malacca cane and the long Cuban cigar, he can brush aside the twinges of an uneasy conscience and sally forth to seduce and conquer like the heroes of old. The mild and melancholy schoolteacher is no more; he is now provisionally a member of Coleman's herd. At first the thought was depressing but once set on his path of conquest, he felt 'duly grateful'. His first victim, Rosie Shearwater, is taken in the true spirit of Rabelaisian complete manhood, but his second encounter raises problems of a different nature.

Emily is a figure of almost perfect innocence. An orphan, the victim of an unhappy sexual experience when young, she shrinks from any form of physical contact. Gumbril's first attempt to make love is disastrous and he considers a more delicate approach. The beard is removed, the Rabelaisian pose is dropped, and Gumbril is momentarily restored to the lost world of his childhood. This episode with its recollections of 'governess carts' and 'barrel-bellied ponies' is over-sentimentalized; nevertheless it provides Gumbril with the first glimpse of what must be described as mystical experience:

It re-establishes itself, an inward quiet, like this outward quiet of grass and trees. It fills one, it grows—a crystal quiet, a growing, expanding crystal. It grows, it becomes more perfect; it is beautiful and terrifying... For one's alone in the crystal and there's no support from outside, there's nothing external and important... There's nothing to laugh at or feel enthusiastic about. But the quiet grows and grows... And at last you are conscious of something approaching; it is almost a faint sound of footsteps. Something inexpressibly lovely and wonderful advances through the crystal, nearer, nearer. (ch. xii)

The experience is closely associated with Emily; she also is 'native to that crystal world'; but the G minor Quintet also strikes a note of liberation:

The spirit is slave to fever and beating blood, at the mercy of an obscure and tyrannous misfortune. But irrelevantly, it elects to dance in triple measure—a mounting skip, a patter of descending feet. (ch. xiii)

'Thought' is already the 'slave of life', but 'God as a sense of warmth in the heart, God as exultation' also has a place in the scheme of things.

The romance with Emily, however, is spun too finely for the 'goat-feet' dance of *Antic Hay*; Huxley loses his touch and the affair rapidly deteriorates into a cottagey idyll. Gumbril, meanwhile, assisted by Myra Viveash, suffers a loss of nerve and retires once more behind his mask of cynicism and wit. With Myra Viveash, Huxley is back on firmer ground. Gumbril had described Emily as 'a case for the text-books of sexual psychology'; Mrs Viveash, too, might have found herself a time-honoured place. She is the spirit of the age, the *femme fatale* of the twenties, whose 'affairs of the heart' invariably end in boredom and frustration. She had made a brief appearance as Anne in *Crome Yellow*; she is to appear again as Lucy Tantamount in *Point Counter Point* and to make a brief and unhappy exit as Mary Amberley in *Eyeless in Gaza*. To Gumbril she is disillusionment personified; and as the musical key shifts from the G minor Quintet to the nightclub dirge, 'What's he to Hecuba?' so Gumbril exchanges the 'quiet places of the mind' for Myra's eternal merry-go-round of pleasure and disenchantment. The 'impossible happiness of being two' is transformed into the 'perfectly united centaur' of Gumbril and Myra revolving aimlessly to the fox-trot of the grinning blackamoors. The *Hamlet* motif is echoed by the chorus; Gumbril has had 'the motive and the cue for passion' and wavered; now he flings himself into a wild bout of self-justification.

'I'm not even responsible for myself.' He imagined a cottagey room, under a roof, with a window near the floor and a sloping ceiling . . . and in the candlelight Emily's candid eyes, her grave and happy mouth. . .

'What's he to Hecuba?'

'Nothing at all', Gumbril clownishly sang. The room, in the cottage, had nothing to do with him. He breathed Mrs. Viveash's memories of Italian jasmines, laid his cheek for a moment against her smooth hair. 'Nothing at all.' Happy clown! (ch. xv)

Still plagued by echoes of former innocence, Gumbril recalls another clown, the inimitable Dan Leno, the comedian of his childhood pantomimes, 'dead now as poor Yorick, no more than a mere skull like anybody else's skull' (ch. xvi). Unwittingly he is rhapsodizing over 'Ophelia's grave'. Emily has already passed out of his life; his protestations are to come too late. It is, perhaps, enough to note that Huxley never returns to romantic love for an antidote to 'meaninglessness'. In *Those Barren Leaves* romanticism is severely castigated; and Calamy, Gumbril's successor, adheres to celibacy as the only acceptable course.

The 'last ride' together of Gumbril and Mrs Viveash, which ends the novel, matches the whole tenor of Gumbril's progress. Their first call is on Lypiatt, whose failure has driven him to the point of suicide. Lypiatt, as the self-elected scourge of the day, is almost a forerunner of Rampion: there is more than an echo of Lawrence in his declamations. Here he is admonishing Mercaptan:

'You disgust me', said Lypiatt, with rising indignation, and making wilder gestures. 'You disgust me—you and your odious little sham eighteenth-century civilization; your piddling little poetry; your art for art's sake instead of for God's sake; your nauseating little copulations without love or passion; your hoggish materialism; your bestial indifference to all that's unhappy and your yelping hatred of all that's great.' (ch. iv)

His philosophy of 'life-worship' carries even stronger overtones of the doctrine of *Point Counter Point*:

'Life', he said, 'life—that's the great essential thing. You've got to get life into your art, otherwise it's nothing. And life only comes out of life, out of passion and feeling; it can't come out of theories.' (ch. vi)

Why Huxley chose to portray Lypiatt as a failure is not obvious. Was he deliberately setting out to satirise Lawrence? There are certainly passages which suggest burlesque: ' "The wind, the great wind that's in me." He struck his forehead. "The wind of life, the wild west wind. I feel it inside me, blowing, blowing" ' (ch. vi). However, in spite of his bombast Lypiatt is, on the whole, drawn sympathetically and he frequently speaks with the voice of the author.[1] His 'ideas' in the context of the novel are positive and are shared to some extent by the redemptive characters, Emily

[1] See 'Breughel', *Along the Road*. On art, Huxley and Lypiatt speak with one and the same voice.

and Gumbril Senior. By presenting Lypiatt as a theatrical show of greatness rather than greatness itself, Huxley seems to be suggesting that the ideals of the past have no currency in the present. Lypiatt, like Emily, is an anachronism, the 'actor of heroic parts' in an age that has dispensed with heroism.

After Lypiatt, Mercaptan is next on the visiting list but he is also engaged—in relating his Lesbian experiences to Mrs Speegle. At Coleman's Gumbril is no more successful; he is just in time to catch a glimpse of Shearwater being cuckolded for the third time. Shearwater, who pays the penalty of regarding marriage as a 'measure of intimate hygiene' and sex as algebraic formula, is the first of Huxley's 'abstracting' scientists. The heresy of the scientific attitude lies in treating the abstractions of scientific analysis as though they were real and in regarding everything else as non-existent. Shearwater's sphere of abstraction has stripped away everything except the physiological; when Gumbril and Mrs Viveash finally discover him he is feverishly pedalling away on a stationary bicycle collecting the drops of his own perspiration. Symbolically coffined in his experimental chamber, surrounded by the products of his vivisection—the cocks with engrafted ovaries, the monkeys rejuvenated by the Steinach process—Shearwater's endless 'ride' underlines Huxley's whole view of the scientist's futile search for value.

What the abstracting scientist lacks is proportion. As Shearwater pedals on his nightmare way, trying to work up the pieces of his life 'into a proportionable whole, into a dome that should hang, light, spacious and high, as though by a miracle, on the empty air', he hears an old man crying out, 'Proportion, proportion' (ch. xxii). The old man of Shearwater's delirium is significantly Gumbril Senior and the imaginary dome belongs to the architect's model of Wren's London. The model, a study in architectural proportion, symbolizes the quality the scientist lacks; while Gumbril Senior, himself, is not unlike one of E. M. Forster's redemptive characters: demonstrating the power of goodness, he exercises a mild but benign influence on all who have contact with him. It is during the 'last ride' that Gumbril learns that his father has parted with his precious model to help an old friend. This single act of goodness causes Gumbril to reflect again:

Beyond good and evil? Below good and evil? The name of earwig. . . The tubby pony trotted. The wild columbines suspended, among the shadows of the hazel copse, hooked spurs, helmets of aerial purple. The Twelfth Sonata of Mozart was insecticide; no earwigs could crawl through that music. Emily's breasts were firm and pointed and she had slept at last without a tremor. In the starlight, good, true and beautiful became one. Write the discovery in books—in books *quos*, in the morning, *legimus cacantes*. (ch. xxi)

This is the measure of Gumbril's progress. God as a sense of warmth about the heart, God as truth; were there bridges to join them? In the starlight they become one, but in the morning? The problem remains unsolved. In *Those Barren Leaves* Calamy was to rephrase the question and hazard an answer. It was not very satisfactory: the final solution was still a long way ahead.

Gumbril's search for value is set against the background of the immediate post-war years. Here the range of Huxley's satire is seen at its most extensive; only in *Point Counter Point* does he again attempt such a wide-scale anatomy of the post-war ethos. The background of the war remains in the memories of Mrs Viveash whose acute sense of loss symbolizes the despair of a generation:

. . . she felt no tears behind her eyes. Grief doesn't kill, love doesn't kill; but time kills everything, kills desire, kills sorrow, kills in the end the mind that feels them; wrinkles and softens the body while it still lives, rots it like a medlar, kills it too at last. Never again, never again. Instead of crying, she laughed, laughed aloud. (ch. xiv)

The war memories linger on in 'the legless soldiers grinding barrel-organs . . . the hawkers of toys stamping their leaky boots in the gutters of the Strand', and the brass bands of unemployed ex-soldiers blowing 'mournfully at all the street corners'; while the plight of the Cockney carter, who had walked to Portsmouth in search of work, reflects the encroaching shadow of unemployment. The traditional sources of amelioration offer nothing in the way of consolation. It is scarcely possible that the Reverend Pelvey, M.A., 'foghorning away from behind the imperial bird' has an answer or even a clue. Orthodox religiosity inspires nothing more spiritual than thoughts of pneumatic seats. Education, by encouraging boys to read bad writers' generalizations, is rotting young minds with a diet of vagueness. The prospects of political reform (voiced, somewhat arbitrarily, by Gumbril's tailor) are equally unpromising. No serious-minded person imagines that revolution will bring liberty. The only point in revolution is that it would provide a change. Meanwhile the upper classes, represented by Bruin Opps, exercise their privileged position by expressing a blind indifference to all except themselves. Love amongst this class has become synonymous with sexual licence; and sexual licence, as Mr Bojanus insists, is akin to slavery. Art and science have fared no better: art has become a market for prints and dismal etchings—a chatter about art for art's sake; science has abstracted itself from the last vestiges of reality. This is a world of dried-up values where, ironically, the only real dynamic is found in business. Mr Boldero is the 'complete man' of *Antic Hay*. In Mr Boldero all the humanities meet: he is the patron of all the arts and sciences, the merchant adventurer of the age, whose empire founded on sweated labour and 'scientific' advertising rules the civilized world.

This breakdown of traditional values is depicted, like Eliot's *Waste Land*, against the variegated backcloth of the London scene of the early twenties. The theme of 'The sunless city' is first introduced by Coleman: this is the city of 'seven million distinct and separate individuals':

Millions of them are now sleeping in an empested atmosphere. Hundreds of thousands of couples are at this moment engaged in mutually caressing one another in a manner too hideous to be thought of. . . Thousands of women are now in the throes of parturition, and of both sexes thousands are dying of the most diverse and appalling diseases, or simply because they have lived too long. Thousands are drunk, thousands have over-eaten, thousands have not had enough to eat. And they are all alive, all unique and separate and sensitive. . . (ch. v)

It is Gumbril's city where old women stand at street corners selling matches, where Her Majesty speaks kindly words to crippled orphans, and murderers are hanged at eight o'clock. It is, more specifically, the city of Mercaptan's Chelsea, and the *dix-huitième* parlour in Sloan Street; of Lypiatt's Tottenham Court Road mews with its rabble of dirty children; of Shearwater's Maida Vale, and the drab respectability of life in Bloxam Gardens. And, finally, it is the city of the tall rachitic house in Paddington, where, hidden behind locked doors, lies Gumbril Senior's model of Wren's London. This is the central symbol of the novel: the capital of utopia. It is a city of wide open spaces and broad streets, of sunlight and cleanliness, of order and grandeur; above all, it is a city of 'proportion' dominated at its central point by a great dome: the dome of St Paul's. This is Wren's London, the city he imagined while walking among the still smouldering ruins of the old:

He offered to build for the imagination and the ambitious spirit of man, so that even the most bestial, vaguely and remotely, as they walked those streets, might feel that they were of the same race—or very nearly—as Michelangelo; that they too might feel themselves, in spirit at least, magnificent, strong and free. He offered them all these things . . . But they preferred to re-erect the old intricate squalor; they preferred the mediaeval darkness and crookedness and beastly irregular quaintness; they preferred holes and crannies and winding tunnels; they preferred foul smells, sunless, stagnant air, phthisis and rickets; they preferred ugliness and pettiness and dirt; they preferred the wretched human scale, the scale of the sickly body, not of the mind. (ch. xi)

The theme of the sunless city is picked up again in the night club scene. The monster of 'the play within the play' is the symbolic child of this huge town whose domes and spires are hidden from the sun: conceived in 'lust and darkness', the product of phthisis and rickets, he is destined to live out his life loveless 'in dirt and impurity'. The contrast, as in *Crome Yellow*, is made between the present reality and an idyllic past. The monster recalls how the young boys and girls of Sparta had wrestled together naked in the sun, pure with 'the chastity of beautiful animals'.

The city of the monster is little more than a caricature of the real city; nevertheless it foreshadows the closing scenes of the novel where Gumbril and Mrs Viveash make their 'Last Ride Together'. Their taxi shuttles backwards and forwards across London, from the scene of Lypiatt's attempted suicide to where Coleman is cuckolding Shearwater, until finally they arrive at the Golgotha Hospital in Southwark. Here, where Shearwater pedals slowly and unremittingly along his futile and endless road, Gumbril and Mrs Viveash look out across the river to where St Paul's—the symbol of 'proportion', of London as it might have been—'floated up as though self-supported in the moonlight'. On the other side of the courtyard in the huge hospital some of the city's 'seven million distinct and separate individuals' are 'dying of the most diverse and appalling diseases'. Here, there is pain without end:

Gumbril and Mrs. Viveash leaned their elbows on the sill. . . Like time the river flowed, stanchlessly, as though from a wound in the world's side. For a long time they were silent. They looked out, without speaking, across the flow of time, at the stars, at the human symbol hanging miraculously in the moonlight. . .

'Tomorrow,' said Gumbril at last, meditatively.

'Tomorrow,' Mrs. Viveash interrupted him, 'will be as awful as to-day.' She breathed it like a truth from beyond the grave prematurely revealed. . . (ch. xxii)

V

Those Barren Leaves (1925)

Huxley's first two novels were primarily vehicles for satire; in neither was there any suggestion of a palliative, unless Gumbril's brief romantic interlude be considered as such. *Those Barren Leaves* continues in the satiric vein but a more serious spirit of inquiry permeates the novel and, more significantly, a tentative solution is offered. That the solution should lie in the form of contemplative mysticism is of particular interest as it foreshadows the main line of Huxley's subsequent development.

In terms of form the novel marks a return to the country-house party formula which Huxley had used so successfully in *Crome Yellow*. The summer palace of the Cybo Malaspina, under the aegis of the histrionic Mrs Aldwinkle, has a truly Peacockian flavour; while the guests make up the now familiar circle of social and artistic dilettanti. The satirical portraiture of the previous novels reappears in a more highly developed form. Mrs Aldwinkle, the ageing *salonnière*, is another Priscilla Wimbush; but while the latter devoted herself to the pursuit of the occult, Mrs Aldwinkle's twin passions are art and love. Unfortunately she has no talent for either and like her predecessor lives a vicarious existence through others. To this end she has acquired the decaying grandeurs of the Cybo Malaspina. The Italian villa, moulded by Mrs Aldwinkle's fertile imagination, has assumed an illustrious past and become a palace dedicated to art and culture and amorous pursuits of the loftiest kind:

. . . what marvellous symposia had been held within those walls—centuries even before they were built—what intellectual feasts! Aquinas, here, had confided to an early Malaspina his secret doubt on the predicability of rollations. . . Dante had insisted on the advantages of having a Platonic mistress whom one never met and who could, when necessary, be identified with Theology. . . Learned Boccaccio had discoursed on the genealogy of the gods. . . Michelangelo had expounded his plans for the façade of San Lorenzo in Florence. Galileo had speculated why it is only up to thirty-two feet that Nature abhors a vacuum. . . And then, what brilliant ladies heightened the lustre of these feasts! Lovely, perennially young, accomplished as the protagonists of Castiglione's *Courtier*, amorous in the extreme—they inspired the men of genius to yet higher flights, they capped their hardiest sallies with a word of feminine grace. (Pt. i, ch. iii)

It was Mrs Aldwinkle's ambition to revive these ancient glories, to see herself as 'a princess, surrounded by a court of poets, philosophers and artists'.

The guests of the Cybo Malaspina can hardly be expected to live up to these flights of fancy. There is Miss Thriplow, the successful female novelist and the star of Mrs Aldwinkle's ring of protégées, whose particular forte is 'genuineness'; and Mrs Aldwinkle's niece, Irene, a younger version of Mary Bracegirdle. Irene Aldwinkle, like her predecessor, has read Havelock Ellis and arrived at similar conclusions on the superfluous nature of chastity. Her problems, however, are not of a sexual nature: she is torn between art and underclothing. 'The struggle between her inclinations and what Aunt Lilian considered good', we are told, 'was prolonged and distressing'. Her lover, Lord Hovendon, is faced with a similar dilemma: immensely rich, he has discovered that there are poor people whose lives are more arduous than his own; converted to Guild Socialism, he now finds the demands of social reform conflict with grouse shooting and courting Irene Aldwinkle. Finally there is Mr Falx, one of Mrs Aldwinkle's 'lions'. In a different age he would have been a minor prophet, a voice of the Lord, but having been born in the previous century and passed 'the years of his early manhood in the profession which, between three and seven, every male child desires to embrace— that of the engine driver—he had become not exactly a prophet, but a Labour leader' (Pt. i, ch. iii). Huxley no doubt lived to regret the engine-driver slight, but Mr Falx is a minor figure and the sketch is in keeping with the light satiric vein running through the early pages of the novel. Later, in compensation, Mr Falx is given the last word on Mrs Aldwinkle's artistic establishment and its pretensions:

... in the heat and darkness of Yorkshire coal-mines, in tea-plantations on the slopes of the Himalaya, in Japanese banks, at the mouth of Mexican oil-wells, in steamers walloping along across the China Sea ... men and women of every race and colour were doing their bit to supply Mrs. Aldwinkle with her income. On the two hundred and seventy thousand pounds of Mrs. Aldwinkle's capital the sun never set. People worked; Mrs. Aldwinkle led the higher life. She for art only, they—albeit unconscious of the privilege—for art in her. (Pt. 1, ch. vi)

This is all very good fun, as the critics have pointed out, and, although these minor conflicts and dissatisfactions foreshadow the main theme of the novel, if Huxley had stopped here, *Those Barren Leaves* would have been little more than another *Crome Yellow*. What changes the whole picture is Huxley's treatment of Mrs Aldwinkle's other great passion: 'compared with it' even art 'hardly existed'. With the 'parallel loves' of Chelifer, Cardan and Calamy, the novel is transformed from a light satire into a morality on love, age and death; the depth of the discussion is deepened and, for the first time, Huxley becomes seriously involved with the problems which are to preoccupy him for the remainder of his life. Further, the first positive reaffirmation of value appears with Calamy's 'conversion' at the close. As we have seen, romantic love offers the only hint of value in the otherwise barren landscape of *Antic Hay*. Gumbril's affair with Emily is a slight but potential source of redemption. Some time after his second novel, however, Huxley became absorbed in Proust, or so it would seem. The Proustian influence is certainly clearly visible in *Those Barren Leaves*,[1] and in this novel romantic love is savaged in all its aspects—only the relatively insignificant Irene and Hovendon remain unscathed. This shift in emphasis undoubtedly prepares

[1] Jocelyn Brooke comments on Huxley's 'Proustian pessimism' in *Those Barren Leaves* and detects Proustian influence in the delineation of character. *Aldous Huxley*, pp. 17–18.

the way for the Laurentian approach of *Point Counter Point*; meanwhile Huxley like Gumbril had come to realize that innocence was no solution. It is not without significance that Calamy picks up the threads where Gumbril left off. *Antic Hay* ended with Gumbril, cynical and disillusioned, departing for the continent: *Those Barren Leaves* begins with Calamy, fresh from his travels, prepared to face the same contemporary scene, but from a different viewpoint.

The theme of romantic love is introduced innocently enough. There is Cardan, the Scogan of *Those Barren Leaves*, deploring its absence in the post-Freudian era:

To those for whom love has become as obvious an affair as eating dinner, for whom there are no blushful mysteries, no reticences, no fancy-fostering concealments, but only plain speaking and the facts of nature—how flat and stale the whole business must become. . . Too much light conversation about the Oedipus complex, and anal erotism is taking the edge off love. (Pt. I, ch. iii)

And there is Mrs Aldwinkle stoutly defending her favourite doctrine against all odds:

One must always follow the spontaneous motions of the heart; it is the divine within us that stirs in the heart. And one must worship Eros so reverently that one can never be content with anything but the most poignant, most passionate manifestations of his power. To be content with a love that has turned in the course of time to mere affection, kindliness and quiet comprehension is almost to blaspheme against the name of Eros. Your true lover . . . leaves the old, paralytic love and turns wholeheartedly to the young passion. (Pt. I, ch. viii)

This is a dangerous doctrine likely to breed its own nemesis, which it duly does, but the irony is not apparent until later. It is Chelifer's following of 'the spontaneous motions of the heart' that strikes the first serious note. Chelifer's Proustian episode represents not only a shift in time—it is related as an autobiographical flashback—it is also a change in key. The affair with Barbara Waters is described in a realistic narrative that owes nothing to Peacock and more than a little to the first volume of Proust's epic.

64

Chelifer first meets Barbara when he is fourteen: the experience is overwhelming. They are separated for a few years until Chelifer returns from the war. They meet again and become lovers, but the process is one of gradual disenchantment as Chelifer becomes aware of her real nature; like Swann he learns that it is possible to be profoundly and slavishly in love with someone for whom he has no esteem. It is only a matter of time before he is able to confirm her infidelity; meanwhile he passes from a state of Denis-like innocence to one of deep cynicism. The result is an abnegation of responsibility reminiscent of Gumbril after he has lost Emily. If Chelifer has no inclination to turn wholeheartedly to young passions, Mrs Aldwinkle has; the ironic twist comes when he is duly washed up at her feet 'like Leander . . . on the sands of Abydos'. Mrs Aldwinkle is able to indulge her twin passions in one and the same person. Chelifer at once becomes the greatest living poet and Mrs Aldwinkle his sole interpreter, while her passion for him begins to assume outsize proportions; she had started loving because she believed in love but the circumstances and the person were the product of her own imagination. Mrs Aldwinkle is the victim of her own illusions and a doctrine which, apart from anything else, makes no allowance for the encroachment of age. The sexual problem had been neatly summed up by Calamy earlier in the novel:

For either you're in love with the woman or you aren't; either you're carried away by your inflamed imagination (for, after all, the person you're really violently in love with is always your own invention and the wildest of fancies) or by your senses and your intellectual curiosity. If you aren't in love, it's a mere experiment in applied physiology, with a few psychological investigations thrown in to make it a little more interesting. But if you are, it means that you become enslaved, involved, dependent on another human being in a way that's positively disgraceful. . . (Pt. I, ch. vii)

Chelifer and Mrs Aldwinkle are both enslaved by their 'inflamed imaginations;' Calamy and Miss Thriplow, who know better, are content to satisfy their intellectual curiosities with 'a few psychological investigations'. The choice lies between Proust on one hand and Freud and Havelock Ellis on the other: both equally unrewarding. For Calamy the final answer is total celibacy, tempered a little by the admission that 'in itself, no doubt, the natural and moderate satisfaction of the sexual instincts is a matter quite indifferent to morality' (Pt. v, ch. iv). The tone lacks conviction: this was mere Sunday-school sermonising as Huxley was well aware. He had no real answer to the problem and in *Point Counter Point* he returned to view it in a fresh light. Lawrence's 'new mythology of nature' was to provide a way out of the impasse, even though it proved only a temporary one.

Those Barren Leaves, as I suggested earlier, is, in spite of the Peacockian elements, a morality on love, age and death. The theme of death's imminence is reserved almost exclusively for Cardan. Cardan, the middle-aged sceptic and rationalist is superficially another Scogan. Like his predecessor he was 'brought up in the simple faith of nineteenth-century materialism' and had believed in 'the ultimate explicability of everything in terms of physics and chemistry' (Pt. i, ch. iii). As the scientific realist he enjoys deflating Mrs Aldwinkle's romantic extravagances. The Shelleyesque clouds, he reminds her, depend for their existence upon the earth's excrementitious dust: 'There are thousands of particles to every cubic centimetre. The water vapour condenses round them in droplets sufficiently large to be visible. Hence the clouds—marvellous and celestial shapes, but with a core of dust. What a symbol of human idealism' (Pt. ii, ch. i). Scogan, the abstracting materialist, had rationalised all the joy out of life: Cardan, however, has a heavier moral burden to bear. Mrs Aldwinkle from being a figure of fun had become one of pathos; like so many of Huxley's portraits of middle age she freezes into a morality figure, an exemplar of wrong behaviour. Cardan is destined to a similar fate. He has lived a full life, has 'drunk well, eaten well and copiously made love', but he has taken no account of the passing of time. Keith, the erudite sensualist of *South Wind*, recognized only one sin, vice or crime on earth and that the vice of old age; as for death, like Mrs Aldwinkle, he hated anything that reminded him of it—it was the one flaw in an uninterrupted life of pleasure. Cardan is likewise unprepared; alone, at nightfall, he meditates on the inevitable end:

Old age, sickness, decrepitude; the bath-chair, the doctor, the bright efficient nurse; and the long agony, the struggle for breath, the thickening darkness, the end, and then. . . (Pt. III, ch. vi)

Cardan is rescued from his gloomy thoughts by the arrival of Grace Elver and her brother, but this is merely another trick that fate has in store for him. Grace Elver, like the 'dog from the skies' in *Eyeless in Gaza*, is the *deus ex machina* that is to shatter Cardan's complacency once and for all. From that moment his life is plagued with uncertainty. On the way to Rome he passes the family vaults of the Volumni; the obese effigies smile as if to say that they enjoyed life and considered death without horror, but a few miles on at Assisi, the tomb of St Claire offers *mementi mori* of a very different kind:

Think of death, says the she-saint, ponder incessantly on the decay of all things, the transience of this sublunary life. Think, think; and in the end life itself will lose all its savour; death will corrupt it; the flesh will seem a shame and a disgustfulness. Think of death hard enough and you will come to deny the beauty and the holiness of life. . . (Pt. IV, ch. ii)

Cardan reflects that when Goethe visited Assisi the only thing he looked at was the portico of a second-rate Roman temple. The wise man does not think of death lest it spoil his pleasure; but the fates give Cardan little opportunity to think of anything else. The 'transience of this sublunary life' is exemplified by the suddenness and violence of Grace Elver's death. Later he recalls the hideous manner in which she died; his thoughts become more generalized and he reflects how inevitably the spirit always succumbs to the body:

Sooner or later every soul is stifled by the sick body; sooner or later there are no more thoughts, but only pain and vomiting and stupor . . . The spirit has no significance; there is only the body. When it is young, the body is beautiful and strong. It grows old, its joints creak, it becomes dry and smelly; it breaks down, the life goes out of it and it rots away. However lovely the feathers on a bird's head, they perish with it; and the spirit, which is a lovelier ornament than any, perishes too. The farce is hideous, thought Mr. Cardan, and in the worst of bad taste. (Pt. IV, ch. ix)

Once again, he wonders how he himself will die.

Huxley had as yet no real answer to Cardan's problem. Calamy, faced with Cardan's gloomiest sentiments on the death of the spirit, points out that salvation is not in the next world; for those who desire it, it is here and now. This is true as far as it goes; but, as Cardan insists, it is really begging the question and, pressed further, Calamy has to fall back on an idealist solution:

Certainly, as things seem to happen, it's as if the body did get hold of the soul and kill it. But the real facts of the case may be entirely different. The body as we know it is an invention of the mind. What is the reality on which the abstracting, symbolizing mind does its work of abstraction and symbolism? It is possible that, at death, we may find out. And in any case, what is death, *really*? (Pt. v, ch. iv)

This was hardly likely to satisfy Cardan. The human mind may have 'invented space, time and matter, picking them out of reality in a quite arbitrary fashion'; but, as Calamy admits, you 'can't help behaving *as if* things really were as they seem to be'. The death of Grace Elver had left no doubt as to that. Rampion, too, was to take the same view in *Point Counter Point* and the later novel is haunted by this problem. Only with *Time Must Have a Stop* could Huxley confidently assert that 'the real facts of the case may be entirely different' and suggest the basis for a belief in survival after death.

Whatever the contemporary reader may have felt about Calamy's answers, it was significant that Huxley was beginning to think seriously about the main biological themes of love, age and death. What, however, was more important at this stage was his treatment of them, the kind of response they were designed to arouse. Both Mrs Aldwinkle and Cardan are cast into a morality mould, exemplars intended to bludgeon the reader into an alternative pattern of behaviour. There are no heroic postures, no redeeming features; in fact, love and death are both presented in such a way as to leave nothing between profound cynicism on one hand and the 'monastic robe' on the other. 'Think of death hard enough and you will come to deny the beauty and holiness of life.' St Claire had become a nun; another faced with the same set of facts might well become a cynic. In *Point Counter Point*, armed with the neo-Laurentian philosophy of *Do What You Will*, Huxley tried to find an alternative route. The attempt was to prove a failure and, faced with the same choice, Anthony Beavis finally accepts the 'monastic robe'. This was to be the pattern of all Huxley's later work: the reactions of Will Farnaby to the facts of love and death are scarcely removed from those of Cardan and Chelifer. The cynicism remains: what ultimately changes is that the 'monastic robe' becomes humanized with the course of time; and in the mystical society of *Island*, 'death' and the 'beauty and holiness of life' are finally reconciled.

The opposing attitudes are dramatised to some extent in the clash between Chelifer and Calamy. Chelifer's cynicism with its accompanying abnegation of responsibility has been frequently pinned on the author. Huxley himself was partly to blame for this: while Chelifer is a convincing character, Calamy simply is not. Chelifer's attitude is a consistent one and we are made aware of its origin. Calamy, as the visitor hero, appears from nowhere; nothing is known of his past except for a few intimations from Mrs Aldwinkle that he was rich, handsome and an amorist who had left London 'at the height of his success and gone travelling round the world to improve his mind'. Then on the strength of the most trivial affair with Miss Thriplow—one of the 'experiments in applied physiology'—the reader is expected to accept his full-blooded conversion to the celibate life. All this points to a structural failure within the novel, and to give Calamy's conversion some conviction one feels that the 'Fragments from the Autobiography' should have, by right, belonged to him rather than to Chelifer. As the novel stands there is everything to justify Chelifer's behaviour and nothing to justify Calamy's.

Moreover Chelifer's viewpoint cannot be entirely dissociated from that of the author. After the disastrous episode with Barbara Waters, Chelifer reflects:

I thought of my passion for universal justice, of my desire that all men should be free, leisured, educated, of my imaginations of a future earth peopled by human beings who should live according to reason. But of what use is leisure, when leisure is occupied with listening-in and going to football matches? freedom, when men voluntarily enslave themselves to politicians like those who now rule the world? education, when the literate read the evening papers and the fiction magazines? And the future; the radiant future—supposing that it should differ from the past . . . what has that to do with me? Nothing whatever. Nothing, nothing, nothing. (Pt. II, ch. v)

There is more evidence of genuine spiritual conflict here than in all Calamy's dallyings with Miss Thriplow; but, more specifically, the passage illustrates Huxley's growing distaste for social reform and anything remotely related to the idea of 'progress'. There was no hint of anything indicative of a political solution in Huxley's first two novels and *Those Barren Leaves*, in spite of the presence of Mr Falx, does nothing to enlarge this view. Whenever the question of social reform is touched on the tone is invariably pessimistic. Chelifer sums up the general mood of the novel: '. . . the millennium which seemed in the days of Godwin not so very remote has receded further and further from us, as each Reform Bill, each victory over entrenched capitalism dashed yet another illusion to the ground' (Pt. II, ch. i). Chelifer's domestic life centred on Miss Carruther's Chelsea boarding-house broadens the social picture and enables Huxley to make some trenchant comments on the life of the middle-class. It is not material poverty that he is concerned with but spiritual poverty. If the plight of the middle-class burgess is one of total degradation, what would be the result of social reform? First of all the worker would be reduced to the same level of wretchedness; with the arrival of the utopian state everyone would be well-off, educated and leisured and everyone would be bored. This equation of material progress with spiritual sterility is considered in some detail in

'Work and Leisure', an essay contemporary to the novel. Huxley's conclusions were the same. Is there any evidence, he asks, that universal leisure will bring into existence a race of people as envisaged by Poincaré, Shaw and Wells? The leisured rich of today suggest the contrary: if all human beings lived according to the same pattern, there would simply be an enormous increase in the demand for all the traditional time-killers and substitutes for thought; and large 'numbers of people, hitherto immune from these mental and moral diseases, would be afflicted by ennui, depression and universal dissatisfaction' (*Along the Road*, Pt. IV). In brief, then, the Cybo Malaspina is the microcosm of the future utopian state, and Mrs Aldwinkle and her friends the ultimate of social reform. This view of the future was not particularly sinister —*Brave New World* was yet to come—but it meant that material progress as a source of potential value was definitely out. The 'monastic robe' remained; and although, as I have suggested, Huxley clearly was not yet ready to explore the conversion theme, Calamy's quest must be regarded as the positive counter to Chelifer's cynicism.

Since Calamy's 'conversion' has a definite bearing on the author's future course, it is worth considering the reasons for his choice in some detail. There is some evidence to suggest that Huxley was sympathetic towards the contemplative life before 1925. In *Limbo*, his first volume of short stories, there is the tale of the Spanish nobleman who 'gave away his lands, quitted his former companions, and turned hermit up in the hills' (*The Death of Lully*); and in *Along the Road* there is a situation which offers an exact parallel to that of Calamy.[1] The author has climbed the mountains above Florence to the monastery of Montesenario; he stands meditating on 'the kingdom of silence and solemn beauty' that lies below:

Here at the heart of it . . . a man might begin to understand something about that part of his being which does not reveal itself in the quotidian commerce of life; which the social contacts do not draw forth, spark-

[1] See John Atkins, *Aldous Huxley* (1957), p. 128.

like, from the sleeping flint that is an untried spirit; that part of him, of whose very existence he is only made aware in solitude and silence. And if there happens to be no silence in his life, if he is never solitary, then he may go down to his grave without a knowledge of its existence, much less an understanding of its nature or realization of its potentialities.

Not only does this foreshadow Calamy's mountain retreat, but the intimations are the same as those which precede his conversion. Meditating on 'the great secret, the beauty, the mystery', he decides there is nothing else in life that holds significance for him: it now seemed obvious to him, but it was also obvious that he couldn't do two things at once; look out into 'the silence beyond the futile noise and bustle—into the mental silence that lies beyond the body' and at the same time partake in the tumult himself (Pt. III, ch. xiii). 'The mental silence beyond the body' has more than an echo of Gumbril's 'quiet places of the mind'; it is apparent that Calamy's mystical leanings had a more solid foundation than the idealist philosophizing at the end of the novel would seem to suggest.

Calamy is presented as an Anthony Beavis in embryo, the victim of a *video meliora proboque*; *deteriora sequor* conflict; this aspect of the novel, however, is never fully realized. What is more interesting is the rationalization of the desire to quit 'the quotidian commerce of life' and explore the 'quiet places of the mind'. Here the arch-rivals, science and religion, are brought together in accord for the first and last time in Huxley's work. In one of the stories in *Little Mexican*, published in the previous year, he had written: 'Now it is possible—it is, indeed, almost necessary—for a man of science to be also a mystic'. Cardan echoes this thought when he complains of the 'disquieting scientific modernism which is now turning the staunchest mathematical physicists into mystics' (Pt. I, ch. iii); while Calamy himself captures something of the excitement prevalent in scientific circles at this time:

The sense that everything's perfectly provisional and temporary—everything, from social institutions to what we've hitherto regarded as the most sacred scientific truths—the feeling that nothing, from the Treaty of Versailles to the rationally explicable universe, is really safe, the intimate conviction that anything may happen, anything may be discovered . . . the artificial creation of life, the proof of continued existence after death—why, it's all infinitely exhilarating. (Pt. 1, ch. iii)

One has only to read Eddington's Gifford Lectures[1] of early 1927 to get the exhilarating sense that in the world of science everything was 'perfectly provisional and temporary'. The mechanistic universe of Scogan and Cardan, which had believed in 'the ultimate explicability of everything in terms of physics and chemistry' was gone forever.

By the time Huxley was writing *Those Barren Leaves* Bohr's theory of admissible quantum orbits had shown that the behaviour of the individual atom could not be determined in accordance with any known laws. This involved a complete break with the deterministic scheme of classical physics. In 1927 Heisenberg's Principle of Indeterminacy was to suggest an element of free will at the heart of the atom itself. In Eddington's words: determinism had 'dropped out altogether in the latest formulations of theoretical physics' and it was doubtful whether it would 'ever be brought back'.[2] What was perhaps even more significant was the now accepted view that physics dealt not with the real nature of things but only with abstracted aspects of them. As Eddington says, the 'recognition that our knowledge of the objects treated in physics consists solely of readings of pointers and other indicators transforms our view of the status of physical knowledge in a fundamental way'.[3] In the first place 'recognising that the physical world is entirely abstract and without "actuality" apart from its linkage to consciousness, we restore consciousness to the fundamental position, instead of representing it as an inessential complication occasionally found in the midst of inorganic nature at a late stage of evolutionary history'.[4] Mind, then, is no longer to be regarded as a mere epiphenomenon of matter. To the question, 'What is matter?' Eddington replies, 'matter is something that Mr.

[1] *The Nature of the Physical World.*   [2] op. cit., p. 294.
[3] op. cit., p. 258.   [4] op. cit., p. 332.

X knows.'[1] From here it was only a short step to insisting that matter exists only in so far as the mind has knowledge of it. Mind had become fundamental and matter merely a derivative of the mind's activity. This view was widespread among the 'mystical physicists' and, according to Joad, not only Eddington and Jeans, but Einstein, Schrödinger and Planck all subscribed to it. Huxley was clearly fascinated by this repudiation of nineteenth-century materialism and its bearing on a mystical solution. Calamy refutes Cardan as follows:

Can you talk of the soul being at the mercy of the body, can you give any kind of an explanation of mind in terms of matter? When you reflect that it's the human mind that has invented space, time and matter, picking them out of reality in a quite arbitrary fashion—can you attempt to explain a thing in terms of something it has invented itself? That's the fundamental question. (Pt. v, ch. iv)

Calamy's meditation on the hand is really a rephrasing of Gumbril's question at the beginning of *Antic Hay*: God as exultation as opposed to God as 2+2=4. 'Was there any chance of their being the same? Were there bridges to join the two worlds?' Calamy, putting forward an idealist solution, concludes, somewhat tentatively, that there was a chance of their being the same:

This shape which interrupts the light—it is enough to think of it for five minutes to perceive that it exists simultaneously in a dozen parallel worlds. It exists as electrical charges; as chemical molecules; as living cells; as part of a moral being, the instrument of good and evil; in the physical world and in mind. And from this one goes on to ask, inevitably, what relationship exists between these different modes of being. What is there in common between life and chemistry; between good and evil and electric charges; between a collection of cells and the consciousness of a caress? It's here that the gulfs begin to open. For there isn't any connection—that one can see, at any rate. Universe lies on the top of universe, layer after layer, distinct and separate. . . And each one has just as much right to exist and to call itself real as any other. And you can't explain one in terms of the others. . . The only hope . . . is that, perhaps, if you went on thinking long enough and hard

[1] op. cit., p. 262.

enough, you might arrive at an explanation. . . Perhaps it's really . . .
all mind, all spirit. The rest is only apparent, an illusion. (Pt. v, ch. i.)

Eddington was to suggest that the 'idea of a universal Mind or
Logos would be . . . a fairly plausible inference from the present
state of scientific theory'.[1] But was it really all as simple as this?
Had the 'mystical physicists' really provided the answer? The
sceptical materialist, Cardan, was to have the last word:

. . . philosophically and even, according to the new physics, scientifically speaking, matter may not be matter, *really*. But the fact
remains that something having all the properties we have always
attributed to matter is perpetually getting in our way, and that our
minds do, in point of fact, fall under the dominion of certain bits of
this matter, known as our bodies, changing as they change and keeping
pace with their decay. (Pt. v, ch. iv)

The idealist tendencies of the 'new physics' were to come under
severe criticism and, as Russell pointed out, the 'progress of
biology, physiology and psychology has made it more probable
than it ever was before that all natural phenomena are governed
by the laws of physics'.[2] Huxley, certainly, never toyed with an
idealist solution again. In *Point Counter Point* Rampion was to
debunk the abstractions of the physicists as irrelevancies; and with
the death of little Phil the soul is once more 'stifled by the sick
body'. In the end Huxley was to accept the fundamental dichotomy of mind and matter, but over and above mind and matter
there was to be the divine Ground, the principle of ultimate reality
immanent in all things.

The approach to the perennial philosophy was, as I suggested in
an earlier chapter, essentially empirical; and the germ of the argument, later to appear in *Ends and Means*, is voiced by Calamy:

. . . the axes chosen by the best observers have always been startlingly
like one another. Gotama, Jesus and Lao-tsze, for example; they lived
sufficiently far from one another in space, time and social position. But
their pictures of reality resemble one another very closely. The nearer

[1] op. cit., p. 338.
[2] Bertrand Russell, *The Scientific Outlook* (1962), p. 125.

a man approaches these in penetration, the more nearly will his axes of moral reference correspond with theirs. (Pt. v, ch. iv)

Here Calamy is on firmer ground and this was to be the route which Huxley was eventually to take. There was, however, one final reason why Calamy's solution could never have been totally satisfactory. In *Proper Studies* Huxley points out that most organized religions were simply a 'de-spiritualization' of the ways of life proposed by Jesus, Gautama and Lao-tsze; that all the founders of the great historical religions, except Confucius, had been solitaries and spirituals. This is the basis of Calamy's justification for his decision to withdraw to the mountain fastness and live the life of a twentieth-century Milarepa. But, as Chelifer insists, has one the moral right 'to ignore what for ninety-nine out of every hundred human beings is reality—even though it mayn't actually be the real thing'? (Pt. v, ch. iv). Calamy replies that one has a right to be what one is. If one is a born mystic, then, that is enough. This could hardly satisfy Huxley for long and two years later, as though in answer to his own question, he takes to task Professor Whitehead and Dean Inge for proposing that 'Solitariness is the real essence of religion' (*Proper Studies*). He admits that it may be superior to social and formalized religion, but the fact remains that it excludes the majority. This is the moral difficulty presented by any mystical solution and in particular the course taken by Calamy: that it is simply physically and psychologically impossible for the majority of mankind. Huxley had no liking for social or formalized religion; he was consistent in his antipathy and so the problem remained unsolved. Not until the publication of *Island*, almost forty years later, was he able to offer the concept of a society in which mysticism played an integral part and was not merely the escape shaft for a privileged minority.

VI

Point Counter Point (1928)

P oint Counter Point recorded a significant stage in Huxley's
development both as a novelist and a moralist. As a literary
form it was his most ambitious attempt to break free of the
restrictions imposed by the house-party formula of *Crome Yellow*
and *Those Barren Leaves* while still retaining the essential features
of the 'novel of ideas'. In terms of moral development it marked
a temporary rejection of the mystical route and a divergence from
what is now generally accepted as the author's main line of evolution. Why, one may ask, was Calamy's solution rejected so
emphatically at this time? Two factors seem to have been largely
contributory. In 1925 Huxley made a tour of the far east, and
early in the following year he renewed his acquaintance with
D. H. Lawrence.[1] This was the beginning of a friendship which
lasted until the latter's death in 1930. Huxley's visit to the east was
on the whole a disappointing affair; in *Jesting Pilate* he confesses:

In Europe . . . and still more, no doubt, in America, the Way of
Gautama has all the appearance of the way of Salvation. One is all for
religion until one visits a really religious country. . . To travel is to
discover that everybody is wrong. The philosophies, the civilizations
which seem, at a distance, so superior to those current at home, all
prove on a close inspection to be in their own way just as hopelessly
imperfect. (Pt. II)

Philip Quarles, the autobiographical character of *Point Counter
Point*, expresses similar feelings while returning from India:

What a comfort it will be to be back in Europe again! And to think

[1] Lawrence wrote from Spotorno to Huxley in India and suggested a meeting
on the latter's return. Their reunion took place in Florence in 1926. They had
previously met during the war when Lawrence was planning his Village of the
Dark God, Ranamin.

there was a time when I read books about yoga and did breathing exercises and tried to persuade myself that I didn't really exist! What a fool! (ch. vi)

Huxley's friendship with Lawrence made a profound impression on him, and only began to lose some of its immediacy after Lawrence's death. He was one of the few people Huxley felt 'real respect and admiration for'; Philip Quarles's notebooks reveal a comparative respect for Rampion. There is little doubt that when *Point Counter Point* was written, Huxley was a confirmed convert to Lawrence's ideas and the novel with its sympathetic portraits of Frieda and Lawrence as Mary and Mark Rampion is in many respects a tribute to their friendship. Huxley's debt to Lawrence was further acknowledged in *Do What You Will*, the volume of essays published in the same year. To what extent Lawrence actually caused Huxley to deviate from his original path is a matter of argument. The strong anti-clerical element prevalent in Huxley's writing at this time was undoubtedly the result of Lawrence's influence; on the other hand, Lawrence merely reinforced Huxley's growing distrust of intellectualism, and *Point Counter Point* and *Brave New World* represent Huxley's most concentrated attack on the scientific attitude and its effect on the modern world.

The outstanding feature of *Point Counter Point*, as a form, lies in the extensive use of parallel plots involving a large number of characters. This method is discussed at some length in one of Philip Quarles's notebook extracts:

A novelist modulates by reduplicating situations and characters. He shows several people falling in love, or dying, or praying in different ways—dissimilars solving the same problem. Or, *vice versa*, similar people confronted with dissimilar problems. In this way you can modulate through all the aspects of your theme, you can write variations in any number of different moods. (ch. xxii)

Both kinds of variation are used effectively in this novel, but as E. K. Brown has noted, neither is as important structurally as the device of repetition: 'The novel opens on a crisis in the life of Walter Bidlake, who turns from the bloodless Marjorie Carling to the predatory Lucy Tantamount. Walter's story is a prelude for the story of his sister, Elinor, the main action of the novel. Elinor turns from the bloodless Philip Quarles to the predatory Everard Webley. Both Walter and Elinor are fearfully hurt, although not in the same way, by the entrance into their lives of the predatory characters. . . Repetition is the dominant device; still if Walter and Elinor are similar, they are not the same, they do not duplicate each other, and the shades of variation, although secondary, are essential to the effect that Huxley achieves.'[1] The crises in the lives of Walter Bidlake and Elinor Quarles provide the main structure of the novel but numerous examples of repetition with minor variations can be drawn from the sub-plot material. Thus John Bidlake and Sidney Quarles, the respective fathers of Walter and Elinor, both indulge in extra-marital relationships. Once again we find dissimilars confronted by the same problem; the variations occur in their respective attitudes. John Bidlake, who is no respecter of conventions, 'sleeps around' with superb indifference to all concerned; Sidney Quarles, in contrast, resorts to subterfuge and guile, conducting his affairs behind a screen of bogus research in the British Museum Library. Moreover the device of repetition, as Quarles's notebook suggests, allows the author to write variations in any number of different moods: thus the pregnancy of the luckless Marjorie Carling is treated with some degree of sympathy; while the pregnancy of Gladys Helmsly, the good-time girl with the Cockney accent, who is Sidney Quarles's mistress, becomes the subject of farce. By this method Huxley introduces a great deal of variety into a few basic situations, while still using the novel essentially as a vehicle for the exposition of ideas.

In spite of the repetitive nature of the plot, it is not strictly contrapuntal; the great variety of incidental matter is related thematically, but there is no overall causal connection between the parallel plots; the characters do not develop or change in any way and there is no final resolution. Huxley, undoubtedly, did himself an injustice by inviting comparison with Gide's *The Coiners* (Philip

[1] *Rhythm in the Novel* (Toronto, 1950), pp. 8–9.

Quarles's notebook entries on the 'musicalization of fiction' echo Edouard's 'what I should like to do is something like the art of fugue-writing'.)[1] As many critics have pointed out, in Gide's novel the theme of counterfeiting is repeated at different levels; the counterpoint enters when these parallels begin to react, and the whole is the successful resolution of an inner conflict. In *Point Counter Point*, as Burgum demonstrates, only 'minor conflicts are resolved in a murder or a rupture of friendship. No development takes place in the totality of relationships. These remain what they were at the beginning, a chaos of contrasts'; it follows, so Burgum concludes, that Huxley's novel is 'an aesthetic failure, since the pattern promised by the title is never achieved'.[2] It is difficult, however, to take Burgum's conclusion seriously; for it to have any validity, the two novels would need to have more in common; as it is, apart from a few minor borrowings the resemblance is largely superficial. The 'novel of ideas', as originated by Peacock, was by its nature a static affair in which ideas took precedence over everything else. By the introduction of multiple plots Huxley created something of a hybrid form, but to judge this by the standards of the conventional novel would be misleading. The counterpoint lies simply in the juxtaposition of parallel plots, character-ideas and related symbolism, and the worst that can be said of *Point Counter Point* is that the title suggests something more ambitious.

The theme is expressed in its simplest form in a line from the Fulke Greville quotation, which serves as an epigraph for the novel, 'Passion and reason, self-division's cause'. The dichotomy between passion and reason has appeared before; it was a latent theme in the *video meliora proboque*; *deteriora sequor* motif of the earlier novels. Now it is affirmed as the essential condition of modern man. Science and Christianity have repressed the bodily instincts, and this has led to an over-development of the mental consciousness. The result has been a psychological degeneration, an almost complete atrophying of one side of the human faculty,

---

[1] André Gide, *The Coiners* (1958), p. 210.

[2] Edwin Berry Burgum, *The Novel and the World's Dilemma*, p. 152.

but the repressed emotions have never been completely extinguished—man, therefore, is a divided being, continually in a state of war with himself. As Rampion explains: 'A man's a creature on a tight-rope, walking delicately, equilibrated, with mind and consciousness and spirit at one end of his balancing pole and body and instinct and all that's unconscious and earthy and mysterious at the other. Balanced' (ch. xxxiv). Modern man, by his 'pathetic belief in rationalism and the absolute supremacy of mental values', has disturbed the balance and invited the principle of nemesis.

The counter theme expresses the Laurentian idea that 'Life is only bearable when the mind and body are in harmony, and there is a natural balance between them'.[1] It is exemplified by the Rampions, the two integrated characters in the novel. The ideal, in Rampion's terms, is to be 'a perfect animal *and* a perfect human', to harmonise reason, feeling and instinct. Barbarism is being one-sided; Christianity has made us barbarians of the soul, and now science is making us barbarians of the intellect. In this context Rampion sees the whole of modern civilization as the fruit of organized professional intellectualism; the scientists are engaged in a futile search for non-human truths, so that by abstracting themselves from the human world of reality they can get a faint glimpse of the universe as it would appear through non-human eyes. The Christians are no better: absolute good and evil 'belong to the [same] class of irrelevant non-human facts' as wave mechanics and relativity. At the root of man's refusal to accept life on a human level lies a fundamental hatred of sex for which the scientist and the Christian are equally responsible. The modern trend to promiscuity is simply another form of sex hatred: 'Christianity turned inside out. The ascetic contempt for the body expressed in a different way' (ch. x). Everyone is perverted by trying to be non-human: 'Non-humanly religious, non-humanly moral, non-humanly intellectual and scientific, non-humanly specialized and efficient. . . . Perverted towards goodness or badness, towards flesh or spirit; but always away from the central

[1] D. H. Lawrence, *À Propos of Lady Chatterley's Lover* (1961), p. 92.

norm, always away from humanity' (ch. xxxiv). The central norm, Rampion's ideal of harmony, is rendered symbolically by his painting of the naked couple embracing against a background of rocks and shrubbery. The painting depicts man and woman restored to their rightful place at the centre of the universe, with physical love 'as the source of light and life and beauty':

These two bodies were the source of the whole illumination of the picture. The rocks and tree trunks in the foreground were silhouetted against the light that issued from them. The precipice behind them was golden with the same light. It touched the lower surface of the leaves above, throwing shadows up into a thickening darkness of greenery. It streamed out of the recess in which they lay . . . creating by its radiance an astounding flora of gigantic roses and zinnias and tulips, with horses and leopards and little antelopes coming and going between the huge flowers. . . (ch. xvi)

In contrast to this symbol of natural harmony, physical love among the characters of *Point Counter Point* has ceased to be anything but a source of frustration and discord. The repression of sensuality has created an inner conflict between passion and reason, and fostered an environment where the extremes of chastity and promiscuity exist side by side. This complex of perverted sexuality is exemplified in the relationships of the Bidlakes, Tantamounts and Quarles. In 'Fashions in Love', an essay in *Do What You Will*, Huxley discusses the two hostile attitudes to love which existed at the time: 'One is the conception evolved by the nineteenth century out of the ideals of Christianity on the one hand and romanticism on the other. The other is that still rather inchoate and negative conception which contemporary youth is in process of forming out of the materials provided by modern psychology.' The twentieth-century conception, which owes its basic attitude to the Ellises and Krafft-Ebings, is a violent reaction to the repressions and taboos of the previous century; its promiscuity, far from acting as a corrective, merely reinforces the fundamental dichotomy in a different way. This idea is worked out in the opening sequence of the novel which depicts a crisis in the life of Walter Bidlake. Walter Bidlake and Marjorie Carling both embody the nineteenth-century conception of love. Walter is the incorrigible romantic whose ideal is based on Shelley's 'Epipsychidion'. He believed that sex was only an irrelevancy to be kept as far as possible in the background. Marjorie, representing the Christian ideal, has been brought up to believe in the ugliness of the animal part of human nature, and the beauty of the spirit. At first all is well. After two years, however, Marjorie's bloodless virtue begins to pall, and Walter's repressed instincts are in open revolt. The new object of his desires is Lucy Tantamount who, nevertheless, epitomizes all the values his conscious reason rejects. Thus Walter is depicted as the first example of the passion–reason conflict. Lucy Tantamount, who is another Myra Viveash, embodies the 'negative conception of contemporary youth' which regards sex as a commonplace activity and a source of amusement. Her emancipation is the freedom to enjoy herself—to ruthlessly have her fun. Moreover her sensuality is detached, an object of her conscious will: she encourages Walter's tenderness only to draw back from him, leaving him unjustified, his guiltiness unpalliated. Lucy is presented here as the antithesis of the Laurentian ideal. As the essayist points out, 'Nothing is more dreadful than a cold, unimpassioned indulgence. And love infallibly becomes cold and unimpassioned when it is too lightly made' (*Do What You Will*).[1] It is not good to have too much liberty and the result of Lucy's 'unimpassioned indulgence', the fate of all Huxley's female reprobates, is boredom, the never-ending search for fresh stimulation. This episode is largely a restatement of Calamy's findings: that there could be no solution to the problem of sexuality while the choice lay between 'romanticism' and detached sensuality. Calamy had settled for the life of the celibate; in *Point Counter Point* Rampion suggests a way out of the dilemma.

The failure in sex relationships can be traced to a similar breakdown in the lives of the previous generation. Here the effect of the division between cerebration and sensuality is stated with allegorical simplicity. Thus Lord Edward is another Shearwater, the

[1] A view endorsed by the much maligned Ellis. See *The Psychology of Sex* (1944), pp. 293–4.

scientist whose over-cerebration has left him with the instincts, intuitions and feelings of a child. As a practising biologist he takes a professional interest in the sexual activities of axolotls and chickens, but any mention of the corresponding activities of human beings leaves him painfully ill at ease. 'Intellectually, in the laboratory, he understood the phenomenon of sex. But in practice and emotionally he was a child, a fossil mid-Victorian child, preserved intact, with all the natural childish timidities and all the taboos acquired from two beloved and very virtuous maiden aunts . . .' (ch. ii). Accordingly his wife seeks consolation with John Bidlake who, in contrast to Lord Edward, is what Rampion would have called a 'barbarian of the senses', a healthy extrovert who made his love 'straightforwardly, naturally, with the good animal gusto of a child of nature' (ch. ii). His deviation away from the central norm is rendered in symbolic terms by his canvas of the 'Bathers', an expression of unadulterated sensuality:

Eight plump and pearly bathers grouped themselves . . . so as to form with their moving bodies and limbs a kind of garland. . . Through this wreath of nacreous flesh (and even their faces were just smiling flesh, not a trace of spirit to distract you from the contemplation of the lovely forms and their relations) the eye travelled on towards a pale bright landscape of softly swelling downland and clouds. (ch. iv)

In contrast to Rampion's painting of the single male and female forms depicting physical love as a source of harmony, Bidlake's canvas points to nothing more than the irresponsible promiscuities of its author. Huxley says in another context, 'Nemesis is the principle of equilibrium. . . . The *Deus prudens*, as Horace calls the divine principle of moderation, dislikes and punishes any exclusive or unbalanced excess' (*Do What You Will*), and John Bidlake's life, which is as devoid of spirituality as the famous 'Bathers', is an unqualified exemplar of 'unbalanced excess'. A Gargantuan figure, 'a great laugher, a great worker, a great eater, drinker and taker of virginities', he has lived his life as though he had only just entered the world and were destined to be eternal. The *Deus prudens* appears in the form of a 'slight obstruction in the pylorus', and in his final state of abjection he is, like Cardan, another morality figure, a warning against a way of life which has made no provision for the encroachment of age and death; as Philip sadly observes, 'His courage, his Gargantuan power, his careless high spirits had been the fruit of a deliberate and life-long ignorance' (ch. xxx).

The wives of John Bidlake and Sidney Quarles both embody aspects of the nineteenth-century concept of love; like Marjorie Carling they are dedicated to a bloodless virtue. Janet Bidlake saw in her husband a 'spiritual compatriot'. Rather than admit to the failure of her marriage, she took refuge in an endless meditation on *maya*, the eternal illusion. Rachel Quarles is similarly disillusioned by marriage and turns to religion as a source of strength. She can never understand how people can get through life without God, and her criticism of the Lucy Tantamount generation is not completely without conviction: 'Everybody strains after happiness, and the result is that nobody's happy' (ch. xxx). As Spandrell remarks to Lucy, 'Putting the bottom in again is one of the traditional occupations of the aged'. The value of Rachel Quarles's contribution, however, is somewhat reduced when she concludes that happiness is a by-product—like coke, and the reader is reminded of another of Huxley's aspirants to the spiritual life, Mary Thriplow. Sidney Quarles, meantime, has been engaged in pursuing his own course of salvation. Quarles Senior is a kind of hypocritical John Bidlake, who like Gide's Oscar Molinier, mistakes his libidinous tendencies for passion; the most striking of his recorded axioms adds an appropriate touch of irony to the passion-reason motif of the novel: 'The key to the problem of sex: passion is sacred, a manifestation of the divinitah' (ch. xxxii).

The attack on intellectualism in *Point Counter Point* is largely embodied in the figure of Philip Quarles, the deliberately auto-biographical character whom Rampion considers 'an intellectual-aesthetic pervert'. Huxley, undoubtedly, thought of himself as a product of excessive intellectualism and although at times the portrait verges on parody it contains a good measure of self-criticism.

To Philip Quarles he attributes all the vices of cerebration. In the daily world of human contacts, Philip is a foreigner who finds it impossible to communicate except through his 'native intellectual language of ideas'. He sees his friends and acquaintances as so many specimens, objects for microscopic examination, to be classified, indexed, and worked-up into material for his fictional zoology. Thus Walter and Lucy become the objects of an interesting exercise on female angler-fishes and their dwarf parasitic males. Elinor, who is the chief victim of Philip's Pyrrhonic detachment, wonders 'whether it was that the habit of secrecy had made it impossible for him to give utterance to his inward feelings, or whether the very capacity to feel had actually been atrophied by consistent silence and repression' (ch. vi). Finally, outraged by his impersonality and lack of warmth, she is driven, almost against her will, into the arms of the importunate Webley. Philip, meanwhile, meets his nemesis in the person of Molly d'Exergillod, one of the vestal virgins of civilization, whose ratiocinative ability matches his own. The effect is chastening: instead of love, he is greeted with analytical anecdotes and philosophic epigrams:

Conscious and civilized, he had been defeated by someone even more civilized than himself. The justice was poetic. But what a warning! Parodies and caricatures are the most penetrating of criticisms. In Molly he perceived a kind of Max Beerbohm version of himself. The spectacle was alarming. (ch. xxviii)

At last he has a notion of what Elinor has had to endure. Describing his own situation in the novel he is planning, he realizes that the measure of freedom he has achieved by the suppression of emotional relationships is false. He has only succeeded in narrowing and desiccating his life; his reason is free, but free to deal with only a small fraction of experience. Rampion is right because he takes into account all the facts and then makes his way of living fit them, instead of trying to make the facts fit in with a preconceived way of life like the Christians and intellectuals. He concludes that 'the course of every intellectual, if he pursues his journey long and unflinchingly enough, ends in the obvious, from which the non-intellectuals have never stirred'. Once the premise has been stated in these terms, the question is how to 'transform a detached intellectual scepticism into a way of harmonious all-round living' (ch. xxvi). This is not only the main problem posed by the novel, it is also the problem which faces all of Huxley's later heroes. Philip Quarles's conversion, at this stage, is little more than a realization of the path he has to follow. It is left to Anthony Beavis and Will Farnaby to transform their lives into the harmony which the conversion theme implies.

Philip Quarles, like Gide's Edouard, is also writing a novel which in theory is related to the real one. Molly d'Exergillod describes Quarles as the 'zoologist of fiction'. It is an appropriate title for he not only thinks in terms of scientific modulations but his chief character is to be a professional zoologist who is writing a novel in his spare time with an approach that will be 'strictly biological'. It is characteristic of Quarles that he should be concerned with those aspects of reality which Rampion has designated as non-human, but it is a striking feature of the larger novel that Huxley has integrated these strictly biological variations into his structure and theme. In one of his later essays he discusses this technique at some length:

The facts and even the peculiar jargon of science can be of great service to the writer whose intention is mainly ironical. Juxtapose two accounts of the same human event, one in terms of pure science, the other in terms of religion, aesthetics, passion, even common sense: their discord will set up the most disquieting reverberations in the mind. Juxtapose, for example, physiology and mysticism . . . acoustics and the music of Bach . . . chemistry and the soul. . . The list of linked incompatibles might be indefinitely prolonged. ('And Wanton Optics Roll the Melting Eye', *Music at Night*)

The 'linked incompatibles' form a characteristic feature of *Point Counter Point*. The intention, as Huxley suggests, is mainly ironical; but, more importantly, the irony points to the basic incompatibility of 'scientific and moral perfectibility', the problem at the heart of the moral dilemma. Here are the biological variations on life and death, the juxta-positions of 'chemistry and the soul', which provide a kind of structural framework to the novel. First, Marjorie Carling's pregnancy as described in Chapter One:

She looked ugly, tired and ill. Six months from now her baby would be born. Something that had been a single cell, a cluster of cells, a little sac of tissue, a kind of worm, a potential fish with gills, stirred in her womb and would one day become a man—a grown man, suffering and enjoying, loving and hating. . . And what had been a blob of jelly within her body would invent a god and worship; what had been a kind of fish would create and, having created, would become the battle-ground of disputing good and evil; what had blindly lived in her as a parasitic worm would look at the stars, would listen to music, would read poetry. A thing would grow into a person, a tiny lump of of stuff would become a human body, a human mind. The astounding process of creation was going on within her; but Marjorie was conscious only of sickness and lassitude . . . and a chronic anxiety about the future, pain of the mind as well as discomfort of the body.

Then, at the end of the novel, there is Webley's corpse described in the first stages of decomposition:

Behind the screen lay the body . . . from the air, the invisible hosts of saprophytics had already begun their unresisted invasion. They would live among the dead cells, they would grow, and prodigiously multiply and in their growing and procreation all the chemical building of the body would be undone, all the intricacies and complications of its matter would be resolved, till by the time their work was finished a few pounds of carbon, a few quarts of water, some lime, a little phosphorus and sulphur, a pinch of iron and silicon, a handful of mixed salts—all scattered and recombined with the surrounding world— would be all that remained of Everard Webley's ambition to rule and his love for Elinor, of his thoughts about politics and his recollections of childhood. . . (ch. xxxiii)

The biological variations on Marjorie's pregnancy and Webley's death offer, as Rampion would have put it, a faint glimpse of the universe as seen through non-human eyes; and, he would have argued, it is a universe which, for all practical purposes, has no relevance to life as it is lived. There is no doubt that Huxley would have sympathized with this view, but it is also evident that the ultimate implications of the scientist's abstractions were more far-reaching than Rampion would have cared to admit. The data of embryonic growth and bacteriological decomposition are harsh incongruities when juxtaposed against Marjorie's anxieties and Webley's frustrated ambition. Their consistent effect is to deny human value, to treat felt experience as the mere off-shoot of a larger biological process: 'the ductless glands secrete among other things our moods, our aspirations, our philosophy of life'. This marks the end of Calamy's 'idealism'; looked at in this way human aspirations are mere epiphenomena of matter. What follows is a marked indifference to all the values which in previous non-scientific eras have given life its intrinsic meaning. To conceive the totality of human experience as a configuration of cell clusters and complex salts is to see life as a biological process with only a biological meaning—the mechanomorphic society of *Brave New World* is the next logical step. It is not the irrelevance of scientific knowledge but its potential threat to value which saddens all Huxley's encounters with science at this time.

The scientific account of the concert was quoted in an earlier chapter where attention was drawn to Peacock's technique of describing a human event in non-human terms.[1] In fact both the Bach suite and the Beethoven quartet serve to illustrate the widening gap between science and morality. Music, in Huxley's novels, is invariably a source of positive value and I have already referred to the Mozart quintet of *Antic Hay*. In *Point Counter Point* the Suite in B Minor and the A Minor Quartet are both presented as supreme manifestations of the spiritual consciousness. In this respect they offer a distinct 'counter' to the biological variations, with which they share a close structural relationship. Here is the Bach concert from Chapter Two:

. . . John Sebastian puts the case. The Rondeau begins, exquisitely and simply melodious, almost a folk-song. It is a young girl singing to herself of love, in solitude, tenderly mournful. A young girl singing

[1] See pp. 16–17 above.

among the hills, with the clouds drifting overhead. . . The thoughts that it provoked in him are the Sarabande that follows the Rondeau. His is a slow and lovely meditation on the beauty (in spite of squalor and stupidity), the profound goodness (in spite of all the evil), the oneness (in spite of such bewildering diversity) of the world. It is a beauty, a goodness, a unity that no intellectual research can discover, that analysis dispels, but of whose reality the spirit is from time to time suddenly and overwhelmingly convinced. . . Is it illusion or the revelation of profoundest truth? Who knows? Pongileoni blew, the fiddlers drew their rosined horse-hair across the stretched intestines of lambs; through the long Sarabande the poet slowly meditated his lovely and consoling certitude.

Once again we have an echo of Gumbril's dilemma: 'God as exultation' as opposed to 'God as $2 + 2 = 4$'. The Rondeau is an expression of goodness too powerful to be ignored, but whether it is an illusion or a revelation of the profoundest truth remains unanswerable. The question for Huxley was a haunting one and casts its shadow across even the greatest intimations of the spirit. James Hinton, the Victorian philosopher, pin-pointed the problem when he observed that if one accepted the world that science reveals as reality then one 'might as well say that the ultimate fact of one of Beethoven's violin quartettes is the scraping of the tails of horses on the intestines of cats'.[1]

The *heilige Dankgesang* of the A Minor Quartet raises the same issues in the closing pages of the novel:

Spiral grooves on a surface of shellac remembered their playing. The artificial memory revolved, a needle travelled in its grooves and through a faint scratching and roaring that mimicked the noises of Beethoven's own deafness, the audible symbols of Beethoven's convictions and emotions quivered out into the air. Slowly, slowly, the melody unfolded itself. The archaic Lydian harmonies hung on the air. It was an unimpassioned music, transparent, pure and crystalline . . . a counterpoint of serenities. . . It was the serenity of the convalescent who wakes from fever and finds himself born again into a realm of beauty. But the fever

[1] Quoted by Alan Willard Brown, *The Metaphysical Society* (New York, 1947), p. 124.

was 'the fever called living' and the rebirth was not into this world; the beauty was unearthly, the convalescent serenity was the peace of God. The interweaving of Lydian melodies was heaven. (ch. xxxvii)

To Spandrell the music is a 'beatific vision', a proof that God existed. Rampion is not so easily swayed. He admits that it is 'the most perfect spiritual abstraction from reality' that he has ever known; but, nevertheless, it is still an abstraction, ultimately, as invalid and irrelevant as the abstractions of science itself. This, of course, is what we would expect of Rampion. Lawrence, in his attack on intellectualism, had grouped the spiritual consciousness with the mental consciousness as a form of perverse cerebration. Christianity and science were equally guilty in suppressing the bodily instincts. Huxley, while accepting the main premises of Lawrence's 'new mythology of nature', was not so certain. He attacked sham spirituality with renewed vigour, but as to the ultimate nature of the spiritual consciousness his attitude remained ambiguous. Even while formulating his doctrine of 'life-worship', it seemed he kept an open mind—for Huxley the basic moral dilemma was still unsolved.

However, it is perhaps a measure of Lawrence's influence that the search for spiritual truth, which Philip Quarles rejects as 'a rather refined and elaborate substitute for genuine living', is undertaken in this novel by the perverted Spandrell. Huxley's great aversion to sham spirituality has often been noted and in this novel it is given full rein. Of the characters with spiritual pretensions, Carling and Burlap are unqualified hypocrites: Carling is the drink-sodden Catholic who versifies the lives of the English saints; Burlap, the fake Messiah, who finds Rampion's paintings too carnal and specialises in seduction by stealth. In contrast to Burlap's hypocrisy and cant, Spandrell is not an entirely unsympathetic figure. In his perverted quest for the Absolute he exemplifies the conflict between 'spirituality' and Rampion's 'life-worship'. Like Baudelaire he is the 'inverted Christian' who tries to realize goodness by offending against it, to know God by denying him. As Huxley says of the French poet in the essay on him in

Do What You Will: 'Only a believer in absolute goodness can consciously pursue the absolute of evil; you cannot be a Satanist without being at the same time, potentially or actually, a Godist. Baudelaire was a Christian inside out, the photographic image in negative of a Father of the Church.' Spandrell's progressive debauchery is then, on one level, the behaviour of a potential believer. God was there but in hiding and the murder of Webley is a final desperate attempt to force Him out of His lair. But God refuses to be forced—the experiment is a failure. To Spandrell God is a joker and his best joke is not being there: 'Neither God nor the devil. For if the devil had been there, God would have been there too' (ch. xxxvi). Spandrell is a living example of Rampion's hypothesis that when man tries to be superhuman he invariably ends up by being sub-human. This is the great vice of Christianity; by postulating a belief in the existence of absolutes it has continuously urged man to seek a more-than-human ideal. The result has been either hypocrisy and cant or a perversion of the natural human instincts. If the concept of God is to have any value at all, it must be as an immanent and not as a transcendent deity. God is neither above nor outside, so Rampion argues. At least not for the purposes of living: God is a 'felt, experienced quality', anything that makes for life, for any vital relation in the world. But Spandrell is not to be convinced: for him absolutes must exist and music is one of them. The *heilige Dankgesang* of the A Minor Quartet is to provide him with a final proof of the existence of God. The novel that began with Bach's intimations of the spirit ends with Beethoven's. Rampion, however, remains adamant. He admits that the music is heaven. 'it is the life of the soul', but it is still an abstraction. And why the need for abstractions? Why can't we be content to be just men? The dialogue is cut short; and, as Spandrell lies dying, the celestial melody draws to a close. Suddenly, there is no more music and all that remains is the sound of the needle on the revolving disc. So the cycle is complete. The dilemma which was raised by the Bach Suite, in the early pages of the novel, finds a last expression in Spandrell's death: the peace of God or the scratching of a needle, an illusion or a revelation of the profoundest truth? Or, as Rampion would insist, 'a kind of cancer, eating up the real, human, natural reality'? (ch. xxxvii). The question remains, providing its own poignant comment on the divided state of man.

Whilst Huxley was deeply involved in the problem of science and morality, he was characteristically less concerned about the political questions of the day. In 1928 he could assert with confidence that the old political issues had receded, and the events of the succeeding years did little to change his opinion. What of the new political issues? Huxley, as I have previously intimated, was never attracted to a political solution and in the clash between communism and fascism which was to engage most of his contemporaries in the thirties, he was content to stand on the sidelines. The new issues, like the old ones, seemed irrelevant to the vital problems of the age. As Rampion insisted, the Communists and the Fascists, the Radicals and the Conservatives, were all bound for the same end, 'all headed for the same psychological impasse'. They all believed in industrialization in one form or another, in organization and the machine.

However, if Huxley refused to commit himself to the political struggle, the conflict between communism and fascism was of too great a contemporary interest to be passed over. It is dramatised in the clash between Illidge, Lord Edward's Marxist assistant, and Everard Webley, the self-appointed Führer of the British Freemen. It is interesting to note how closely Webley's attacks on democracy reflect Huxley's own views expressed a year earlier in *Proper Studies*. Both Huxley and Lawrence were accused of fascist tendencies and, in fairness to their critics, it must be admitted that both favoured the leader-principle. Some of Lawrence's ideas have a decidedly authoritarian ring when considered in retrospect. On the nature of the body politic, for instance, he remarks that 'The next relation has got to be a relationship of men towards men in a spirit of unfathomable trust and responsibility, service and leadership, obedience and pure authority. Men have got to choose their leaders and obey them to the death. And it must be a system of culminating aristocracy, society tapering like a pyramid

93

to the supreme leader.'[1] Huxley's view, although not so extreme favoured 'any system which secured intelligent men with a talent for government to do the ruling' and his concept of 'a ruling aristocracy of mind' echoes Webley's principle that the best men should rule irrespective of class or origin. However, by 1928, Huxley was fully aware of the dangers latent in fascism. Webley, with his collection of old swords and firearms, his medallion heads of Caesar and Alexander the Great, is portrayed as a petty demagogue. Philip Quarles easily recognizes Webley's self-aggrandisement as a lust for power, another step towards reducing human beings to automatism. It was becoming increasingly clear that the extremes of capitalism and socialism were, each in its own way, the political heirs of nineteenth-century mechanism; scientific determinism by undermining the idea of individual responsibility was unconsciously paving the way for *Brave New World*, the society of mechanised slaves, where totalitarian politics and applied science were to be wedded in an indissoluble union.

If Webley illustrates, rather superficially perhaps, the demagogue's drive to power, Illidge represents its complementary aspect, the revolutionary's urge to destruction. Illidge, as a scientist and a revolutionary Marxist of working-class origin, furnishes another variant on the passion-reason motif. Committed to nineteenth-century materialism as he is, his principles make him reject any scientific theory less than fifty years old. Spandrell explains his dilemma to Lucy: it is impossible to be a true communist without at the same time being a mechanist. A communist has to believe in the fundamentals of space, mass and time and that all the rest is mere illusion. Mach, Einstein and Eddington were all undermining his simple faith.[2] Illidge, in fact, in spite of his claim to reason, is basically irrational in his beliefs and behaviour. Too sensitive about what the parsons would have called his 'station in life', his aggressive politics mask a deep sense of inferiority; his social conscience is at the roots emotional, a

[1] *Fantasia of the Unconscious*, p. 210.

[2] Illidge's fears were also shared by Lenin. See Susan Stebbing, *Philosophy and the Physicists* (New York, 1958), pp. xi–xii.

deep and lasting hatred for the products of wealth and leisure. As a symbol of working-class aspirations, he exemplifies Rampion's analogy between the repressed instincts and the repressed classes: 'It's poor against rich in the state. In the individual, it's the oppressed body and instincts against the intellect' (ch. xi). The revolution in the body politic, like the repressed instincts in the individual, expresses an inner urge to destroy, just as Webley becomes the focal point of Illidge's irrational hatred. The final revolution, Rampion argues, will not be revolution for a humanistic cause, but revolution as an end in itself, 'Smashing for smashing's sake', a psychological revolt against all the circumstances which make life in a materially-civilized society untenable.

In *Do What You Will*, Huxley outlines the main doctrine of the life-worshipper which lies behind Rampion's pronouncements:

The life-worshipper's aim is to achieve a vital equilibrium, not by drawing in his diversities, not by moderating his exuberances (for Exuberance, in the words of Blake, is Beauty), but by giving them rein one against the other. His is the equilibrium of balanced excesses. . . ('Pascal')

An earlier essay in the same volume attributes this view to the Athenian Greeks:

What Pericles took for granted was briefly this: that men should accept their natures as they found them. Man has a mind: very well, let him think. Senses that enjoy: let him be sensual. Instincts: they are there to be satisfied. Passions: it does a man good to succumb to them from time to time. Imagination, a feeling for beauty, a sense of awe: let him create, let him surround himself with lovely forms, let him worship. Man is multifarious, inconsistent, self-contradictory: the Greeks accepted the fact and lived multifariously, inconsistently and contradictorily. ('Spinoza's Worm')

The nemesis which overtakes the characters in *Point Counter Point* is the result of their failure to harmonize passion and reason; by living excessively in one direction they have reduced themselves to incarnate functions of the intellect, the spirit or the senses. Thus, if Marjorie Carling had lived with her instincts as well as her spirit, Walter would never have been drawn to Lucy; or if John Bidlake had cultivated his spiritual as well as his sensual consciousness, death would not have seemed such a fearful thing. Only Rampion, it is implied, has succeeded in giving play to all the vital functions which complete the life-worshipper's ideal of harmony. It is here that the novel breaks down: the anatomy is convincing; the synthesis is not. Rampion is continually praised for living his ideas but the reader is given no evidence of it. Critics generally, including Lawrence himself, have observed that Rampion merely sits around and talks: 'the most boring character in the book—a gas-bag'.[1] The failure to animate the life-worshipper's doctrine disturbs the whole moral balance of the novel, a weakness of which Huxley himself may have been aware when he talked of 'the implied or specified "counter" which . . . tempered, *or at least was intended to temper*, the harshness of the "points" ' (*Music at Night*, my italics). The fact is, I believe, that the 'counter' does not temper the harshness of the 'points', and this is further apparent if one considers Philip Quarles's problem of how to transform his detached intellectual scepticism into a way of harmonious living. It is not so much that the novel fails to provide an answer but that it suggests there is no answer. Spandrell's doctrine of 'Nothing ever happens to a man except what is like him' denies the possibility of change; and this peculiarly negative aspect is exemplified by the underlying pattern of determinism which runs counter to the moral theme of the novel. Spandrell sees his own pattern of determinism as a 'providential conspiracy'—he was damned from the start. As I suggested earlier, Spandrell's story reads like a Freudian case-book history; from the moment that his youthful happiness is shattered by his mother's second marriage his life is tainted. He can only break the stranglehold of his complex in death. Philip Quarles presents a different case but the deterministic pattern is equally pronounced. Congenitally indifferent to others, a childhood accident has raised an artificial barrier between himself and the rest of the world and guaranteed

[1] *The Letters of D. H. Lawrence*, edited by Aldous Huxley (1934), p. 758.

the life of quiet detachment to which he was already disposed by nature. When he resolves to break the pattern and assist in the up-bringing of little Phil, the latter's unexpected death deprives him of the motive. There is no longer any incentive to change his way of life, even if change were possible, and the reader is left with the feeling that all will go on as before.

An even more sinister threat to any presupposition of free will is that aspect of psychological determinism which reveals the mind and spirit as the prisoners of an alien and hostile body.[1] Once again it is the knowledge that science brings which presents a threat to value. Marjorie's sickness and lassitude in the early pages of the novel stem from a three-month-old pregnancy: a month later she is blissfully experiencing the peace of God. (As Huxley points out in a different context, 'Mme. Guyon's ecstasies were most frequent and most spiritually significant in the fourth month of her pregnancies'.) Happiness is a by-product, not of pursuing salvation but of the beating of the foetal heart, of changes in the circulation. John Bidlake's buoyant personality is at the mercy of 'a slight obstruction in the pylorus'; Illidge's social advancement depended, among other things, on a shopkeeper's son having tubercle bacilli in the lymph system; while Webley's love and ambition fade away in a few pounds of carbon, one or two quarts of water and a handful of chemicals. The mind is the plaything of the body, and the body, as the death of little Phil so ruthlessly insists, is the freak of chance. Elinor, faced with the death of her lover and seeing her child gratuitously tortured before her eyes, feels that 'the very possession of a body is a cynical comment on the soul and all its ways. It is a piece of cynicism, however, which the soul must accept, whether it likes it or no' (ch. xxxv). It is 'the wearisome condition of humanity', not Rampion's vision of har-mony, which has the final word; for the moralist *Point Counter Point* offers no resolution.

[1] More specifically Behaviourism which ignores the concepts of mind and consciousness and relates all human activity directly to the bodily functions.

VII

Brave New World (1932)

Huxley has been compared to H. G. Wells as a popularizer of scientific ideas and as a revolutionary and prophetic writer. Both certainly can be considered as prophets in their own right, but if Wells is the prophet of scientific optimism Huxley is without doubt its prophet of gloom. In his utopia of the early twenties *Men Like Gods*, Wells depicts a modern world-state in which private ownership, religious worship and parental control have been replaced by socialism, scientific humanism and education by the state, where eugenics and birth control have produced a society that nurtures freedom and tolerance. All the elements of control exercised by the Wellsian world-state are to be found in *Brave New World*, but whereas Wells sees technological progress leading to a new millennium—a race of athletic chemists and mathematical physicists, Huxley envisages the birth of a scientific dictatorship in which the last traces of individuality have been ruthlessly stamped out. In *The Shape of Things to Come* Wells dismisses Huxley's view as an alarmist fantasy; he accepts scientific totalitarianism as a necessary evil which will ultimately wither away as man becomes more enlightened. Accordingly, at the hypothetical conference of Mégève set in the year 2059, his guardians of the future world-state dismiss themselves with the proclamation that the need for repressions and disciplines has passed, and that everyone is free to express himself to the limit of his potentialities. This act of benevolence on the part of the ruling guardians and the revolution of the educational élite which leads up to it would have seemed to Huxley highly improbable. He would have agreed with Wells that under a scientific dictator 'education will really work' but, as he points out, in *Brave New World Revisited* the result will be 'that most men and women will grow up to love their servitude and will never dream of revolution'; he concludes that 'there seems to be no good reason why a thoroughly scientific dictatorship should ever be overthrown' (ch. xii). *Brave New World* is the portrait of such a dictatorship.

In the office of the World Controller for Western Europe lies a copy of 'My Life and Work, by Our Ford'. It is no coincidence that 'Our Ford' is both the patron saint and prophet of Huxley's new world-state. 'Fordism', he wrote in a contemporary essay, 'demands that we should sacrifice the animal man (and along with the animal large portions of the thinking, spiritual man) not indeed to God, but to the Machine. There is no place in the factory, or in that larger factory which is the modern industrialized world, for animals on the one hand, or for artists, mystics, or even, finally, individuals on the other. Of all the ascetic religions Fordism is that which demands the cruellest mutilations of the human psyche—demands the cruellest mutilations and offers the smallest spiritual returns' ('The Puritan', *Music at Night*). Fordism, the philosophy of applied science and industrialism, is the religion of *Brave New World*. By the double process of genetic manipulation and post-natal conditioning the World Controllers have succeeded in producing a race which loves its servitude, a race of standardized machine-minders for standardized machines who will never challenge their authority. The animal, thinking and spiritual man has been sacrificed in his entirety.

At the beginning of *Brave New World*, the Director of Hatcheries and Conditioning describes Bokanovsky's process, whereby 'an average of nearly eleven thousand brothers and sisters in a hundred and fifty batches of identical twins' could be produced from a single ovary, as one of the major instruments of social stability. The problem of selective breeding has been a favourite subject of scientific speculation since the beginning of the century: the scientist in Lowes Dickinson's *A Modern Symposium* (first published in 1905) affirms that 'it may be desirable for government to undertake the complete regulation of marriage'. And Huxley concluded, following Wells, that general progress was only possible upon two conditions: that the heritable qualities of the population be improved and that the population be reduced. Eugenic reform, however, raises its own problems: in a society of superior individuals only a chosen few could be permitted to make full use of their powers because no society provides openings for more than a limited number of superior people. Wells solved this problem by allowing his utopian inhabitants to rule and be ruled, to do highbrow and lowbrow work in turns, but Huxley was characteristically sceptical of such a solution; governments only rule effectively because most people are not very intelligent, dread responsibility and desire nothing better than to be told what to do. The World Controllers of *Brave New World* held similar views and created a highly stable, differentiated society by means of ectogenesis, in which both eugenics and dysgenics were practised systematically at the same time:

In one set of bottles biologically superior ova, fertilized by biologically superior sperm, were given the best possible pre-natal treatment and were finally decanted as Betas, Alphas and even Alpha Pluses. In another, much more numerous set of bottles, biologically inferior ova, fertilized by biologically inferior sperm, were subjected to the Bokanovsky Process (ninety-six identical twins out of a single egg) and treated pre-natally with alcohol and other protein poisons. The creatures finally decanted were almost sub-human; but they were capable of performing unskilled work. . . (*Brave New World Revisited*, ch. ii)

Those decanted as Alphas and Alpha Pluses were destined for a higher education (Eton was reserved exclusively for Alpha caste boys and girls) and posts of responsibility; while the lower and more numerous castes manned the benches of industry, where each process was carried out as far as possible by a single Bokanovsky group. By controlled ectogenesis and the Bokanovsky Process the population of the planet was fixed at two thousand million inhabitants with only ten thousand names between them.

The Bokanovsky Process and pre-natal treatment of the embryos insured that the future inhabitants of *Brave New World* were decanted as socialized human beings, but this was merely a beginning. After birth infants were subjected to an intensive course of behaviourist and hypnopaedic conditioning, primarily designed to make their minds endorse the already predestined judgment of their bodies. As the Director of Hatcheries explained, 'that is the secret of happiness and virtue—liking what you've *got* to do. All conditioning aims at that: making people like their unescapable social destiny' (ch. i). In John B. Watson's classic study of behaviourism, the American psychologist describes techniques for establishing conditioned reflexes in infants. One series of experiments shows how an eleven-month-old baby, who is perfectly at ease with tame white rodents, can be conditioned to a fear response, simply by striking a steel bar with a hammer every time he approaches the proximity of the animals. After this has been repeated seven times, the mere sight of a rodent or any related animal is sufficient to produce intense fear and dismay.[1] In the Neo-Pavlovian Conditioning Rooms at the Infant Nurseries, eight-month-old, khaki-clad Delta babies are treated by identical techniques: encouraged to approach bowls of roses and brightly-coloured nursery quartos, they are subjected simultaneously to the loud ringing of alarm bells and electric shocks. After two hundred repetitions, books and loud noises, flowers and electric shocks are indissolubly wedded: 'They'll grow up with what the psychologists used to call an 'instinctive' hatred of books and flowers. Reflexes unalterably conditioned, They'll be safe from books and botany all their lives' (ch. ii).

In *Brave New World Revisited* Huxley discusses Wetterstrand's successful hypnotic treatment of sleeping children and concludes that, under proper conditions, hypnopaedia or sleep teaching actually works about as well as hypnosis. The Controllers of *Brave New World* have taken full advantage of the fact. The Director of Hatcheries called hypnopaedia 'the greatest moralizing and socializing force of all time'. Wordless conditioning had its value, but it was relatively crude and limited when it came to the finer distinctions; for that there had to be words but words without reason. Therefore part of the moral education of Beta children

[1] *Behaviourism* (Chicago, 1959), pp. 159–64.

consisted in 'lessons' in elementary class consciousness. While the children slept a voice under every pillow softly whispered:

'Alpha children wear grey. They work much harder than we do, because they're so frightfully clever. I'm really awfully glad I'm a Beta, because I don't work so hard. And then we are much better than the Gammas and Deltas. Gammas are stupid. They all wear green, and Delta children wear khaki. Oh no, I *don't* want to play with Delta children. And Epsilons are still worse. They're too stupid to be able . . . (ch. ii)

Finally, as the Director sums up, 'the child's mind *is* these suggestions, and the sum of the suggestions *is* the child's mind. And not the child's mind only. The adult's mind too—all his life long' (ch. ii).

After ectogenesis and conditioning, Soma[1] was the most powerful instrument of authority in the hands of the Controllers of the World-State. Huxley had already speculated on the invention of a new drug, a more efficient and less harmful substitute for alcohol and cocaine; he considered that if he were a millionaire, he would endow a band of research workers to look for the ideal intoxicant. The rulers of *Brave New World*, with a similar object in mind, had subsidized two thousand pharmacologists and biochemists to search for the perfect drug. Soma was the product of six years' research; euphoric, narcotic, pleasantly hallucinant, it had all the advantages of alcohol and none of the defects, but there the resemblance ended. To the inhabitants of Huxley's utopia the Soma habit was not a private vice but a political institution. The World Controllers encouraged the systematic drugging of their own citizens for the benefit of the state.

The daily Soma ration was an insurance against personal maladjustment, social unrest and the spread of subversive ideas. Religion, Karl Marx declared, is the opium of the people. In the Brave New World this situation was reversed. Opium, or rather Soma, was the people's

[1] The original Soma from which Huxley took the name of this hypothetical drug was an unknown plant used by the ancient Aryan invaders of India in one of the most solemn of their religious rites.

religion. Like religion, the drug had power to console and compensate, it called up visions of another, better world, it offered hope, strengthened faith and promoted charity. (*Brave New World Revisited*, ch. viii)

Huxley, comparing his novel with *1984*, observes that in the latter a strict code of sexual morality is imposed on the party hierarchy. The society of Orwell's fable is permanently at war and therefore aims to keep its subjects in a constant state of tension. A puritanical approach to sex is therefore a major instrument of policy. The World-State, however, of *Brave New World* is one in which war has been eliminated and the first aim of its rulers is to keep their subjects from making trouble. Together with Soma, sexual licence, made practical by the abolition of the family, is one of the chief means of guaranteeing the inhabitants against any kind of destructive or creative emotional tension. The appalling dangers of family life had first been pointed out by Our Ford or 'Our Freud, as, for some inscrutable reason, he chose to call himself whenever he spoke of psychological matters' (ch. iii). Once the world had been full of every kind of perversion from chastity to sadism; but the World Controllers had realized that an industrial civilization depended on self-indulgence. Chastity meant passion and neurasthenia, and passion and neurasthenia meant instability, which, in turn, meant a constant threat to civilization. Therefore life for the Brave New Worlders was made emotionally easy; in short, people were saved from having any emotions at all. No one was allowed to love anyone too much; there were no temptations to resist, and if something unpleasant were to happen, there was always Soma. Legalized sexual freedom was made possible by every device known to applied science. Contraceptive precautions were prescribed by the regulations while years of 'intensive hypnopaedia and, from twelve to seventeen, Malthusian drill three times a week had made the taking of these precautions almost as automatic and inevitable as blinking' (ch. v).

Soma and licensed promiscuity would probably have been sufficient in themselves to prevent the Brave New Worlders from taking any active interest in the realities of the social and political situation; circuses, however, are a traditional aid to dictators, and the Controllers of the World-State were no exception. Instead of spending their leisure hours working out the practical implications of the theory of relativity, like their predecessors in *Men Like Gods*, Huxley's utopians were provided with a series of non-stop distractions guaranteed to ward off boredom and discourage idle speculation about the nature of things. Any frustrated religious instincts were provided for by the Ford's Day Solidarity Services, where, in a crude parody of the Holy Communion, dedicated Soma Tablets and the loving cup of ice-cream Soma were passed round. By these means the Controllers insured that the Brave New Worlders loved their servitude and never dreamt of revolution.

In *Brave New World* the imprisonment of the human spirit by science is almost complete; human values have totally disappeared, natural impulses allowed to atrophy until the inhabitants react like automata. Only in the remote Indian Reservation, which, owing to a poor climate and a lack of natural resources, has not been worth civilizing, have the normal values of humanity survived. There, surrounded by electrified fencing, some sixty thousand Indians and half-breeds still practise marriage, rear families and preserve the religious traditions of the past. One among them, John, is the natural born son of a Brave New Worlder, Linda, who had been left behind during one of the infrequent expeditions from outside. John, brought up as an Indian, taught to read Shakespeare and to listen to his mother's stories of the Other Place, is Huxley's device for introducing an outsider with relatively normal values into his world of scientifically conditioned inhabitants. (Wells used a similar device when he introduced the Earthlings into the utopia of *Men Like Gods*, although his intention was, of course, the exact opposite of Huxley's.) John, and through him, Shakespeare, becomes the symbol of the human spirit, opposed to Fordism and applied science:

. . . the Savage has the weakness and the strength of a personality not 'artificially made'. He wants to love, but to love for ever. He wants to work, but to work with effort and in the sweat of his brow. He wants to live, but to live dangerously. He wants to rejoice, but he wants also to suffer. He wants life with its fulness, but he wants also death with its tragedy. All the wonders of material civilisation leave him cold, because he remembers that:

'Ariel could put a girdle round the earth in forty minutes.'[1]

Above all, he wants God, goodness and sin—he claims the right to be unhappy, to which the World-Controller adds the final ironic comment: 'Not to mention the right to grow old and ugly and impotent, the right to have syphilis and cancer; the right to have too little to eat; the right to be lousy; the right to live in a constant apprehension of what may happen tomorrow; the right to catch typhoid; the right to be tortured by unspeakable pains of every kind' (ch. xvii). The Savage claims them all; but, as the World Controller insists, the price of freedom is inordinately high. In the end, the Savage's resistance amounts to little more than an heroic gesture. He rejects the world which no longer seems brave or beauteous. The burden is inevitably too great; like Lypiatt, in his extremity, he has no other recourse but to end his life in a fit of despair.

At a first glance the Savage, with his insatiable desire for experience, appears as an embodiment of the 'life-worshipper's' creed. His peculiar blend of the primitive and the civilized points to Rampion's 'balanced opposites'; against this his *'penitente* ferocity'*, the savagery with which he greets Lenina's sensual advances, is far from the 'life-worshipper's' ideal. Whatever Huxley's intentions were, it would be unwise to push the equation too far. It is the Brave New Worlders who give John the title of the Savage, but it is important to note that the irony is double-edged. Humanity's last living representative owes his allegiance to a creed that is half fertility cult and half *penitente* ferocity. The Indians are far from being 'noble' and, if 'civilization is sterilization', savagery means goitre and flagellation. And John, in spite of his Shakespearean upbringing, is still very much a savage. As Huxley himself admitted, the choice lay 'between insanity on the one hand and lunacy on the other'—the insanity of the scientific utopia or the

[1] M. D. Petre, *The Hibbert Journal*, XXXI (October 1932), p. 70.

lunacy of the primitive cult (Foreword to *Brave New World*). The failure of the Savage to find a real alternative suggests, in spite of the many echoes of 'life worship', that Huxley was moving away from the doctrine of *Do What You Will*. There was as yet nothing to take its place and, although the introduction of Maine de Biran late in the novel anticipates a renewed interest in the life of the spirit, the contemplative solution still lay ahead. Thirty years later, in *Island*, Huxley was to offer a real alternative, another utopia, in which science and technology would be used not to enslave man but to further his salvation.

John, in his redemptive role, has two potential converts among the Brave New Worlders, Bernard Marx and Helmholtz Watson. Both are Alpha Pluses. The Alphas of the scientific society are all products of excessive cerebration: 'Adults intellectually and during working hours. . . Infants where feeling and desire are concerned'. The terms are familiar: this kind of 'unbalanced excess' is the typical defect of the 'scientific' character. Bernard, however, whose predicament recalls that of Philip Quarles, is something of an odd man out even among the Brave New Worlders. An Alpha Plus, he has the physique of a Gamma -Minus (it is said that alcohol had been put into his blood surrogate by mistake). His inadequacy nurtures a sense of revolt: but more important, Bernard's grievances are not merely anti-social; behind his revolt stems a genuine impulse to extend his range of feeling— to know what it would be like if he were not enslaved by his conditioning:

On their way back across the Channel, Bernard insisted on stopping his propeller and hovering on his helicopter screws within a hundred feet of the waves. . .

'Look,' he commanded.

'But it's horrible', said Lenina, shrinking back from the window. She was appalled by the rushing emptiness of the night, by the black foam-flecked water heaving beneath them, by the pale face of the moon, so haggard and distracted among the hastening clouds. 'Let's turn on the radio. Quick.' She reached for the dialling knob on the dashboard and turned it at random. . .

'I want to look at the sea in peace', he said. 'One can't even look with that beastly noise going on.'

'But it's lovely. And I don't want to look.'

'But I do', he insisted. 'It makes me feel as though . . .' he hesitated, searching for words with which to express himself, 'as though I were more *me*, if you see what I mean. More on my own, not so completely a part of something else. Not just a cell in the social body.' (ch. vi)

Bernard's problem, like that of Philip Quarles, is how to be an adult all the time, not just intellectually but with his senses as well. This is the 'life-worshipper's' problem—to achieve the harmony of Rampion's 'balanced opposites'.

Helmholtz Watson's sense of dissatisfaction springs, less plausibly, from having too much ability. This, like Bernard's physical defect, isolates him from his fellow men. A successful lecturer, an indefatigable lover and an Escalator-Squash champion, he has nevertheless realized that sport, women and communal activities are not enough. Bernard and Helmholtz are too conditioned to present a serious threat to the values of the Brave New World, but, together with John, they form a core of resistance within the deterministic society. John precipitates his friends into something approaching open revolt; the three are arrested and Bernard and Helmholtz duly sent into exile. The only positive result of John's bid for freedom is expressed in a moment of genuine affection when the three meet for the last time: 'There was a silence. In spite of their sadness—because of it, even; for their sadness was the symptom of their love for one another—the three young men were happy' (ch. xviii).

In a society where sexual licence has supplanted love, feelings of desire are virtually unknown. Both Bernard and Helmholtz try to make themselves more 'human' by practising self-denial. Bernard wants to examine the effect of arresting his impulses; Helmholtz finds the effects of abstinence worthwhile but exceedingly odd. For Bernard the process is little short of the rediscovery of free will. 'Thought' is still 'the slave of life' but, he concludes, the process appears to be reversible:

A physical shortcoming could produce a kind of mental excess. The process, it seemed, was reversible. Mental excess could produce, for its own purposes, the voluntary blindness and deafness of deliberate solitude, the artificial impotence of asceticism. (ch. iv)

This is the first step to redemption; it denotes a crack in the iron-bound determinism which overshadowed the protagonists of *Point Counter Point*, and looks ahead to Anthony Beavis's discovery in *Eyeless in Gaza* that the conditioned reflexes could themselves be reconditioned.

By introducing Shakespeare to the World-State, the Savage brings the first taste of culture into a cultureless society. Following Ford's dictum that 'History is bunk', all the art and knowledge of the past has been suppressed—only a few pre-Fordian books remain locked in the safe in the World Controller's study. No one was encouraged to indulge in solitary amusements. When the Savage suggests *Othello* as an alternative to 'Three Weeks in a Helicopter', the Controller points out that no one would understand it. Tragedies depend on an environment which lacks social stability. Now, the world is stable:

People are happy; they get what they want, and they never want what they can't get. They're well off; they're safe; they're never ill; they're not afraid of death; they're blissfully ignorant of passion and old age; they're plagued with no mothers or fathers; they've got no wives, or children, or lovers to feel strongly about; they're so conditioned that they practically can't help behaving as they ought to behave. And if anything should go wrong, there's *soma*. (ch. xvi)

Othello is admittedly better than the feelies but a price must be paid for stability. The choice lay between happiness and what people used to call high art. The high art has been sacrificed; but, as the Controller admits, actual happiness never looks exciting and 'being contented has none of the glamour of a good fight against misfortune, none of the picturesqueness of a struggle with temptation, or a fatal overthrow by passion or doubt. Happiness is never grand' (ch. xvi).

To the Savage in his search for spiritual values, the brand of 'happiness' offered by the World-State is inevitably inadequate, and the death of Linda serves to emphasize the intrinsic nature of the conflict between two essentially incompatible ways of life. When Linda is brought back among the Brave New Worlders no one wishes to see her, ostensibly because she is not a real savage, but really because she has aged. At forty-four, she has lost her youth, and not one of the citizens of civilization can look on her without a feeling of nausea. In the World-State old age has been conquered and with it all the mental attitudes of senility. Men who in the old days would have spent their time in retirement, reading, thinking, and turning to religion, now work and make love. There is no rest from pleasure, not a moment to sit down and think. Preservation from disease and biochemical adjustments keep them permanently youthful until, at the age of sixty, they suddenly break down and death is immediate. In this world of youth the ageing Linda has no place and her return to civilization becomes, in effect, one prolonged Soma holiday. A few months later she lies in the special hospital for the dying, surrounded by every distraction that applied science can invent. The Savage's desire to be with her at the end defies all the conventions of the scientific society. Brave New Worlders have no close relationships; the individual as an individual has ceased to matter. Further, the act of dying has been stripped of all significance. Intensive conditioning from the age of eighteen months—every tot spent two mornings a week in a Hospital for the Dying; all the best toys were kept there, with special helpings of chocolate cream on death days—has robbed death of its terrors. Soma and synthetic melodies do the rest. The Savage, who sees death in a rather different light, tries to restore Linda to consciousness, but she is dreaming happily of Popé, her Indian lover.

He squeezed her limp hand almost with violence, as though he would force her to come back from this dream of ignoble pleasures, from these base and hateful memories—back into the present, back into reality; the appalling present, the awful reality—but sublime, but significant, but desperately important precisely because of the imminence of that which made them so fearful. (ch. xiv)

This is the first intimation of the importance which Huxley was to attach to the act of dying. In the last novels, holy living and holy dying become an integral part of Huxley's philosophy,[1] and death is seen as the culminating point of human experience. To the Brave New Worlders death has no more spiritual significance than life, and as such is merely an unpleasant termination to what is otherwise a state of unqualified contentment.

By abolishing old age and the fear of death, the rulers of *Brave New World* feel that they have not only eradicated spiritual values, but have further removed all need for God. The World Controller quotes Maine de Biran (one of the few surviving authors in his collection of pre-Fordian volumes) to prove his point:

. . . the religious sentiment tends to develop as we grow older; to develop because, as the passions grow calm, as the fancy and sensibilities are less excited and less excitable, our reason becomes less troubled in its working . . . whereupon God emerges as from behind a cloud; our soul feels, sees, turns towards the source of all light; turns naturally and inevitably; for now that all that gave to the world of sensations its life and charm has begun to leak away from us . . . we feel the need to lean on something that abides, something that will never play us false—a reality, an absolute and everlasting truth. Yes, we inevitably turn to God; for this religious sentiment is of its nature so pure, so delightful to the soul that experiences it, that it makes up to us for all our other losses. (ch. xvii)

For the citizens of the World-State there are no losses to compensate for; there is no need for a substitute for youthful desires when youthful desires remain to the end, therefore religious sentiment is rendered superfluous. And, if there is no need for God, then the values which human beings normally reverence are likewise irrelevant; self-denial and chastity, nobility and patience are also superfluous. There is no need for any civilized man to bear anything that is unpleasant. God and moral values are incompatible with machinery, scientific medicine and universal happiness.

[1] The deaths of Eustace Barnack and Lakshmi are central to the themes of *Time Must Have a Stop* and *Island*.

In the World-State man has been enslaved by science, or as the hypnopaedic platitude puts it, 'science is everything'. But, while everything owes its origin to science, science itself has been paradoxically relegated to the limbo of the past along with culture, religion and every other worthwhile object of human endeavour. It is ironic that science, which has given the stablest equilibrium in history, should itself be regarded as a potential menace, and that all scientific progress should have been frozen since the establishment of the World-State. But it was Whitehead who said, in warning against the dangers inherent in the scientific method, 'A self-satisfied rationalism is in effect a form of anti-rationalism. It means an arbitrary halt at a particular set of abstractions'.[1] This is what has happened in *Brave New World*, where a self-satisfied rationalism has called an arbitrary halt at ectogenesis, behaviourism and hypnopaedia. The result is anti-rational in the extreme. The cause of this lies in the intrinsic nature of science itself. Wells foresaw a scientific utopia based on science as a love of truth and knowledge for its own sake; in Huxley's utopia, science has degenerated into an instrument of power. Today it would seem that Huxley's vision is the truer one. The kind of knowledge that science provides inevitably extends man's power over the physical world. Science therefore can pursue knowledge for its own sake, as Wells envisaged; or alternatively it can pursue knowledge for the sake of power. In the twentieth century, science has increasingly become identified with the pursuit of power. Russell, commenting on this tendency, drew a similar conclusion when he noted that 'We may seek knowledge of an object because we love the object or because we wish to have power over it' and that 'The scientific society of the future . . . is one in which the power impulse has completely overwhelmed the impulse of love.'[2] In *Brave New World* not only has the pursuit of all intuitive knowledge disappeared, but science itself has become incompatible with truth. Russell's summing-up which might well have served as a text for this novel, states: 'The scientific society in its pure form . . . is incompatible with the pursuit of truth, with love, with art,

[1] *Science and the Modern World*, p. 250.   [2] *The Scientific Outlook*, pp. 269–73.

with spontaneous delight, with every ideal that men have hitherto cherished. . . It is not knowledge that is the source of these
dangers. Knowledge is good and ignorance is evil. . . Nor is it
power in and for itself that is the source of danger. What is
dangerous is power wielded for the sake of power, not power
wielded for the sake of genuine good'.[1]

The epigraph to *Brave New World*, a quotation from Nicolas
Berdiaeff, posed a question:

Les utopies apparaissent comme bien plus réalisables qu'on ne le
croyait autrefois. Et nous nous trouvons actuellement devant une
question autrement angoissante: Comment éviter leur réalisation
définitive?

Huxley's fable makes no attempt to provide an answer; however,
in *Brave New World Revisited*, he returns to this point. Arguing
the case for individual freedom, he emphasizes the importance of
heredity in the life of the individual and society. Every individual
is biologically unique and unlike other individuals. Freedom and
tolerance are therefore necessary if human beings are to develop
to their full potential. Many years earlier in *Beyond the Mexique
Bay*, he had stressed the significance of 'freedom' in primitive
societies:

Man's biological success was due to the fact that he never specialized.
Unfitted by his physique to do any one thing to perfection, he was
forced to develop the means for doing everything reasonably well.
Civilization reverses the evolutionary process. . . Primitives are men
who have never succumbed to the suicidal ambition to resemble ants.
Generalization—this is the great, the vitally important lesson they have
to teach the specialists of the civilised world.

It follows that any education for freedom must stress 'the facts of
human diversity and genetic uniqueness', together with 'the value
of charity and compassion, based upon the old familiar fact, lately
rediscovered by modern psychiatry—the fact that, whatever their
mental and physical diversity, love is as necessary to human beings
as food and shelter; and finally the value of intelligence, without

[1] op. cit., p. 274.

which love is impotent and freedom unattainable' (*Brave New World Revisited*, ch. xi). As for society, the only way to avoid the threat of a future scientific utopia is to decentralize; science tends progressively to group men into larger and larger units with a proportionate loss of individual freedom—to counter this it is necessary to form small self-governing communities, freed from the restrictions of Big Business and Big Government, where people can work together as individuals and not as the embodiment of specialized functions. To persist on our present course is to invite disaster:

When we think presumptuously that we are, or shall become in some future Utopian state, 'men like gods', then in fact we are in mortal danger of becoming devils, capable only (however exalted our 'ideals' may be, however beautifully worked out our plans and blue-prints) of ruining our world and destroying ourselves. ('Man and Reality', *Vedanta for the Western World*)

The triumph of humanism, Huxley prophesies, will prove the ultimate defeat of humanity.

VIII

Eyeless in Gaza (1936)

In 'Uncle Spenser', one of his short stories of the early twenties,
Huxley wrote 'Some day, it may be, the successful novelist will
write about man's relation to God.' *Eyeless in Gaza*, Huxley's
'conversion' novel, was in every sense a beginning. Huxley's
return to contemplative mysticism, in the context of 1936, was
totally unexpected. Alexander Henderson, whose critical work on
the writer had been published in the previous year, had expressed
the hope that 'Much would be done to remove the imperfections
of English Communism if our own Brahmins, men of the quality
of Huxley and Aldington and E. M. Forster, would look more
carefully into Communism and consider whether they cannot,
after all, find it worthy of support. They would in all probability
discover, as André Gide did, that they could support it.'[1] In actual
fact Huxley had already come under the influence of Gerald
Heard, whom he had first met in 1930.[2] Dr Miller, the first of
Huxley's 'men of good will', was undoubtedly a portrait of
Heard; while the events recorded in Anthony Beavis's journal
relate directly to Heard and Huxley's activities in the Rev. H.
R. L. Sheppard's peace movement and must have occurred at
approximately the time when they were written. Their common
interests were further reflected in the two parallel tracts, Huxley's
Ends and Means, and Heard's *The Third Morality*, both published in
1937.

In terms of form, *Eyeless in Gaza* represents Huxley's most complete departure from the original 'novel of ideas'. To dramatize
the conversion theme it was necessary to show a character at
different stages of his career; and, in contrast to the earlier novels,
Eyeless in Gaza spans a period of over thirty years from the hero's

[1] *Aldous Huxley*, p. 196. [2] See Ronald W. Clark, *The Huxleys* (1968), pp. 231–2

boyhood to middle life. Instead of a chronological sequence, there is a counterpoint of four narratives describing different epochs of Anthony Beavis's life; the earliest shows him as a schoolboy at the turn of the century shortly after his mother's death; next, as an adolescent at Oxford in the years immediately preceding the first world war, when his irresponsibility leads to the death of his best friend; then, in London during the late nineteen-twenties, when his career is well established; and finally between 1933 and 1935, when he comes to the crisis which makes him reject his previous life and seek a new one. The various episodes are woven together so that the novel shifts backwards and forwards in time; thus a scene from 1926 is followed immediately by one of 1902, an event from 1914 by one of 1933 and so on. In spite of this, there is a general forward movement in time throughout the novel as a whole; the first half concentrates on the events of the years 1902 to 1926, while the latter half is largely devoted to the events of the years 1927 to 1935, which include Anthony Beavis's Diary. The separate narratives are, of course, related in a chronological order.

The opening chapters give a clue to the method. The novel begins on the occasion of Anthony's forty-second birthday, the day which is to change the whole course of his existence. Anthony, who is having an affair with Helen Ledwidge, the wife of one of his former schoolfellows, has accidentally discovered a heap of snapshots. Depicting scenes from his early life, they evoke memories of his mother and father, Mary Amberley (his first mistress), and by implication his dead friend, Brian Foxe. Their significance becomes clear as the chapter unfolds. Anthony, like Philip Quarles, is the sceptic of a scientific age, the detached philosopher, 'the preoccupied man of science who doesn't see the things that to everyone else are obvious' (ch. i). What is patently obvious, in this case, is Anthony's share in Helen's unhappiness. He has no time for emotions and responsibilities; he has denied his ability to love for what he believes to be freedom and in consequence Helen exists for him only in a context of pleasure. His love, as she puts it herself, is really a swindle, a trick for getting something for nothing. Anthony's attitude to Helen typifies his attitude to life;

at the cost of denying his responsibility to others, his freedom is complete, complete that is except for the superfluous memories, 'the corpses' that turn up inopportunely to remind him of the past. The faded snapshots, then, symbolize all the buried past Anthony would rather forget. Later, when he is making love to Helen on the sun-roof, the memories come swarming back: 'The thirty-five years of his conscious life made themselves immediately known to him as a chaos—a pack of snapshots in the hands of a lunatic'. There is no order, no purpose: somewhere in the back of his mind a lunatic shuffled the pack of cards and dealt them out at random. In spite of Freud, it was all a matter of chance:

Unless, it now rather disquietingly occurred to him, unless of course the reason were not before the event, but after it. . . What if that picture gallery had been recorded and stored away in the cellars of his mind for the sole and express purpose of being brought up into consciousness at this present moment? Brought up, today, when he was forty-two and secure, forty-two and fixed, unchangeably himself, brought up along with those critical years of his adolescence, along with the woman who had been his teacher, his first mistress, and was now a hardly human creature festering to death, alone, in a dirty burrow? And what if that absurd childish game with the flints had had a point, a profound purpose, which was simply to be recollected here on this blazing roof, now as his lips made contact with Helen's sun-warmed flesh? In order that he might be forced, in the midst of this act of detached and irresponsible sensuality, to think of Brian and of the things that Brian had lived for; yes, and had died for—died for, another image suddenly reminded him, at the foot of just such a cliff as that beneath which they had played as children in the chalk pit. Yes, even Brian's suicide, he now realized, with horror even the poor huddled body on the rocks, was mysteriously implicit in this hot skin. (ch. iii)

To allay these disquieting thoughts he begins to count the movements of his hand as he caresses Helen's warm body and, by an easy transition, the reader is taken back to 1902, when Anthony as a child is counting the wayside advertisements from the train window on the way to his mother's funeral.

The method is now apparent: from this point the chapters unfold like the heap of snapshots and the images of Anthony's memory—without chronology. The story of the growth of the hero from boyhood to his discovery in middle life that his imagined freedom is no freedom at all is presented through the episodes, the spots in time which are significant to his moral development; his conversion is only complete when he has finally accepted responsibility for the past events which he has formerly denied. The return to the experience of the past, beginning with the snapshots and memories on his forty-second birthday, is thus the start of a process which eventually restores meaning to his life. In spite of this, most critics felt when the novel appeared that the method was unjustified. It must be admitted that the device of the time shift is too mechanical; that the events of the past are recorded from outside by an impersonal narrator, whereas the treatment of time in the first chapter suggests a psychological method more after the manner of Virginia Woolf's *Mrs Dalloway*, in which the 'remembrance of things past' takes place in the mind of the protagonist. However, an early critic observed that the method does serve 'to increase the suspense, because the chief event in the story, the suicide, which chronologically comes early, is not completely related until the end'.[1] Furthermore, the presence of the journal or diary necessitated some method of this kind; placed at the end of the novel it would have confronted the reader with a huge indigestible framework of ideas, like the second epilogue to *War and Peace*. For the purposes of analysis, on the other hand, it is convenient to unravel the main narrative and restore the chronology, beginning with the events of Anthony's boyhood.

The first of the snapshots is one of Anthony's mother taken shortly before her death, the young woman who stood in a garden at the turn of the century 'like a ghost at cockcrow'. As Anthony wrote later in his journal, 'most infantile and adolescent histories are disastrous'; perhaps Anthony's was more disastrous than most. Certainly, his Hamlet's eye view of his father's second

[1] George Stevens, 'Aldous Huxley's Man of Good Will', *Saturday Review of Literature*, 11 July 1936, p. 4.

marriage is still with him in middle life. The snapshot inscribed 'Grindelwald 1912', showing his father, stepmother and two half-sisters carrying alpenstocks against the dim background of the mountains, has deeper associations going back to the months immediately after his mother's funeral. 'I would wish my days to be separated each from each by unnatural impiety,' he exclaims as he puts the picture down (ch. i). The misquotation is an echo of his father, recalling a conversation, just five months to the day after his mother's death:

'Today's the second', said his father in the same slow voice.

Anthony felt apprehensive. If his father knew the date, why had he asked?

'It's exactly five months today', Mr. Beavis went on.

Five months? And then, with a sudden sickening drop of the heart, Anthony realized what his father was talking about. The Second of November, the Second of April. It was five months since she had died.

'Each second of the month—one tried to keep the day sacred.'

Anthony nodded and turned his eyes away with a sense of guilty discomfort.

'Bound each to each by natural piety', said Mr. Beavis. (ch. ix)

The first trip to the Bernese Oberland with Anthony's future step-mother took place only three months later; and Anthony's atti-tude to his father was irrevocably fixed. 'The dramas of memory', as he observed later, 'are always Hamlet in modern dress'. The marriage for the sake of the motherless child is portrayed in vivid terms by Anthony's uncle:

The house positively reeked of matrimony. It was asphyxiating! And there sat John, fairly basking in those invisible radiations of dark female warmth, inhaling the stuffiness with a quivering nostril, deeply contented, revoltingly happy! Like a marmot . . . a marmot with its female, crowded fur to fur in their subterranean burrow. Yes, the house was just like a burrow—a burrow . . . and that unhappy little Anthony like a changeling from the world of fresh air, caught and dragged down and imprisoned in the marmot warren. (ch. xv)

His father's hypocrisy and repulsive sentimentalism foster a cynicism towards marriage and all it implies. He is to rationalize the attitude in terms of his work; later he admits that he could have accepted Helen's love; he could have even loved in return, but he had deliberately chosen to be free, to remain free for the sake of his writing. Finally, he comes to realize that his own position is as false as the one he has rejected; that having spent his whole life reacting away from his father's standards, he had become precisely what his father was—'a man in a burrow'. In his case the burrow happened to be intermittently adulterous instead of connubial. If Anthony's revolt against the connubial burrow has its origin in his father's second marriage, his scepticism towards religion and its ethical offshoots is also a family inheritance. For his father there could be no immortality after Darwin; his uncle, James Beavis, held similar views—he had grown up as a Bradlaugh atheist who ought to have been blissfully happy parading his cosmic defiance. Needless to say he was not. Much to his brother's horrified amazement, he died with all the consolations of the Catholic faith.

The first challenge to the standards Anthony has acquired from his father and uncle comes from the liberal Christianity of Mrs Foxe and her son, Brian. Brian, the child of an unsatisfactory marriage, has no father and his close relationship with his mother has disastrous consequences. The main function of Brian and his mother, however, is to serve as a foil to Anthony's cynicism. Brian's emotional temperament and nervous disposition prove an easy target for his friend's detached and sceptical view of life. Their relationship is worked out symbolically in the movement of the tiny, three-masted schooner with paper sails that spans the guttering between the two boys' bedrooms. It has been carved by Brian and, like their friendship, is a little 'lop-sided'. Brian has been consoling Anthony over his mother's death:

Balanced precariously in the tall embrasure of the windows, the two children stood there for a long time in silence. The cheeks of both of them were cold with tears; but on Anthony's wrist the grip of that consoling hand was obstinately violent, like a drowning man's.

Suddenly, with a thin rattling of withered leaves, a gust of wind came swelling up out of the darkness. The little three-master started, as though it had been woken out of sleep, and noiselessly, with an air of purposeful haste, began to glide, stern-foremost, along the gutter. (ch. vi)

A few years later the roles are reversed. It is Brian who now stands in need of consolation but this time Anthony fails to span the gap between them. He frees himself from the 'obstinately violent' hand, even though it means his friend's death. Brian's grip, then as always, is a stranglehold on his conscience.

Brian's immediate role, however, is to restore some significance to the natural order of things in the face of Anthony's negation. Tutored by Mrs Foxe's radical Christianity, he tries to explain that it is God who counts, not the church; it is caring for people that really matters. Anthony resists; his uncle does not believe in God and for that matter he doesn't either. But in spite of Anthony's defiance, the figure of his friend remains before him, an unwelcome example of the behaviour he should imitate, continually awakening an unpleasant and repressed sense of guilt. When Brian protests about the ragging of young Ledwidge,

. . . they all laughed—none more derisively than Anthony. For Anthony had had time to feel ashamed of his shame; time to refuse to think about that hole in Lollingdon churchyard; time, too, to find himself all of a sudden almost hating old Horse-Face. 'For being so disgustingly pi', he would have said, if somebody had asked him to explain his hatred. But the real reason was deeper, obscurer. If he hated Horse-Face, it was because Horse-Face was so extraordinarily decent; because Horse-Face had the courage of convictions which Anthony felt should also be *his* convictions—which, indeed, would be his convictions, if only he could bring himself to have the courage of them. (ch. vi)

Anthony's sense of moral guilt is bound up with his desire to forget 'the hole in Lollingdon churchyard'. Every act of moral cowardice is a betrayal of his dead mother—it is Hamlet in modern dress again; and on an ethical plane this is the central theme of the novel; the gap between belief and action, between knowledge and experience and the problem of transforming one into the other. Or as Anthony writes on the first page of his journal: 'Five words sum up every biography. *Video meliora proboque: deteriora sequor.* Like all other human beings, I know what I ought to do, but continue to do what I know I oughtn't to do' (ch. ii). Rachel Foxe imposes herself on Anthony as a kind of spiritual substitute for his mother, one he bitterly resents; and after her son's death she continues to act as the keeper of a conscience he would rather ignore. But for the moment her reading from Renan's *Life of Jesus*, during the Easter holidays, has the effect of a momentary conversion: 'The tears came into Anthony's eyes as he listened, and he felt an unspeakable longing to be good, to do something fine and noble' (ch. ix).

The second section of the novel covers the years 1912–14, when Anthony and Brian are at Oxford; his affair with Helen's mother, Mary Amberley, and his share in Brian's death. The forces exerting themselves on Anthony during his childhood, Mrs Foxe's Christianity on the one hand and his uncle's agnosticism on the other, are now replaced by Brian's Fabianism, with its implicit commitment to something 'fine and noble', and Gerry Watchett and his aristocratic friends. Anthony's view of life has hardened somewhat and any form of moral obligation is seen as a threat to his concept of personal freedom. He rejects Brian's Shavian equation of poverty with evil and the organization of society so that the individual couldn't commit sins because he refuses to bind himself. He professes a belief in the fundamental theory of mysticism, but he doesn't want to achieve anything—he is quite content only to know about the way of perfection. While recognizing that known truth is not the same as experienced truth, he does not consider the experience to be worth the price he would have to pay for it. When Brian points out that one has to be a prisoner to become free, Anthony is forced to admit that he is, in fact, a prisoner of knowledge; but he will always be ready to stay in that prison. The irony is not immediately apparent. To Brian the implication is of a moral rather than a spiritual nature. It is too much of a luxury, an exploitation of one's privileges; for him

Fabianism is only a beginning. He meant to go on with philosophy and literature and history until he was thirty. Then it would be time to do something else, something more direct in getting at people, in realizing the Kingdom of God. Anthony's reply is one of automatic ridicule, but after Brian has gone he feels ashamed and humiliated. It was a brainless response.

Nevertheless, the fundamental weakness in Anthony's character triumphs; Brian and the Fabians are left to their own resources and Anthony joins Gerry and his friends. Anthony's emancipation, or what he likes to think of as emancipation, is largely intellectual; the irresponsibility of the young aristocrats belongs to a social and economic order of which he has no part. They do, however, represent an aspect of freedom to which he would readily aspire:

They faced life, not diffidently and apologetically, as Anthony faced it, not wistfully, from behind invisible bars, but with the serenely insolent assurance of those who know that God intended them to enjoy themselves and had decreed the unfailing acquiescence of their fellows in all their desires. (ch. ix)

But they, like Anthony, have their own prison. In a later conversation with Staithes, he suggests that people with money or power are freer or at least less completely conditioned by their environment than the poor. This is somewhat naïve and, as Staithes is quick to point out, if he really knew rich and powerful people, he would soon feel differently. However, in spite of this, we find Anthony writing in a notebook entry for 1933, that personal freedom can only exist in the political context of an aristocrat or plutocratic society. But in fairness one must add that he was beginning to have doubts.

To return to Anthony and Brian: for a time the slight Mephistophelian influence that Anthony exerts over Brian—he had introduced him to Baudelaire, 'the words that remained in the memory like a crime'—is more than counterbalanced by Anthony's sense of shame and betrayal. Mrs Foxe, whose pseudo-scientific Christianity is beyond 'the pale of rationality', still strikes an unpleasant chord in his conscience. This delicate balance is upset by the advent of Mary Amberley, who Anthony has not seen since his mother's funeral. Mary Amberley, 'the very embodiment of desirability', was the subject of one of the snapshots taken in 1912. She belongs with the 'femme fatale' sketches of the earlier novels, Mrs Viveash and Lucy Tantamount, whose chief function is to deprive the hero of all normal concepts of morality. Mrs Amberley is no exception; she has all the ruthlessness of her predecessors and under her guidance Anthony's cynicism is allowed full rein. As he tells Helen, when looking at the snapshots, she delivered him from the worst perils of 'Darkest Switzerland' —she also delivers him from the perils of darkest Fabianism. He becomes the 'enlightened and scientific vivisector' of Brian's adolescence:

'Poor old Brian!' By his tone, by the use of the patronizing adjective, Anthony established his position of superiority, asserted his right . . . to anatomize and examine. Yes, poor old Brian! That maniacal pre-occupation of his with chastity! Chastity—the most unnatural of all the sexual perversions. . . Mary's appreciative smile acted on him like a spur to fresh efforts. Fresh efforts, of course, at Brian's expense. But at the moment, that didn't occur to him. (ch. xxvii)

The same image is used to describe Helen's flirtation with Hugh Ledwidge: 'It was an experiment, made in a spirit of hilarious scientific enquiry. She was a vivisector—licensed by perfection, justified by happiness' (ch. xx). In his eulogy to Crébillon le Fils, written in 1925, Huxley had elaborated on the spirit of detachment applied to sexual behaviour:

. . . Crébillon's attitude towards the phenomena of sex seems to me precisely that of the true scientific investigator. . . He contrives to forget that love is a matter of the most intimate human concern. . . Making a clean sweep of all prejudices, he sets to work, coolly and with detachment, as though the subject of his investigations were something as remote, as utterly divorced from good and evil, as spiral nebulae, liver flukes, or the aurora borealis. (*The Olive Tree*)

It is clear from *Point Counter Point* that Huxley saw this as one of the dominant attitudes of the time and, like Lawrence, he felt it was to be deplored. In Anthony it is a vice; from a detached observation it becomes a detached participation. He recognizes that his seduction of Joan is the result of a momentary sensuality; while his reply to Joan's innocent question about Iago, 'Men don't tell themselves that the wrong they're doing is wrong. Either they do it without thinking. Or else they invent reasons for believing it's right' (ch. xxxiii), simply reflects on the sheer irresponsibility of his behaviour. But, in spite of this, he vacillates right to the end; his final refusal to take any responsibility comes when Brian confesses his own sensual weakness for Joan and asks his friend's advice. Anthony concludes that the decision had made itself and he evades the issue once and for all by telling Brian that he ought to come to terms with reality, the same meaningless platitude he is to offer many years later to Mary Amberley, financially ruined and addicted to morphia.

Anthony's refusal to face reality is brought home to him in the light of Mrs Foxe's admission of guilt, the acceptance of her own share of responsibility for Brian's suicide. For a brief moment Anthony had been determined to tell the truth, but now he was pinned irrevocably to his own lie. The bars of Anthony's cage are forged to his own design: knowledge, detached sensuality, and the role of the vivisecting comedian; so that when Miller tells him that 'what we're all looking for is some way of getting beyond our own vomit', some way of getting beyond 'this piddling, two-penny-halfpenny personality . . . with all its wretched little virtues and vices, all its silly cravings and silly pretensions', Anthony translates it into terms of his own immediate experience:

Some way, Anthony was thinking, of getting beyond the books, beyond the perfumed and resilient flesh of women, beyond fear and sloth, beyond the painful but secretly flattering vision of the world as menagerie and asylum. (ch. xlix)

Of the three spots of time recalled in the sun-roof scene, the last belongs to Helen, the incident at the midwife's in the rue de la Tombe-Issoire. This forms the climax of the third section of the novel which describes the events of the years 1926–28 and is largely devoted to the lives of Helen and Mary Amberley. Helen is perhaps the most attractive and successful piece of characterization in the novel. She inherits some of her mother's qualities, her flippant sense of humour, her ability to give herself completely to the sensation of the moment:

Dancing, she lost her life in order to save it; lost her identity and became something greater than herself; lost her perplexities and self-hatreds in a bright harmonious certitude; lost her bad character and was made perfect; lost the regretted past, the apprehended future, and gained a timeless present of consummate happiness. (ch. xviii)

In her irresponsible flirtation with Hugh Ledwige she resembles Mary Amberley, but she is more sensitive and intelligent—her handling of Hugh's party to launch 'The Invisible Lover' is one of the humorous high spots of the novel. Further she shows some development, from her disastrous marriage to Hugh to a fuller and more mature relationship with Ekki Giesebrecht. But her progress, like her mother's, is one of increasing bondage and disillusionment. Her momentary vision of 'a timeless present of consummate happiness', like Mary's divine moment in the shadow of the Pascin nudes, is of the same order of experience as the St Matthew Passion or the Hammerclavier Sonata: they give a taste of the next world, but they are not enough. What is enough, is one of the questions Huxley is trying to answer, but clearly any form of sensual experience is suspect. Anthony in his drunken dissertation on St Thomas and mystical experience concludes that

Even St. Thomas is forced to admit that no mind can see the divine substance unless it is divorced from bodily senses, either by death or by some rapture. Some rapture, mark you! But a rapture is always a rapture, whatever it's due to. Whether it's champagne, or saying OM, or squinting at your nose, or looking at a crucifix, or making love. . . (ch. x)

But a rapture is not always a rapture; the Baroque Saints may be portrayed writhing in ecstasies of physical passion, but this is a direct misrepresentation of fact. Mere sensuality is wrong, whether

it is Anthony's detached amusement or Helen's joyous abandon-
ment, because it invariably results in enslavement to the self; and
this leads to irresponsibility and moral degradation. Physical
passion can be made compatible with responsibility, Anthony
decides, but 'only when it ceases to be an end in itself and becomes a means towards the unification through love of two
separate individuals' (ch. xv). This is suggestive of the Laurentian
relationship of *Point Counter Point*, but again there is no active
demonstration of it within the novel (Anthony himself settles for
celibacy as the only safe course); and it is not until *Island* that
Huxley is able to offer a satisfactory compromise between sensuality and the claims of moral rectitude.

The failure of Helen's sensual life, her progressive disillusionment and enslavement to the self are expressed symbolically in
three closely related scenes: the theft of the kidney, the death of
her kitten, and her subsequent seduction by her mother's lover;
there is finally the climax in the rue de la Tombe-Issoire where
desire, shame and physical revulsion become fused together in a
nightmare of delirium. On the couch in Mme Bonifay's sitting-
room, she sees Gerry making love to her again:

And Gerry was there, sitting on the edge of her bed, kissing her,
stroking her shoulders, her breasts. 'But Gerry, you mustn't! . . . Gerry,
don't!' But when she tried to push him away, he was like a block of
granite, immovable; and all the time his hands, his lips were releasing
soft moths of quick and fluttering pleasure under her skin. . . (ch.
xxxix)

Later she imagines herself with her sister, Joyce, and her baby:

She took the baby from Joyce, she pressed him close against her body,
she bent her head so as to be able to kiss those adorable little fingers.
But the thing she held in her arms was the dying kitten, was those
kidneys at the butcher's, was the horrible thing which she had opened
her eyes to see Mme. Bonifay nonchalantly picking up and carrying
away in a tin to the kitchen.

On returning to consciousness, she likens herself to the dying
kitten, reduced 'to a dirty little rag of limp flesh, transformed from

a bright living creature into something repellent, into the likeness of kidneys, of that unspeakable thing that Mme. Bonifay . . .' For a brief while with Ekki she escapes from this enslavement to the self but after his death everything is the same as before; her continuing allegiance to communism is little more than an emotional projection of her feelings for her lover, and a hatred for his torturers. A year after Ekki's disappearance, she is wishing that they had taken her too, instead of leaving her there, 'rotting away, like a piece of dirt on a rubbish heap. Like a dead kitten' (ch. liv). Her words were spoken with a vehement disgust. Such is the measure of Helen's progress. In his essay on Swift, Huxley notes that, considered as comments on reality, Gulliver and Prometheus, for all their astonishing difference, have a common origin—'the refusal on the part of their authors to accept the physical reality of the world' (*Do What You Will*). Intense disgust with physiological phenomena is always associated, in Huxley, with a refusal to face reality. Almost all the characters in the novel are guilty in their respective ways. For Helen and Anthony life is a constant evasion of facts, while Brian's refusal to come to terms with his physical passion has disastrous consequences. John Beavis and Hugh Ledwidge make their protest by deliberately mimicking the attitudes of childhood. John Beavis takes refuge in an abject and repulsive kind of sentimentalism; while the 'invisible lover', like the author of the *Journal to Stella*, desires Helen to be a bodiless abstraction, and is furious with her for being otherwise.

Further, the thematic symbols associated with Anthony and Helen are always presented in a moral context and intense feelings of disgust are invariably linked with a sense of guilt and shame. Implicit in their physical revulsion is a feeling of betrayal, whether it be the hole in Lollingdon churchyard, Helen's unborn child, or 'the millions going cold and hungry'. The refusal to face up to physical reality is just another way of evading responsibility, of refusing to accept the full consequences of one's thoughts, feelings and actions, and in the final analysis, the fact of death itself. For, on another level, the associated symbolism depicts decay and mortality;[1] as Helen was carrying her kitten across the lawn, she thought how

. . . it was not only the declining sun that made everything seem so solemnly and richly beautiful; it was also the thought of the passing days, of human limitations, of the final unescapable dissolution. . . The tears came into her eyes; she pressed the sleeping kitten more closely to her breast. (ch. xxiv)

Helen, like the other main characters in *Eyeless in Gaza*, approximates to one of W. Sheldon's physiological types referred to in *Ends and Means*. She is the viscerotonic, whose experience of life is largely emotional; Anthony, the cerebrotonic, the intellectual who can only express himself in terms of ideas; while Staithes is the somatotonic, the man of action. Each is a prisoner of his predominating tendency; Helen of her emotions, Anthony of his knowledge, and Staithes of his futile schemes to reform himself and the world. Staithes, in fact, is hardly a character at all. There is little to connect the rugby playing type at Bulstrode with the Fabian at Oxford or the misanthropist who reads *Timon*. But his function as a mouthpiece is important; as the man of action he voices the theme of political as opposed to personal freedom. It is perhaps an indication of Huxley's desire to answer his left-wing critics that Anthony, while preoccupied with his own concept of personal freedom, is always opposed by someone expounding its political counterpart. The banner of political reform is handed on through the novel from Mrs Foxe's Liberalism to Brian's Fabianism; from Staithes's revolutionary Marxism to Ekki's Communism, to fade away finally with Ekki's death and Helen's disenchantment. The political theme is never realized dramatically; the abortive Mexican revolution merely promotes discussion and provides Miller with an excuse to propound his ideas. Nevertheless it is essential to the working out of the theme; in the end, under Miller's guidance, the concepts of personal and political freedom are resolved into one. Meanwhile Staithes carries the main burden of political disillusionment: as a Marxist revolutionary, he is

[1] It will be recalled that to Mrs Viveash kidneys were a *memento mori*.

opposed to Gerry Watchett's aristocratic 'ideal'; but by the third phase of the novel his fervour has turned to cynicism. Revolution is all right in the preliminary stages when it is just a matter of getting rid of the people at the top. But afterwards, he argues, echoing Chelifer's more pessimistic strictures on the utopian society, if society is changed, what then? 'More wireless sets, more chocolates, more beauty parlours, more girls with better contraceptives . . .' (ch. xxii). In brief, simply more opportunities to be piggish. Staithes's puritanical dislike of pleasure, like Chelifer's, invites criticism; but this, of course, was only one side of the utopian picture—*Brave New World* had already provided the other. Staithe's Mexican expedition with his destructive slogan of 'Revolution for my sake' is the final measure of his disenchantment.

The fourth narrative phase returns to the events of the opening chapters of the novel, and the occasion of Anthony's forty-second birthday. This section describes the events which change the pattern of Anthony's life and lead to his conversion at the hands of Miller. Anthony, who is making love to Helen on the sunroof, has returned to his detached sensualities to avoid the unpleasant implications of the past. Into this context, 'the dog from the skies' appears like the thunderbolt of a wrathful Jehovah. The carcase of the fox terrier is a unifying symbol: it partakes of the same qualities as the thematic symbols associated with Helen—like the kitten it is 'another dirty little rag of limp flesh, transformed from a bright living creature into something repellent', and it is another object evoking a deep sense of physical disgust allied with feelings of guilt and shame. In his meditation on unity, Anthony integrates it into his total experience of physical reality: fear, shame, guilt and disgust are unified in 'the drunken Mexican's pistol . . . the dark dried blood on that mangled face among the rocks, the fresh blood spattered scarlet over Helen's naked body, the drops oozing from the raw contusion of Mark's knee' (ch. liv). Further, like the other associated symbols, it depicts mortality; Anthony compares the fly-covered carcase with Brian's battered body at the cliff's foot, and Helen links it with death. At Hugh's party Staithes asks Croyland whether he found that even *Macbeth*, even the Mass in D, or the El Greco *Assumption* were adequate against death, to which Helen adds with irony that 'Father Hopkins won't keep dogs off'. Finally, it is almost literally the *deus ex machina*—dog 'interpreted kabbalistically backwards, signifies God'. The other thematic symbols are woven into the narrative: the almost 'shapeless carcase' appears from nowhere with the moral force of a heavenly visitation:

Anthony opened his eyes for just long enough to see that the aeroplane was almost immediately above them, then shut them again, dazzled by the intense blue of the sky.

'These damned machines!' he said. Then, with a little laugh, 'They'll have a nice God's-eye view of us here', he added.

Helen did not answer; but behind her closed eyelids she smiled. Pop-eyed and with an obscene and gloating disapproval! The vision of that heavenly visitant was irresistibly comic. (ch. xii)

Then comes the thunderbolt of the angry Jehovah: like the snap-shots, it is another corpse that turned up very opportunely to shatter Anthony's complacency, and force him to re-examine once more the burden of the past.

This scene has been described as the moral pivot of the novel.[1] Certainly Anthony is never the same again. His first genuine feeling is one of pity followed by 'an almost violent movement of love' as he sees the hurt and suffering Helen as a human being for the very first time. It is too late. Helen after her baptism of blood has resolved to leave. As she is going both pause to examine a butterfly settled on a cluster of buddleia:

The spread wings were tremulous as though from an uncontrollable excess of life, of passionate energy. Rapidly, ravenously, but with an extraordinary precision of purposeful movement, the creature plunged its uncoiled proboscis into the tiny trumpet-shaped flowers that composed the cluster. . . Again, again, to the very quick of the expectant flowers, deep to the sheathed and hidden sources of that hot intoxi-

[1] Elizabeth Bowen, *Collected Impressions* (1950), p. 147.

cating sweetness! Again, again, with what a tireless concupiscence, what an intense passion of aimed and accurate greed. (ch. xii)

It is too much for Helen to watch; she flicks it away and departs almost at once. The moral is obvious to both of them. That night Anthony has a nightmare, a familiar dream that had haunted him since boyhood; now, it has a 'vague but horrible connection with the dog'. As he lies awake afterwards he is faced with 'a huge accumulation of neglected memories. . . Those snapshots. His mother and Mary Amberley. Brian in the chalk pit, evoked by that salty smell of sun-warmed flesh, and again dead at the cliff's foot, among the flies—like that dog . . .' (ch. xii).

A few days later, in the course of another sleepless night, Anthony reads Lawrence's *The Man Who Died*. At long intervals the distant crowing of a cock and the cicadas, endlessly repeating the proclamation of their existence, remind him, like the butterfly, of the irresponsible stream of energy of natural life. For Lawrence the animal purpose had seemed enough, had seemed better than 'the squalid relationships of human beings advanced half-way to consciousness, still only partially civilized' (ch. xxvi), but then Lawrence had never looked through a microscope.[1] He recalls a film of the fertilization of a rabbit's ovum: 'the horror of that display of sub-mental passion, of violent and impersonal egotism! Intolerable, unless one could think of it only as raw material and available energy', raw material that could be worked-up for other ulterior purposes. Anthony suddenly realizes that his own pursuit of knowledge, which he had once thought of as an end in itself, was only the means, was only a part of the evolutionary process like the spermatozoa struggling towards their goal, as definitely raw material as life itself, to be worked-up, but

[1] Huxley comments on *The Plumed Serpent*, ' . . . in the end, we are asked to renounce daylight and fresh air and immerse ourselves in "the grand sea of the living blood". . . We cannot accept the invitation. Lawrence's own incomparable descriptions of the horror of unadulterated blood have made it impossible. It was impossible even for himself; he could not accept his own invitation' (*Beyond the Mexique Bay*). This was written in 1934 following Huxley's visit to Central America. Lawrence's influence was already beginning to wane.

to what end? He knows what the finished product would have to be and with one part of his being he revolts against the knowledge; but with another he is miserably reflecting that he would never be able to succeed. He has no idea where or how to begin and, in the end, he is afraid of making a fool of himself. A few hours later he is telling Staithes that since the death of Brian his life has been without purpose. He had rejected the concept of an integrated personality, for

'how can there be freedom—so long as the "you" persists?. A "you" has got to be consistent and responsible, has got to make choices and commit itself. But if one gets rid of the "you", one gets rid of responsibility and the need for consistency. One's free as a succession of un-conditioned, uncommitted states without past or future, except in so far as one can't voluntarily get rid of one's memories and anticipations.' (ch. xxvi)

This was an essential part of the doctrine of *Do What You Will*, a kind of philosophical extension of Lawrence's 'non-stable ego', which Anthony had described some seven years earlier:

It was left to Blake to rationalize psychological atomism into a philosophical system. Man, according to Blake (and, after him, according to Proust, according to Lawrence), is simply a succession of states. Good and evil can be predicated only of states, not of individuals, who in fact don't exist, except as the places where the states occur. It is the end of personality in the old sense of the word. (ch. xi)

Or as one critic put it, the chief contention of *Do What You Will* was that there was no persisting self, and 'there being no persisting self there is of course, no Universe—none, that is, of which any consistent truth can be predicated'.[1] For Anthony this had become a doctrine of irresponsibility but, as he admits to Staithes, the memory is the rub. The lunatic who shuffles the cards at the back of his mind has the last word. It is Miller who provides the answer: there is a moral order 'where every event has its cause and produces its effect—where the card's forced upon you by the con-

[1] E. P. Hart, *New Adelphi*, XIII (November 1936), p. 101.

juror, but only because your previous actions have forced the conjuror to force it upon you' (ch. xlix), or as the author of the *Dhammapada* wrote, 'All that we are is the result of what we have thought'. This is the last of *Do What You Will* and the beginning of the neo-Buddhism of *Ends and Means*.

On Anthony's return to London, he accidentally meets Helen and Ekki Giesebrecht; her happiness with her new lover is an immediate reminder of his own sense of failure. To return to his old way of life is now out of the question and he decides to throw in his lot with Staithes and go to Mexico. The Mexican expedition provides Anthony with a series of experiences, paralleling those of Helen, which reveal the true nature of his imagined freedom; like Helen, he has no answer to the problem of physical suffering. The first incident which reveals his inadequacy occurs at Puerto san Felipe where the daughter of the agent lies sick with meningitis. The screaming child with her head rolling from side to side reminds him of Helen on the sun-roof; there he observed 'the symptoms of that death-bed in which he had his part as assassin and fellow-victim', Helen's face twisted in grief like one of Van der Weyden's Holy women at the foot of the Cross (ch. iii). It was all one and the same: 'Tortured by pleasure, tortured by pain. At the mercy of one's skin and mucus, at the mercy of those thin threads of nerve', and there was nothing whatever one could do about it (ch. xli). There are further examples of Anthony's inadequacy: the incident in the bar at the Hotel at Tapatlan and the amputation of Staithes' leg have a common background for which Huxley once coined the phrase, 'the human vomedy'. The first suggestion of something more positive comes when Anthony observes Staithes's face, serene and almost smiling, under the chloroform; it was the face of one who had made himself free.

But in fact, Anthony reflected, in fact he had had his freedom forced upon him by this evil-smelling vapour. Was it possible to be one's own liberator? There were snares; but also there was a way of walking out of them. Prisons; but they could be opened. And if the torture-chambers could never be abolished, perhaps the torturers could be made to seem irrelevant. (ch. xlix)

'Was it possible to be one's own liberator?' Helen on the sun-roof, the screaming child, Staithes under the anaesthetic—all stretched out supine on their beds of torment, suggest no answer. Only the picture of the martyrdom of St Erasmus in the museum at Basel indicates the way:

An executioner in a fifteenth-century costume, with a pale shell-pink codpiece, was methodically turning the handle of a winch . . . winding the saint's intestines, yard after yard, out of a gash in the emaciated belly, while the victim lay back, as if on a sofa, making himself thoroughly comfortable and looking up into the sky with an expression of unruffled equanimity. (ch. liii)

For Anthony the final moment of truth occurs when Staithes quotes Rochester. Suddenly, he is faced with the realization:

> After a search so painful and so long
> That all his life he had been in the wrong.

He resolves to go and make himself look ridiculous with Miller.

The final section of the novel covers the events of the twelve months following Anthony's return to London with Miller. It is written in the form of a diary and serves as a record of Anthony's spiritual growth. Self-knowledge, he declares, is an essential preliminary to self-change. The journal was the first step. It begins and concludes with a confession and repudiation of his past way of life:[1] the way of 'detached sensualities' and 'sterilised ideas'. His life's work had been:

A picture of futility, apparently objective, scientific, but composed, I realize, in order to justify my own way of life. If men had always behaved either like half-wits or baboons, if they couldn't behave otherwise, then I was justified in sitting comfortably in the stalls with my opera-glasses. (ch. ii)

He himself had chosen to regard the whole process as either pointless or a practical joke; as he admits in the closing chapter of the novel, it had been a deliberate act of the will. This avowal is to

---

[1] This is a structural feature of the novel: the two confessions belong to the second and final chapters respectively.

some extent autobiographical and is paralleled by a similar confession in *Ends and Means* where, posing the question of 'significance', Huxley says that, like so many of his contemporaries, he took it for granted that there was no meaning; but as he also concedes, most ignorance is vincible ignorance. We don't know because we don't want to know. The knowledge, as Anthony so frequently insists, had always been there, but knowledge is not enough. The problem, as always, is how to transform it into a practical way of life. This is the function of Dr Miller, the first of Huxley's exemplary characters who were to point the way.

James Miller, as it has previously been suggested, is essentially a mouthpiece for the ideas of Gerald Heard. In *The Third Morality* (1937), Heard outlines the training he considers necessary to fit the facts of the 'new cosmology'. The three physical means consist of diet, psycho-physical re-education and co-ordination on the lines propounded by F. M. Alexander, and lastly control of the respiration. These functions, although generally subconscious, can be brought into full consciousness and re-ordered to produce a better pattern of basic psycho-physical behaviour.[1] Bodily training is to be practised in conjunction with meditation, the fundamental technique of Hindu and Buddhist mysticism whereby the individual achieves a state of self-awareness and non-attachment. Here are the main features of Dr Miller's system: 'a non-theological praxis of meditation which he would like . . . to couple with training, along F. M. Alexander's lines, in use of the self, beginning with physical control and achieving through it (since mind and body are one) control of impulses and feelings' (ch. ii). To which Huxley has added the form of pacifism known as passive or nonviolent resistance; this is the political correlative of the ethic of non-attachment.

The idea that there is a persisting self which can be re-educated represents an important advance in Huxley's thought. Anthony, we recall, had finally reached the point of rejecting the concept of the self as a 'succession of unconditioned, uncommitted states'. This marked Huxley's final break with Rampion's or Lawrence's

[1] See pp. 276–7.

doctrine of 'life-worship'. Just how far Huxley had committed himself to this theory it is hard to say; less one might suppose than most critics have imagined. In *Point Counter Point*, the characters far from being free as a 'succession of states' were at the mercy of their bodily functions—the very existence of the body was a cynical comment on the soul; and there was little to suggest that any kind of radical change were possible. In fact, it is precisely this lack of freedom, so painfully manifest in Helen and Anthony, that lies behind so much of Huxley's pessimism. Bernard's cry of 'what would it be like . . . if I were free—not enslaved by my conditioning' is not restricted to the confines of *Brave New World*. It would have seemed indeed at times that Huxley had succumbed to the Behaviourist view that 'mind is merely an epiphenomenon of matter'. Anthony certainly sees the mind as determined by the body, 'at the mercy of one's skin and mucus', at least he does so before he meets Miller. Then in the journal a new note of optimism appears:

Conditioned reflex. What a lot of satisfaction I got out of old Pavlov when first I read him. The ultimate de-bunking of all human pretensions. We were all dogs and bitches together. . . No nonsense about free will, goodness, truth and all the rest. Each age has its psychological revolutionaries. . . The nineteenth century had to begin again. Marx and the Darwinians. Who are still with us—Marx obsessively so. Meanwhile the twentieth century has produced yet another lot of de-bunkers—Freud and, when he began to flag, Pavlov and the Behaviourists. Conditioned reflex: it seemed, I remember, to put the lid on everything. Whereas actually, of course, it merely re-stated the doctrine of free-will. For if reflexes can be conditioned, then, obviously, they can be re-conditioned. Learning to use the self properly, when one has been using it badly—what is it but re-conditioning one's reflexes? (ch. vii)

This is the secret of F. M. Alexander's method. In his introduction to Alexander's *The Use of the Self*, John Dewey writes: 'The school of Pavloff has made current the idea of conditioned reflexes. Mr. Alexander's work extends and corrects the idea. It proves that there are certain basic, central organic habits and attitudes which condition *every* act we perform, every use we make of ourselves. . . This discovery corrects the ordinary conception of the conditioned reflex. The latter as usually understood renders an individual a passive puppet to be played upon by external manipulations. The discovery of a central control which conditions all other reactions brings the conditioning factor under conscious direction and enables the individual through his own co-ordinated activities to take possession of his own potentialities. It converts the fact of conditioned reflexes from a principle of external enslavement into a means of vital freedom.'[1] In *Ends and Means* Huxley goes further and states that the physical attributes achieved by Alexander's method lead ultimately to greater mental and moral self-awareness and self-control. This was a completely new concept of the conditioned reflex, the importance of which need hardly be emphasized here.

Meditation can also be conceived as another method of self-education, a further means of gaining greater self-awareness and self-control; but it is, of course, more than this: it has always been the primary means of achieving what Huxley has called man's final end and purpose, the unitive knowledge of the Godhead, or as he puts it somewhat more tentatively in *Ends and Means*, 'the direct intuition of, and union with, an ultimate spiritual reality that is perceived as simultaneously beyond the self and in some way within it' (ch. xiv). Miller, like Heard, wanted meditation practice to be strictly 'non-theological' to attract the widest possible following and, as Anthony insists, meditation in no way necessitates the belief in a personal Deity: 'God may or may not exist. But there is the empirical fact that contemplation of the divinity—of goodness in its most unqualified form—is a method of realizing that goodness to some slight degree in one's life. . .' (ch. xliv). Whether one believes in a personal God or not is a matter of taste. The psychological results will be the same.

In the final chapter, Anthony's meditation on unity draws together the threads of the novel; it is a movement away from individual separateness to a merging with the spiritual reality of

[1] *The Use of the Self* (1946), p. xxi.

the universe. It begins with the physical facts of Anthony's life, the importunate memories that pinpoint his weaknesses and failures; it dwells on the 'almost nightmarish vision of a more-than-Bergsonian life force' of the sub-microscopic world; then it spirals upwards to higher forms of life and existence, moving away from evil—all that emphasizes the separate self, towards goodness, love and compassion. 'Step by step towards the experience of being no longer wholly separate, but united at the depths with other lives, with the rest of being', to merge finally in an ultimate vision of peace, unity and liberation:

Peace from pride and hatred and anger, peace from cravings and aversions, peace from all the separating frenzies. Peace through liberation, for peace is achieved freedom. Freedom and at the same time truth. The truth of unity actually experienced. . . Peace in this profound subaqueous night, peace in this silence, this still emptiness where there is no more time, where there are no more images, no more words. . . For now there is only the darkness expanding and deepening, deepening into light: there is only this final peace, this consciousness of being no more separate, this illumination . . .[1]

The personal and political themes merge together at the point where the individual takes responsibility. Personal and political freedom are compatible in the form of non-violent resistance or 'positive pacifism'. Here again, the material is largely autobiographical. Huxley's pamphlet, *What Are You Going to do About It?*, the case for constructive peace, was published in the summer of 1936. Asking for recruits for the Rev. H. R. L. Sheppard's peace movement,[2] Huxley warned that the formation of another subscription-collecting, literature-distributing and pledge-signing society would not be enough. The constructive peace movement

[1] Gerald Heard, *The Third Morality*, p. 258, states: 'The first contemplation must be of the unifying life to which the individual belongs and into which he may be delivered by pushing through and beyond his individualistic arbitrary frontiers.'

[2] The Peace Pledge Movement which included such well-known figures as Bertrand Russell, Middleton Murry, Siegfried Sassoon, George Lansbury and Donald Soper.

had to be all these things; but it also had to be a kind of religious order in which the members were dedicated to a definite way of life. The organization would take the form of an affiliation of small groups of five to ten individuals, such as those adopted by the early Christians, the Quakers, the Wesleyans and the Communists. Intensive training would be necessary because peace and social justice can only be realized by means that are just and pacific. And human beings will only behave justly and pacifically if they have been trained to do so. Miller, who had learned his technique of non-violence as a field anthropologist, provides Anthony with a practical demonstration while addressing the meeting at Tower Hill, when he allows himself to be assaulted by an angry heckler; but it is clear that Huxley envisaged far more of the peace movement than mere resistance to hostile crowds. In *Ends and Means* he foresees trained groups that would 'go out into the world' where they would organize non-violent resistance to domestic oppression, and intercede between hostile armies.

All other means of social reform will ultimately fail because they do not make sufficient allowances for the freedom of the individual. Brian's Fabian concept of a society organized 'so well the individual couldn't commit sins' is limited because preventative ethics are not enough. Prevention is good but it cannot eliminate the necessity for a cure. One is external to the individual, the other, the individual teaching of right use, gets rid of the cause of maladjustment and therefore of the occasions giving rise to bad behaviour. What is needed is a method of achieving progress from within as well as from without. Progress, not only as a citizen, a machine-minder and machine-user, but also as a human being. Staithes rejected communism because he thought the ultimate end unworthy: 'Millions and millions of soft, piggish Babbitts, ruled by a small minority of ambitious Staitheses' (ch. xxii), but Anthony rejects it because he believes that the means would finally defeat the ends: 'One of the first discoveries . . . one makes', he tells Helen, 'is that organized hatred and violence aren't the best means for securing justice and peace' (ch. liv). If reform is to be regarded simply as a matter of politics, then it seems one must approve and practise liquidation; governments with comprehensive plans for the betterment of society have invariably been governments that have used torture, but a solution is possible if one thinks in terms of individual men and women. All the evils of society are performed not in the name of individuals but in the name of the nation. In the end, Anthony concluded, there is 'no remedy except to become aware of one's interests as a human being' (ch. xxxv).

IX

After Many a Summer (1939)

In 1937, accompanied by Gerald Heard, Huxley left England for the United States. There were many reasons for his departure: the civil war in Spain and the formation of the Popular Front had created a climate unfavourable to pacifism; the outbreak of a widespread conflict in Europe now seemed inevitable and once the fighting had started there was little the pacifist propagandist could hope to achieve. *After Many a Summer*, written shortly after Huxley's arrival in America, reflects something of the frustration of the time, the sense of impending disaster, of 'humanity tearing toward perdition',[1] when the best that the man of goodwill could do was to withdraw and forge the blueprints for a better world. This was Huxley's intention in *After Many a Summer*: to work on 'the technics of a better system', to lay the foundations for a future society which would incorporate all the neglected wisdom of the past. In this he shared a common object with Gerald Heard, whose *Pain, Sex and Time* had been published earlier in the same year. Heard, in his new hypothesis of evolution, advocated the formation of small self-subsisting communities where techniques for psychological advancement could be explored in an atmosphere free from the distractions of civilization. *After Many a Summer*, while not exactly 'a fictional twin to Heard's tract',[2] advanced the claims of the contemplative life as the main cure for an unregenerate world. It is clear that both authors saw in the small religiously orientated community the mainstay of sanity and survival in a world now seemingly bent on

[1] See Edgar Johnson, *Kenyon Review*, II (Summer, 1940), p. 353.
[2] William York Tindall, *Forces in Modern British Literature* (New York, 1956), p. 174.

self-destruction. The keynote of both works was one of with-drawal and retrenchment.

For *After Many a Summer* Huxley returned to the country-house party formula of the early novels (the *locus* is Jo Stoyte's ferro-concrete fortress situated outside Hollywood); and in both form and style *After Many a Summer* is more reminiscent of *Antic Hay* than any of its predecessors. This lack of interest in form, which characterises all Huxley's later work, was accompanied by an increasing preoccupation with the didactic content of the novel; and at this point, as most critics have observed, the moralist began to take precedence over the novelist. There is no doubt that the urgency of the times contributed to this shift in emphasis, which was further reflected in Huxley's violent and prejudiced attack on the 'so-called good literature'. What was wrong with most conventional plays and novels, he argued, was that they lacked a 'unifying philosophy': they were just 'a huge collection of facts about lust and greed, fear and ambition, duty and affec-tion; just facts, and imaginary facts at that, with no co-ordinating philosophy superior to common sense and the local system of conventions. . . .' Further, by condoning the values of a decadent society literature helped indirectly to perpetuate the main causes of human misery:

. . . it accepted the conventional scale of values; it respected power and position; it admired success; it treated as though they were reason-able the mainly lunatic preoccupations of statesmen, lovers, business men, social climbers, parents. . . It helped to perpetuate misery by explicitly or implicitly approving the thoughts and feelings and prac-tices which could not fail to result in misery. (Pt. II, ch. v)

This sounds like a reply to those critics who had attacked the overt moralizing of *Eyeless in Gaza*; but Huxley undoubtedly felt that literature in general had failed in its moral purpose, that of wean-ing the public from patterns of behaviour which were unequivo-cally bad and of providing alternative patterns which were as unequivocally good. 'Literary example', he had written in *Ends and Means*, 'is a powerful instrument for the moulding of character', adding that there was 'a great need for literary artists as the educators of a new type of human being' (ch. xii).

What kind of novel was the literary educator to write? In *After Many a Summer* there is the advice that in a really corrupt society the only safe attitude is one of steady unflagging cynicism. For Huxley 'cynicism' in the moral context of literature meant satire. There is no surprise, therefore, when he concludes that a good satire, in so far as it refuses to accept the values condoned by the 'so-called good literature' is more truthful and profitable than a good tragedy. That he had his own novel in mind is evident, for he goes on to criticize *Candide* for offering nothing better in the way of a palliative than the 'ideal of harmlessness'. Whatever it may lack in other respects, *After Many a Summer* is a good satire in that it both rejects the accredited standards of the day and is firmly grounded in a 'unifying philosophy' superior to Voltaire's 'ideal of harmlessness'. By subscribing to a satirical sketch of pre-war materialism with an exemplary hero preaching a doctrine of enlightenment, Huxley had committed himself to the task of the 'literary educator' in no uncertain manner.

To consider the satirical elements first. The setting of *After Many a Summer* is California during the last months of the Spanish Civil War, when the newspaper hoardings headline Franco's drive on Barcelona. The contemporary American scene is given much the same treatment as the London of the nineteen-twenties in *Antic Hay*. This is the sick society, the unregenerate world of debased spirituality and *ersatz* values. The Los Angeles streets mirror the *Zeitgeist* in a bewildering profusion of drug stores, hamburger bars and giant billboards. Religious faiths have proliferated but their temples rear up in the unfamiliar guise of alien creeds: Primitive Methodist churches built in the style of the Cartuja at Granada, synagogues disguised as Hagia Sophia, Christian Science churches with pillars and pediments, like banks. Billboards equate the divine with commerce, sexuality and the occult: offers of 'Cash loans in Fifteen Minutes' brush shoulders with admonitions to 'Go to Church and Feel Better All the Week'; prognostications of the coming of the Saviour compete with the expectations of 'Abiding Youth with Thrillphorm Brassieres'. But this medley of startling juxtapositions is only a prelude; the real centre of what Pete Boone calls 'the absurd, insane, diabolical confusion of it all' is Jo Stoyte's ungainly monument to material success, the pseudo-Gothic fortress in the environs of Hollywood. Here in a kind of cultural motley all the furnishings of the civilized world are thrown together in a meaningless profusion, a symbol of a world in which everything cancels everything else out. A manifestation of the mental disorder of its occupants, Stoyte's castle is 'like walking into the mind of a lunatic' where 'every item is perfectly irrelevant to every other item'; it is the perfect 'embodiment of an imbecile's no-track mind'.

In the great hall of the castle, lit by hidden searchlights, El Greco's 'Crucifixion of St Peter' and Rubens's full-length portrait of Hélène Fourment dressed only in a bearskin cape, confront each other from opposite ends of the cavernous room; the ectoplasm of the inverted saint and the creams and warm pinks of Flemish nudity, two 'shining symbols, incomparably powerful and expressive—but', Huxley insists, '. . . of what?' (Pt. I, ch. iii). There was a similar juxtaposition of the spiritual and the sensual at the castle approach: the replica of the Grotto of Lourdes and the bronze nymph of Giambologna spouting streams of water from her polished breasts. In fact, the novel fairly bristles with motifs of this kind, symbolizing, no doubt, what Huxley calls the 'chronic civil war between passion and prudence and, on a higher level of awareness and ethical sensibility, between egotism and dawning spirituality' (*The Perennial Philosophy*, ch. vii). This is the 'wearisome condition of humanity', but what typifies the American scene is the confusion arising out of a vain attempt to enjoy the best of both worlds. The *reductio ad absurdum* of this principle is embodied in Jo Stoyte's Personality Cemetery. The Beverley Pantheon, with its Perpetual Wurlitzer reminiscent of the Hospital for the Dying in *Brave New World* in its deliberate attempt to evade the reality of death, is almost literally a temple of worship to all the gods of pleasure—from the replicas of 'Le Baiser' to the Bride's Apartment, Hollywood style. Only in the Children's

Corner does the Infant Jesus appear alongside a medley of Peter Pan, alabaster babies and bronze rabbits. With the basic idea of injecting sex-appeal into death, all representations of grief, age, mortality, and the suffering of Christ, everything possibly suggestive of the spiritual life has been ruthlessly suppressed. 'Death is swallowed up in victory', proclaim the scrolls, but 'the victory no longer of the spirit but of the body, the well-fed body, for ever youthful, immortally athletic, indefatigably sexy' (Pt. I, ch. ii). On the surface the somatotonic revolution is complete but underlying it a harsher reality speaks: the well-fed body is not, alas, for ever, youthful, nor immortally athletic, nor indefatigably sexy; it is bald, long-sighted, short-winded, edentate, chronically constipated, its digestion capricious and its potency falling off; it is pepped up with synthetic hormones, and in its horror of the approaching end it turns to science in a futile search for longevity. Herein lies the moral of Huxley's tale: 'Man cannot live in a chronic state of negation: the voids of thought and feeling must be filled, and if we reject the divine, its place will inevitably be taken by some idolatrous *ersatz*' (*Themes and Variations*). The *ersatz*, in this case, is only too painfully inadequate.

The personages of *After Many a Summer* typify the frustrations arising from the pursuit of the 'idolatrous *ersatz*': there is Jeremy Pordage weltering in a luxuriance of Bloomsbury aestheticism; Virginia Maunciple, Stoyte's child mistress, Catholic and promiscuous; Pete Boone with his American college boy brand of Marxist idealism; and Stoyte himself, the rapacious tycoon, whose hunger for possession has decimated every corner of the civilized globe. Stoyte's whole life is one long attempt to fill the vast void of his personality: wealth, culture, sexuality and religion—each in turn offers its brief moment of consolation and then shrinks away before the recurring horror of his death-fixation. In the pursuit of riches Stoyte has become an adept hand at accruing advantages from both worlds. The tycoon exploits the glut of transient labour to force wages down to a near-starvation level; while the philanthropist endows universities and finances the finest children's hospital in the state. But, in his extremity, neither

the prospect of another million nor the excited occupants of the
Stoyte Home for Sick Children bring relief.

Ironically, the chief benefactor of Stoyte's acquisitive instinct is
Jeremy Pordage, the foreigner on the American scene. Almost all
the characters of *After Many a Summer* cling to what Propter calls
'the idiot world of the *homme moyen sensuel*—the world where the
irrelevances consist of newspapers and baseball, of sex and worry,
of advertising and money and halitosis and keeping up with the
Joneses' (Pt. I, ch. xii). Jeremy, however, being both a scholar
and an Englishman, a product of Trinity College, Cambridge,
inhabits a private universe where the irrelevances are of a classier
variety:

. . . the daily walk with Mr. Gladstone, the Yorkshire terrier. And the
library; the works of Voltaire in eighty-three volumes; the inexhaustible treasure of Horace Walpole; and for a change the *Divine Comedy*;
and then, in case you might be tempted to take the Middle Ages too
seriously, Salimbene's autobiography and the Miller's Tale. And sometimes calls in the afternoon—the Rector, Lady Fredegond with her ear-
trumpet, Mr. Veal. And political discussions—except that in these last
months, since the *Anschluss* and Munich, one had found that political
discussion was one of the unpleasant things it was wise to avoid. And
the weekly journey to London, with lunch at the Reform . . . and
Vespers at Westminster Cathedral, if they happened to be singing
Palestrina; and every alternate week, between five and six-thirty, an
hour and a half with Mae or Doris in their flat in Maida Vale. Infinite
squalor in a little room, as he liked to call it; abysmally delightful.
(Pt. I, ch. viii)

The patchwork of mutual irrelevances which make up Jeremy's
mind provide a kind of analogue to the castle; and, while Stoyte
has neither the slightest understanding nor regard for the possessions accumulated in his name, Jeremy soon discovers his spiritual
home among the cultural bric-à-brac. It is the fulfilment of the
scholar escapist's dream where there were no issues and nothing
led anywhere: a universe of infinite cosiness, 'of hermetically
bottled art and learning, of culture for its own sake'.

Stoyte is neither a scholar nor a gentleman and if his manifold possessions bring no consolation to their indifferent owner, his experiment in sensuality proves equally barren. Stoyte's child mistress, Virginia Maunciple, epitomises the incongruities of her environment: like those American girls who appeared to be absorbed in silent prayer but in reality were only ruminating on gum, Virginia has the air of 'being hardly adolescent, of not having reached the age of consent' while, at the same time, being a mature ex-show girl of twenty-two and Stoyte's mistress. Paying a token tribute to the conventions, she accepts without question the double morality of the Los Angeles billboards; her sensibility outraged by the spouting breasts of Giambologna's nymph, she takes a salacious pleasure in Nerciat and the *Cent-Vingt Jours de Sodome*. A practising Catholic, she entertains a miniature shrine in her bedroom, an effigy of Our Lady brilliantly illuminated by a system of concealed electric bulbs. Nevertheless her relationship with 'Uncle Jo' calls forth no moral scruples. In the world in which she lived 'it was axiomatic that a man who could make a million dollars must be wonderful. Parents, friends, teachers, newspapers, radio advertisements—explicitly or by implication, all were unanimous in proclaiming his wonderfulness' (Pt. i, ch. iv). To be such a man's mistress could scarcely be wrong; to be unfaithful to him might have its disadvantages but it scarcely stepped beyond the bounds of propriety. Father O'Reilly would, of course, disapprove, but Our Lady would be a lot more understanding and forgiving than he was. Virginia's caprice, however, proves her undoing; sexuality, she discovers, has more attributes than moonlight and soft music.

Stoyte, meanwhile, deprived of his source of 'purest father love' and 'violent eroticism', is alone with his miseries. Religion might have helped him, but what to Virginia is a mixed blessing, to Stoyte is pure poison. Stoyte, in fact, is almost a sacrificial victim to the proliferation of faiths: his late wife, Prudence McGladdery Stoyte, whom he curses for reminding him of death by her insistence that there wasn't any, had been a Christian Scientist; his maternal grandmother, on the other hand, had lived and died a Plymouth Sister and, as a result, his memory is haunted by the text which had hung over his childhood bed: 'IT IS A TERRIBLE THING TO FALL INTO THE HANDS OF THE LIVING GOD.' Prudence's 'God is love. There is no death' has become a kind of talisman which he murmurs to himself in moments of doubt, but it pales alongside the childhood threat now ineradicably stamped on his mind. For all his cupidity, Stoyte is hardly a personification of greed; in the grip of a horrible death-fixation he emerges, like Cardan or John Bidlake, another of Huxley's morality figures, a frightened and self-pitying old man tottering on the brink of the grave:

In the world he had been reduced to inhabiting, millions were irrelevant. For what could millions do to allay his miseries? The miseries of an old, tired, empty man; of a man who had no end in life but himself, no philosophy, no knowledge but of his own interests, no appreciations, not even any friends—only a daughter-mistress, a concubine-child, frantically desired, cherished to the point of idolatry. And now this being, on whom he had relied to give significance to his life, had begun to fail him. He had come to doubt her fidelity . . . he was in a situation with which he did not know how to deal, hopelessly bewildered. And always, in the background of his mind, there floated an image of that circular marble room, with Rodin's image of desire at the centre, and that white slab in the pavement at its base—the slab that would some day have his name engraved upon it: Joseph Panton Stoyte, and the dates of his birth and death. And along with that inscription went another, in orange letters on a coal-black ground: 'It is a terrible thing to fall into the hands of the living God.' (Pt. II, ch. iii)

In the unregenerate world the sum of human misery is a constant. The plight of Stoyte is reflected in the plight of that other former capitalist and slave-trader, the Fifth Earl of Gonister, who, almost two centuries earlier had written:

From solitude in the Womb, we emerge into solitude among our Fellows, and return again to solitude within the Grave. We pass our lives in the attempt to mitigate that solitude. . . We reiterate the act of love; but . . . propinquity is never fusion. The most intimate contact is only of Surfaces, and we couple, as I have seen the condemned Prisoners at Newgate coupling with their Trulls, between the bars of our cages. . . The reality of Solitude is the same in all men, there being no mitigation of it, except in Forgetfulness, Stupidity or Illusion; but a man's sense of Solitude is proportionate to the sense and fact of his Power. In any set of circumstances, the more Power we have, the more intensely do we feel our solitude. (Pt. II, ch. iv)

Stoyte, like the Fifth Earl before him, seeks reprieve from his darkest fears in the faint hope of longevity; but, whereas the Fifth Earl seeks mitigation in carp, Stoyte's faith, rather less happily, is placed in the person of Dr Obispo.

Dr Obispo and Mr Propter, representing the conflicting ideologies in the novel, are symbolic manifestations of the material, spiritual motifs referred to earlier. Delineated with an almost allegorical simplicity, they hover around Stoyte like the good and evil angels round a tottering Faustus, Obispo tempting with his promise of rejuvenation, while Propter offers the more permanent, if less immediate, attractions of enlightenment. Dr Obispo, a ruthless 'go-getter', is a crude personification of scientific materialism. Like Ivor Lombard of *Crome Yellow* and Gerry Watchett of *Eyeless in Gaza*, he typifies the kind of self-interest which guarantees survival in a society where morality is confused and values are in decline. The product of an environment in which the only criterion of success is material gain, he entertains no illusions about progress, human happiness or ultimate truth; religion is a morass of meaningless words, and literature the result of bad doctoring— thiamin chloride and testosterone, he boasts, would have strangled romantic poetry at birth. Propter, in his own way, is equally single-minded, but to a less worldly end. In *The Perennial Philosophy*, Huxley asks why it is that in the whole repertory of epic drama and the novel there are hardly any representations of true theocentric saints. The trouble with saints is that they are all incessantly preoccupied with only one subject—spiritual Reality; and as for their actions—these are as monotonously uniform as their thoughts. For these reasons the saintly figure is unlikely to provide the novelty and diversity of character required by the average reader. In spite of this, Huxley's fullest portrait of a contemplative mystic is not without merit. It is true that he is 'incessantly preoccupied' with one topic, spiritual Reality; but, while outlining Huxley's contemplative philosophy, his monologues also provide a fitting commentary on the idolatrous pursuits of the others. A 'bit of an Ancient Mariner', as Jeremy suggests, he is in no sense like Rampion, a mere mouthpiece for ideas; with his colony of transients in the making he not only preaches good works but is seen to do them. Probably the real danger of saintly figures, and this was a failing of Dr Miller's, is that they appear overbearing and patronising in their attitude to their weaker brethren. Propter, though behaving in a consistently selfless, patient and charitable manner, is relatively free from this fault. His character is such that he makes no converts; his impact on the others is marginal, yet he remains 'intensely *there*, more present, so to speak, radiating more life than anyone else' (Pt. I, ch. ix). For this reason, he is, perhaps, the most successful and likeable of all Huxley's men of goodwill.

The 'unifying philosophy' of *After Many a Summer*, Propter's gospel of enlightenment, contains Huxley's most complete fictional rendering of contemplative mysticism and its relation to the political and social problems of the time outside of *Island*[1] and unlike the latter, it is largely based on Christian sources. The first main statement emerges from Propter's meditation on Cardinal Bérulle's definition of man: 'A nothingness surrounded by God, indigent and capable of God, filled with God, if he so desires'. Man is a 'nothingness' because his personality is illusory; his 'all-important ego' is 'a fiction, a kind of nightmare, a frantically agitated nothingness' (Pt. I, ch. viii). To conceive the ego as something permanent is the height of human folly:

Madness consists . . . in thinking of oneself as a soul, a coherent and enduring human entity. But . . . there is nothing on the human level

---

[1] This was, in fact, Huxley's first attempt at rationalizing a mystical philosophy; the completer non-fictional versions, *Grey Eminence* and *The Perennial Philosophy*, come later.

except a swarm of constellated impulses and sentiments and notions; a swarm brought together by the accidents of heredity and language; a swarm of incongruous and often contradictory thoughts and desires. Memory and the slowly changing body constitute a kind of spatio-temporal cage, within which the swarm is enclosed. To talk of it as though it were a coherent and enduring 'soul' is madness. On the strictly human level there is no such thing as a soul. (Pt. II, ch. x)

This description of man's nature owes more than a little to the Buddhist doctrine of *Anatta* or Not-Self, as it is called, which, in turn, bears a close resemblance, in Western philosophy, to 'Hume's denial of the existence of the ego as an entity distinct from mental processes'.[1] What Huxley wishes to stress, however, is the emptiness of the posturings of the ego and the danger inherent in the identification of man's essential nature with his illusory personality.

Man, then, is a 'nothingness' but he is also 'indigent and capable of God', capable of being filled with God if he fulfills certain requirements the foremost of which is to love God, in the words of Molinos, as He is in Himself and not as he exists in the imagination. But 'Dios en si' cannot be comprehended by a consciousness dominated by the ego. There is no personal God, no God who can be worshipped on a purely human level; there is only 'God in himself' unknowable to the personal human mind. The unitive knowledge of God, then, can only be realized by what the Christian mystics call 'self-naughting' or 'dying to self', or as it is expressed in *The Perennial Philosophy*, 'Spiritual progress is through the growing knowledge of the self as nothing and of the Godhead as all-embracing Reality' (ch. ix). The insistence on a separative self is the most formidable obstacle to spiritual Reality,[2] nevertheless man is free to be 'filled with God, if he so desires'. On the strictly human level every psychological pattern is

---

[1] See Edward Conze, *Buddhism* (New York, 1959), pp. 19–20.

[2] 'All the mystics agree that the stripping off of the I, the Me, the Mine, utter renouncement, or "self-naughting"—self-abandonment to the direction of a larger Will—is an imperative condition of the attainment of the unitive life.' Evelyn Underhill, *Mysticism* (1960), p. 425.

determined, but it is in man's power to pass from the level
of the absence of God to God's presence:

No iron necessity condemns the individual to the futile torment of
being merely human. Even the swarm we call the soul has it in its
power temporarily to inhibit its insane activity, to absent itself, if only
for a moment, in order that, if only for a moment, God may be present.
But let eternity experience itself, let God be sufficiently often present in
the absence of human desires and feelings and preoccupations: the
result will be a transformation of the life which must be lived, in the
intervals, on the human level. . . Bondage gives place to liberty—for
choices are no longer dictated by the chance occurrences of earlier history, but are made teleologically and in the light of a direct insight into
the nature of things. Violence and mere inertia give place to peace—
for violence is the manic, and inertia the depressive, phase of that cyclic
insanity, which consists in regarding the ego or its social projections as
real entities. Peace is the serene activity which springs from the knowledge that our 'souls' are illusory and their creations insane, that all
beings are potentially united in eternity. (Pt. II, ch. x)

This is the essence of Propter's teaching centred on the quotations
from Bérulle and Molinos. (The theology of the seventeenth century was one of Huxley's special interests and led to the two studies
of the Counter Reformation, Grey Eminence and The Devils of
Loudun).

At the beginning of Propter's long discourse on spiritual reality
he makes the assertion that time is evil. The theme of time unites
the plot with the didactic elements of the novel: there is the
implied moral choice between the psychological eternity of the
mystic and the promised longevity of the scientist. The result of
choosing existence in time is evolutionary regression, the simian
paradise that awaits Obispo and Stoyte in the cellars at Gonister.
This suggests a polarity of time in terms of good and evil: psychological eternity is what Propter calls 'timeless good'; existence in
time, as the story of the Fifth Earl illustrates, is potentially evil.
In Propter's words: 'Time is potential evil, and craving converts the potentiality into actual evil'; goodness exists only
outside time, 'a temporal act can never be more than potentially

good, with a potentiality . . . that can't be actualized except out
of time' (Pt. 1, ch. ix). This was the kind of thinking that
aroused the hostility of the critics, although, in fact, Christian
mystics had voiced similar ideas. John Scotus thought that 'to enter
the time-process must be to contract a certain admixture of un-
reality or evil', while Eckhart expresses the same idea in stronger
terms: '. . . time, which is what keeps the light from reaching us.
There is no greater obstacle to God than time. Not only time but
temporalities, not only temporal things but temporal affections;
not only temporal affections, but the very taint and aroma of
time.'[1] In *The Perennial Philosophy* Huxley holds to this view;
criticizing the Hebrew-Christian tradition of the Fall, he asserts
that the act of creation, of incarnation in time, was 'not merely the
prelude and necessary condition of the Fall; to some extent it *is*
the Fall'; and, further, that in the Hindu and Buddhist renderings
of the perennial philosophy, 'pain and evil are inseparable from
individual existence in a world of time' (ch. xi). On the level of
time and craving, then, nothing can be achieved but evil and
Propter concludes that on the strictly human level the world is
beyond hope. All this sounds very much like the kind of quietist
doctrine of which Huxley has been accused by his left-wing
critics.[2] If existence in time is evil, then, clearly there is no point in
trying to ameliorate the human condition; but, of course, Huxley
would never have lent credence to this view. Propter concedes that
he would call an act good if it enhanced the liberation of those
concerned in it and his whole life is devoted to 'good' acts of this
kind. Again, as Huxley himself realized, 'Man must live in time
in order to be able to advance into eternity' (*The Perennial Philosophy*, ch. vii), or, in T. S. Eliot's phrase, 'Only through time
time is conquered'.

The real obstacle to any kind of human progress lies in the fact
that, whereas things are good or bad depending on whether they
facilitate liberation, most human activities merely intensify the

[1] Quoted by Rudolph Otto, *Mysticism East and West* (New York, 1959), p. 66.
[2] Burgum, for example, accuses him of justifying an 'indifference to the suffering of others'. See *The Novel and the World's Dilemma*, p. 142.

obsession with the personality. Even on the highest level the artist's ideal of beauty and the scientist's ideal of truth are merely projections on an enormously large scale of certain aspects of the personality. What appears to be selflessness is really another aspect of bondage, the sacrifice of one part of the ego to another part. This is true of all self-sacrifice, however devoted and heroic it may appear. Pete Boone's ideal of loyalty and comradeship in the trenches (a backward glance at the International Brigade), in terms of ultimate good, is as futile as Stoyte's acquisitiveness and Jeremy's aestheticism. Self-sacrifice to anything except the highest cause merely results in a further projection of the ego. As for the effect of science and art on others: most of art is 'the mental equivalent of alcohol and cantharides', while science has through its applications increased human bondage more than it has diminished it and is likely to go on increasing it. Every improvement in armaments increases the sum of national fear and hatred and makes it more difficult for people to forget 'those horrible projections of themselves they call their ideals of patriotism, heroism, glory and all the rest'. Even the more harmless pursuits of science are, in the end, scarcely less destructive, What do they result in? 'The multiplication of possessable objects; the invention of new instruments of stimulation; the dissemination of new wants through propaganda aimed at equating possession with well-being and incessant stimulation with happiness' (Pt. i, ch. ix). This, like so many of Propter's utterances, has more than a touch of exasperation about it (not unlike Rampion, or even Lawrence himself), and expresses a view which Huxley was later to modify. In an appendix to *The Devils of Loudun* he admits that without what he calls 'horizontal self-transcendence', man's capacity for self-identification with ideas, feelings and causes, there would be no civilization. The problem is how to have the good without the evil, the high civilization without the saturation bombing. It is not enough to identify ourselves with socialism or capitalism, art or science, or any given church or religion.

Civilization demands from the individual devoted self-identification with the highest of human causes. But if this self-identification with what is human is *not accompanied by* a conscious and consistent effort to achieve upward self-transcendence into the universal life of the Spirit, the goods achieved will always be mingled with counterbalancing evils.

This represents Huxley's final position expressed in *Island*. It is implicit, however, that such a state of psychological harmony could never exist outside a contemplative society.

If 'horizontal self-transcendence' only increases the sum of human bondage, then it is clear that 'downward self-transcendence', the only fitting description of Virginia's sexual adventures must be proportionately worse. Sex, like drugs, is a powerful aid to self-transcendence and, in *The Devils of Loudun*, Huxley describes two kinds of sexuality: an elementary sexuality which is innocent and an elementary sexuality which is morally squalid. Both of these have the power to carry the individual beyond his normal insulated self. The first is the property of D. H. Lawrence; the second and commoner variety is that of Genêt, which 'takes those who indulge in it to a lower level of sub-humanity . . . and leaves the memory, of a completer alienation, than does the first. Hence, for all those who feel the urge to escape from their imprisoning identity, the perennial attraction of debauchery . . .' Stoyte's child mistress provides an example of the second variety:

Virginia had been one of those, happy in limitation, not sufficiently conscious of her personal self to realize its ugliness and inadequacy, or the fundamental wretchedness of the human state. And yet, when Dr. Obispo had scientifically engineered her escape into an erotic epilepsy more excruciatingly intense than anything she had known before or even imagined possible, Virginia realized that, after all, there was something in her existence that required alleviating, and that this headlong plunge through an intenser, utterly alien consciousness into the darkness of a total oblivion was precisely the alleviation it required.

But, like all the other addictions . . . the addiction to pleasure tends to aggravate the condition it temporarily alleviates. (Pt. II, ch. ii.)

Habit-forming sex, like habit-forming drugs, is evil because it ultimately intensifies the attachment to the personality. After every bout of self-annihilation there is a return to consciousness, to a more complete separateness, and a more acute sense of the self;

the condition it set out to alleviate is merely heightened and, contrary to Virginia's hopes, satiation can never bring relief.

But addiction is not the only negative form of sexuality; it is also evil when it becomes an instrument of the will. Here, Dr Obispo serves to illustrate the second moral generalization on sexual behaviour. The scientific truth about love, according to Obispo, is 'that it consisted essentially of tumescence and detumescence'; but, as he admits, there were personal reasons for his wishing to treat the whole business scientifically for 'it was a fact that he personally found an added pleasure in the imposition of his will upon the partner he had chosen' (Pt. i, ch. x). This kind of sadism is a greater evil than mere addiction. The very act of imposing the will on another is to insist on the separateness of the ego; in *Ends and Means* Huxley remarks that 'by refusing to respect the other's personality, the domineering lover makes it impossible for the . . . victim to pay attention to that "*infini que vous portez en vous*". Addiction degrades only the addict. The lust for power harms not only the person who lusts, but also the person or persons at whose expense the lust is satisfied. Non-attachment becomes impossible for both parties' (ch. xv). The full force of the moral is registered when the Fifth Earl and his former housekeeper are discovered enacting a grotesque parody of Virginia and Obispo in the cellars at Gonister—a particular piece of indulgence which is already over a hundred years old. 'Making Love is an even more innocent employment than making Money', the Fifth Earl had written, with unintentional irony, over a century earlier. In *After Many a Summer* making love is, if anything, a little less innocent than making money; but between the activities of Stoyte and the machinations of Obispo there is little to choose. The sexual merry-go-round, which began with the human-like apes on the terrace and ends with the ape-like humans in the cellars, is completed by Pete Boone's adolescent infatuation, Jeremy's fortnightly visits to his two superannuated prostitutes and Stoyte's semi-incestuous passion for his child-mistress. It is difficult not to sympathize with John Wain's exasperated outburst: 'What on earth has this got to do with the life of a normally poised human being?'[1] It is doubtful whether Huxley would ever have conceded the existence of a sexually normal being. Gerald Heard quotes Havelock Ellis as saying, 'There cannot now be natural sex—self-consciousness has made it impossible'.[2] Propter insists on the same point so that Pete Boone finally comes to accept his passion as harmful to all concerned. In *Ends and Means* Huxley admits that sex is not always addiction nor always used as an instrument of domination; it is also presumably the Laurentian innocence referred to above. But, in spite of this, he consistently presents sexuality as squalid and it is not until his last novel that he is able to envisage it universally in a more positive light.

It follows then, from Propter's teaching, that 'if individuality is not absolute, if personalities are illusory fragments of a self-will disastrously blind to the reality of a more-than-personal consciousness . . . all of every human being's efforts must be directed, in the last resort, to the actualization of that more-than-personal consciousness' (Pt. I, ch. viii). Of the characters in *After Many a Summer* only Propter applies himself to the desired end—Pete Boone's premature efforts being cut short by Stoyte's fatal bullet; but both Huxley and Gerald Heard had come to realize that the 'actualization of that more-than-personal consciousness' could not readily be effected within the confines of a modern industrial society. In the words of Gerald Heard, both the capitalist and the socialist countries 'compel those who see that neither the present individual nor the present state can be the end, to show clearly not only the goal but the steps leading to it: to live a complete way of life which has not only its right psychology but an economy which agrees with and is the outcome of that psychology'.[3] The only economy compatible with the contemplative life was that of the small self-subsisting community and, although Propter's colony of transients could hardly be considered a parallel to Heard's proposed society of neo-Brahmins, it was clearly intended as a prototype of what both writers had in mind. The first essential of the

---

[1] 'Tracts against Materialism', *London Magazine*, II (August 1955), p. 60.
[2] *Pain, Sex and Time*, p. 219.
[3] op. cit., p. 236.

ideal community was that it should be as economically independent as possible; economic independence was the only
guarantee of political independence. Democratic institutions are
valuable because the 'more you respect a personality, the better
its chance of discovering that all personality is a prison' (Pt. I,
ch. ix), but democratic institutions are dependent upon people
supporting themselves. Here lies the crux of Propter's quarrel
with the capitalist Stoyte: according to Propter, both socialism
and capitalism are committed to policies of economic enslavement; the idea that progress depends upon organization, 'that you
can't be happy unless you're entirely dependent on government
or centralized business', has destroyed American democracy (Pt.
I, ch. x). Stoyte's treatment of the migrant labourers, who have
been deprived of their economic independence, illustrates this
principle—the less self-support, the less democracy. Politically,
what Propter advocates then is a return to Jeffersonian democracy
but, as he points out, to live again under the old constitution one
has first to recreate the conditions under which it was first made
and this necessitates that every man should be to a large extent his
own employer. Huxley was convinced that this was not as im-
practical as it sounds, and in the introduction to J. D. Unwin's
Hopousia, he wrote:

Recent technological advances have made [centralization] the last word
but one. For example, planners still talk about the desirability of great
hydroelectric projects, oblivious of the fact that the enormous first cost
of the dams and power lines makes the electricity they produce much
more expensive than the current that can be generated in any back
yard by the new baby Diesel power plants. And, of course, electricity
is not the only commodity that can now be produced more cheaply in
the home or the local workshop than in the factory. For example, the
great steam mills at our ports produce flour very cheaply; but any
housewife who wishes can now have better flour at a lower cost by
passing wheat through a tiny electric mill in her own kitchen. Again,
a local workshop with electric current and perhaps a hundred pounds'
worth of machinery can turn out wooden furniture almost as rapidly
as, and certainly more cheaply than, a great factory. . . Borsodi has

calculated that, in the present state of technological development, about two-thirds of all productive processes can be carried out in the home or the small workshop more economically than in the mass-producing factory...[1]

Propter's scheme for the transients: the use of solar energy to run electric generators, electric mills for grinding flour, carpenters' shops for making greenhouses and furniture for the migrant families—all these are based on Borsodi's ideas. This was the basis of Huxley's ideal community: small, self-subsisting, economically independent, and devoted to the practice of meditation and good works. It was not, of course, fully realized in *After Many a Summer*; but, over twenty years later, Huxley was to return to the subject and in the island community of Pala the ideal was finally conceived. On the question of whether people will be prepared to co-operate in such a scheme, Propter sounds a cautionary note: the sad truth, he observes, is that doing 'good on any but the tiniest scale requires more intelligence than most people possess' (Pt. I, ch. xi). Similar thoughts are echoed in *Grey Eminence* where, talking of the relationship between religion and politics, Huxley insists that good by its very nature 'cannot be mass-produced in an unregenerate society'; that 'if it is to remain at all pure and unmixed, good must be worked for upon the margin of society' (ch. x). This is the best that can be hoped for under the present dispensation. All that the man of goodwill can do is to reiterate the truths of the past three thousand years and 'do active work on the technics of a better system' with the few who will collaborate. Political reform cannot be expected to produce much in the way of improvement unless large numbers of individuals undertake to change their personalities by the only known method that really works—that of the contemplative mystic; hope, he sadly concludes, begins only when human beings start to realize that the kingdom of heaven is within.

[1] Gerald Heard makes an identical comment. See *Pain, Sex and Time*, pp. 237–8. Their common source was Borsodi's *School of Living*.

X

Time Must Have a Stop (1945)

In *Time Must Have a Stop* the conversion theme reappears once more with Sebastian Barnack, the self-centred adolescent, who through irresponsible behaviour condemns the innocent Bruno Rontini to political incarceration; later, like Anthony Beavis, he comes to accept responsibility and make amends for his error. However, as a study of Sebastian's moral progress *Time Must Have a Stop* is unrewarding. Critics have pointed out the structural hiatus: the crucial moment of conversion is avoided and the novel makes 'a huge jump from Sebastian the precocious, cowardly, inhibited schoolboy to Sebastian the mature, meditative man, already far advanced in the practice of spiritual discrimination'.[1] On the other hand, Sebastian's conversion is clearly subordinate to the main theme of the novel and is reserved for the epilogue. It seems pointless to over-emphasize this aspect of the plot, as many critics have done, and then accuse the author of a structural failure.[2] Huxley's prime object in *Time Must Have a Stop* was to elucidate the *bardo* or after-death existence of Eustace Barnack; and although the epilogue has a peripheral function in that it serves to illuminate the 'unifying philosophy' (in much the same way as Tolstoy's two epilogues to *War and Peace*) the novel can, nevertheless, be considered as a complete entity without it.

The critical reception of *Time Must Have a Stop* was largely one of unqualified mystification: one reviewer spoke of 'this immensely interesting, rather confusing, rather confused book';[3]

---

[1] Christopher Isherwood, 'The Problem of the Religious Novel', *Vedanta for Modern Man* (1952), p. 248.

[2] D. S. Savage, for example, accuses Huxley of being incapable of 'revealing the inner processes by which human beings come to inward maturity'. See *The Withered Branch* (1950), p. 154. This kind of criticism applied to *Time Must Have a Stop* is largely irrelevant.

[3] Anna Kavan, *Horizon*, XII (July 1945), p. 69.

another referred to 'the baffling mystical abstractions of Mr. Huxley's new faith', concluding that 'much of its mystic message is incomprehensible'.[1] Many reviewers wisely ignored the *bardo* experience altogether. The confusion was understandable. The *Bardo Thödol* was not as widely read then as it is today and it is difficult to imagine what could be made of Eustace's after-death experiences without, at least, some knowledge of Huxley's source material. The *Bardo Thödol* or *Tibetan Book of the Dead* (first published in translation in 1927) is a Mahayana Buddhist text describing the intermediate state between death and rebirth. It was originally conceived as a breviary to be recited by the priest on the occasion of death and it is probably the most comprehensive treatise on the art of dying extant today. There are innumerable references to the *Bardo* throughout Huxley's works: for Jeremy Pordage in *After Many a Summer* it was one of the 'significant books' next to Patanjali and the Pseudo-Dionysius. This was Huxley's own view and by dramatizing its essential message in *Time Must Have a Stop* he was attempting to revive interest in what he considered to be another important aspect of the neglected wisdom of the past.

There is something of an obsession with death in almost all of Huxley's novels. Characters who come to a violent and sudden end are commonplace: Grace Elver, little Phil and Pete Boone are all victims of what seems to be a pointless harrying of the innocent. As if in answer to Huxley's critics (the gratuitous horror of Little Phil's death in *Point Counter Point* had met with almost universal censure), Propter, in *After Many a Summer*, comments on the seeming pointlessness of sudden and premature death; he concludes that 'to a being who is in fact the slave of circumstances there's nothing specially irrelevant' about it; on the contrary, it is the sort of event that is characteristic of the universe in which we live (Pt. III, ch. i). That man is a victim of circumstance, that life is 'time's fool' is something Huxley always insisted on. At first this insistence is wholly negative but it becomes, in the end, an urgent plea to act on those levels where free will does operate. The first

[1] Orville Prescott, *Yale Review*, xxxiv (Autumn 1944), p. 189.

intimation of a more positive approach to the problem of death is met in *Brave New World* when the Savage laments, not so much the fact that Linda is dying, but that she is dying in an artificially induced coma. It is clear that there is an alternative and this is also implicit in Bruno's condemnation of the contemporary 'scientific' attitude to death: 'Ignore death up to the last moment; then, when it can't be ignored any longer, have yourself squirted full of morphia and shuffle off in a coma. Thoroughly sensible, humane and scientific. . .' (ch. xxvi). In *Island* Huxley finally gives an active demonstration of what he understands by the art of dying; but in *Time Must Have a Stop* he is primarily concerned with the unregenerate who die without forethought. For someone who is prepared, it is implied, there would be nothing to record. The fate of Eustace Barnack is offered as a parable on this theme.

Eustace Barnack is one of Huxley's unrepentant good-livers— more of a mediaeval vice than a character. A cultivated hedonist, he has accrued wealth by marriage to a rich widow and furnished his luxurious Florentine villa on the proceeds. When the novel begins he is already ravaged by a lifetime of excess: his face like a rubber mask, 'flabby and soft and unwholesomely blotched'; the eyes yellow and bloodshot, the mouth loose and damp, a com- bination of 'senility and babyishness, of the infantile with the epicurean' (ch. iv). The portrait is augmented in the following chapter where Sebastian, fascinated, watches his uncle lighting the massive Romeo and Juliet:

First the ritual of piercing; then, as he raised the cigar to his mouth, the smile of happy anticipation. Damply, lovingly, the lips closed over the butt; the match was ignited; he pulled at the flame. And suddenly Sebastian was reminded of his cousin Marjorie's baby, nuzzling with blind concupiscence for the nipple, seizing it at last between the soft prehensile flaps of its little mouth and working away, working away in a noiseless frenzy of enjoyment.

The cigar is at once a symbol of sensual indulgence and infantile retrogression: 'blind concupiscence' and 'working away in a noiseless frenzy of enjoyment' have the right sexual overtones, and are not unlike the phrases used to describe Sebastian's night with Veronica; but it is the 'combination of senility and babyishness, of the infantile with the epicurean' which is stressed. At the close of the novel, Sebastian, thinking of his father, points the moral. The world was full of old men 'playing at being in their thirties or even in their teens when they ought to have been preparing for death, ought to have been trying to unearth the spiritual reality which they had spent a lifetime burying under a mountain of garbage', but, he concludes, this was 'an age that had invented Peter Pan and raised the monstrosity of arrested development to the rank of an ideal'; like his brother, Eustace is a case of arrested development, of someone 'old but an infant', destined to end his life, 'not as a ripened human being, but as an aged foetus' (ch. xxx).

There is nothing in the least gratuitous about the ending of Eustace Barnack. His last day is thick with hints and warnings which Eustace chooses to ignore; from the midnight snack of anchovies and stout to the last fatal cigar less than twenty-four hours later it is a close study of persistent evasion and unbroken self-gratification. There is even an air of lazy indulgence about the Florentine morning: the clouds over Monte Morello are like 'the backsides of Correggio's cherubs at Parma'; the hyacinths, 'carved jewels in the sunlight, white jade and lapis lazuli and pale-pink coral'. This is perfectly matched by Eustace's choice of apparel for the day: the pearl-grey suit and the 'delicious salmon-pink' tie from Sulka's; the rose for the buttonhole is a 'virginal white bud', the grapes, which adorn the table, 'hot-house'—all faintly suggestive of the sickly-sweet odour of the sick-room. The first ample meal of the day is rounded off by 'the delicate lusciousness' of a Larranaga *claros*—a dangerous habit as the doctors have repeatedly warned him; but 'these little fellows were so mild that it would take a dozen of them to produce the same effect as one of his big Romeo and Juliets'. The first real intimation of future events occurs when Eustace discovers Veronica reading Sir Oliver Lodge's *Raymond* to Mrs Gamble. Veronica welcomes the interruption:

'But it's a pleasure', she said, 'to get back from all these ghosts to a bit of solid flesh.'

She lingered a little over the final consonant. As 'flesh-sh', the word took on a meatier significance.

Like an Ingres madonna, Eustace reflected, as he twinkled back at her. Smooth and serene . . . and yet with all the sex left in—and perhaps even a little added.

'Too, too solid, I'm afraid.'

Chuckling, he patted the smooth convexity of his pearl-grey waistcoat. (ch. vi)

Mrs Gamble however dints the armour of Eustace's complacency by the timely rejoinder that no fat man ever lived to enjoy his three score years and ten.

This light-hearted brush between Sir Oliver Lodge's 'spirits' and the 'too, too solid flesh' sets the tone for what is to follow. Eustace is soon to share the fate of Raymond; the literary reference is exact, for Mrs Gamble has already obtained the name of a medium. In the chapters that follow the antithesis between the spiritual and the sensual is elaborated in a series of scenes in which Eustace is alternately 'tempted' and then offered salvation. The first temptation scene takes place at Weyl Frères, where Eustace is confronted by Mme Weyl: 'Pearly, golden, deliciously pink and plump, how had this sumptuous young creature escaped from the Rubens canvas which was so obviously her home?' Then, more sinister, M. Weyl himself:

[Weyl] was silent for a moment: then, changing his expression to the libidinous leer of a slave-dealer peddling Circassians to an ageing pasha, he started to undo the strings of the portfolio. The hands, Eustace noticed, were deft and powerful, their backs furred with a growth of soft black hair, their short fingers exquisitely manicured. With a flourish M. Weyl threw back the heavy flap of cardboard.

'Look!'

The tone was triumphant and assured. At the sight of those newly budded paps, the incomparable navel, no pasha, however jaded, could possibly resist. (ch. vii)

The jaded pasha raises only the faintest show of resistance and fourteen thousand lire exchange hands. The next scene is one of sharp contrast. In Bruno Rontini's cavernous little bookshop, Eustace is faced by one of Bruno's young disciples, the ascetic Carlo Malpighi. Once again he is talked into making a purchase, but this time it is a battered little volume costing only twenty-five lire:

Eustace put up his monocle, opened the book at random, and read aloud:

'Grace did not fail thee, but thou wast wanting to grace. God did not deprive thee of the operation of his love, but thou didst deprive his love of thy co-operation. God would never have rejected thee, if thou hadst not rejected him.'

'Golly!' He turned back to the title page. 'Treatise of the Love of God by St. François de Sales', he read. (ch. vii)

Eustace's 'wanting to grace' is only too apparent: the 'Treatise of the Love of God' is firmly rejected. During the afternoon it accompanies Eustace on one of his sexual adventures, and St François de Sales finds a place on Mimi's bedside table. The contrasting scenes are almost literal representations of the choice that ultimately confronts Eustace in the *bardo* world: the way of M. Weyl and his Flemish Venus, or the way of Bruno. In the second séance he recognizes the Weyls as 'enormously significant and important' and it is they who are destined to become the source of his deliverance from the persistent entreaties of the light.

After a lunch of creamed breasts of turkey, during which Paul de Vries tries to convince him of the validity of psychic and spiritual fields, Eustace starts his afternoon. The pattern of the morning is largely repeated. Temptation this time rears its head in the character of Mimi, 'the caricature of a pretty little tart in a comic paper'; and Eustace readily succumbs to a piece of sensual indulgence that is not without its element of perversity. Infantile regression, it appears, is more than a matter of Romeo and Juliets. The antithetical scene begins once more in Bruno's bookshop where Bruno himself this time tries to break through the shell of Eustace's complacency. The conversation turns to the death of

Eustace's wife, Amy. Bruno insists that she wasn't to be pitied: 'You don't have to feel sorry for people who are prepared for death'. Eustace refuses to be baited: if there was no immortality, there was simply nothing to prepare for; one didn't want to believe in annihilation, one just accepted the facts. Which meant, Bruno asserts, that one accepted the inferences drawn from one set of facts and ignored the rest; ignored them because one really wanted to believe that life was a tale told by an idiot. As Bruno sees that Eustace is irretrievably lost, he touches him lightly on the arm and a channel of grace is immediately established between the two. For Eustace the experience is analogous to his first glimpse of the Light in the *bardo* world:

Eustace started. Something strange was happening. It was as though the slats of a Venetian blind had suddenly been turned so as to admit the sunlight and the expanse of the summer sky. Unobstructed, an enormous and blissful brightness streamed into him. But with the brightness came the memory of what Bruno had said in the shop: 'To be forgiven . . . forgiven for being what you are.' With a mixture of anger and fear, he jerked his arm away.
'What *are* you doing?' he asked sharply. (ch. x)

There was always a sufficiency of grace if one were prepared to co-operate with it. Eustace is not; for all practical purposes he is spiritually dead, 'coffined away from the light'.

Eustace's last hours are devoted to a characteristic mixture of gross gormandizing, mild obscenity and aesthetic niceties. After a prolonged dinner—'the beauty of holiness', he tells Sebastian is a banquet executed with all the 'solemn perfection of High Mass at the Madeleine'—he settles down to reminisce over the third brandy and the now inevitable Romeo and Juliet:

'Half-past ten', Eustace proclaimed. ' "Time, time and half a time. The innocent and the beautiful have no enemy but time".' He gave vent to a belch. 'That's what I like about champagne—it makes one so poetical. All the lovely refuse of fifty years of indiscriminate reading comes floating to the surface. O *lente, lente, currite noctis equi!*' (ch. xii)

A few moments later the echoes of Faust's soliloquy take on a more urgent tone. Christ's name is evoked in vain and Eustace is gasping his last breath on the tiled floor of the w.c.: 'there was no air; only a smell of cigar smoke'.

The second half of the novel, based on Eustace's experiences on the *bardo* plane, owes its conception to *The Tibetan Book of the Dead*. The *Bardo Thödol* is divided into three parts, all of which are easily recognizable in Huxley's novel: first, the Chikhai Bardo which describes the happenings immediately after death; then, the Chönyid Bardo which deals with karmic visions and hallucinations; and finally, the Sidpa Bardo which is concerned with the events leading up to reincarnation. In the Chikhai Bardo the deceased is faced with what the Mahayana Buddhists call the Dharma-Kāya, or the Clear Light of the Void. This is symbolic of the purest and highest state of spiritual being which Huxley identifies with the divine Ground or immanent Godhead of the Christian mystics. If, through a lack of spiritual insight, the dead person is unable to recognize the light as the manifestation of his own spiritual consciousness, karmic illusions begin to cloud his vision, the light is obscured and he enters the second bardo. In the Chönyid Bardo he is subjected to what Evans-Wentz calls 'a solemn and mighty panorama' of 'the consciousness-content of his personality'.[1] This will vary according to the life and religious beliefs of the individual concerned: thus, the Chönyid Bardo in *The Tibetan Book of the Dead* simply describes what is assumed will be the *bardo* visualizations of a Mahayanist devotee of the time. (Eustace's experiences are, of course, somewhat different and here the source material is left behind.) Once again, if the deceased is spiritually immature and unable to recognize the fantasy world confronting him as the product of his own consciousness he will pass into the third and last *bardo*. In the Sidpa Bardo the dead person becomes aware that he no longer has a corporeal body and the desire for a new incarnation begins to dominate his consciousness. As a sign of approaching rebirth he sees visions of copulation and, depending on his state of spiritual grace, he is reborn into an earthly womb and a new life commences. As Jung points out in

[1] W. Y. Evans-Wentz, *The Tibetan Book of the Dead* (New York, 1960), p. 29.

his psychological commentary: 'The supreme vision comes not at
the end of the *Bardo*, but right at the beginning, in the moment of
death; what happens afterward is an ever-deepening descent into
illusion and obscuration, down to the ultimate degradation of a
new physical birth. The spiritual climax is reached at the moment
when life ends. Human life, therefore, is the vehicle of the highest
perfection it is possible to attain; it alone generates the *karma* that
makes it possible for the dead man to abide in the perpetual light
of the Voidness without clinging to any object, and thus to rest on
the hub of the wheel of rebirth, freed from all illusion of genesis
and decay. Life in the *Bardo* brings no eternal rewards or punish-
ments, but merely a descent into a new life which shall bear the
individual nearer to his final goal. But this eschatological goal is
what he himself brings to birth as the last and highest fruit of the
labours and aspirations of earthly existence'.[1] This is the essential
teaching of *Time Must Have a Stop*.

Chapter Thirteen, which so confounded the critics of this novel
is, then, simply a dramatization of Eustace's immediate after-death
experiences in the Chikhai Bardo. Eustace's first consciousness on
the *bardo* plane is that of a growing awareness of absence:

Awareness not of a name or person, not of things present, not of
memories of the past, not even of here or there—for there was no place,
only an existence whose single dimension was this knowledge of being
ownerless and without possessions and alone.

The awareness knew only itself, and itself only as the absence of
something else.

Then gradually the awareness becomes an awareness of light. The
light brings with it a sense of reassurance, a denial of absence
which slowly changes into a growing knowledge of joy and bliss.
This is Eustace's encounter with the Dharma Kāya, the Clear
Light of the Void:

And through ever-lengthening durations the light kept brightening
from beauty into beauty. And the joy of knowing, the joy of being

[1] Evans-Wentz, op. cit., li.

known, increased with every increment of that embracing and inter-
penetrating beauty.

Brighter, brighter, through succeeding durations, that expanded at
last into an eternity of joy.

An eternity of radiant knowledge, of bliss unchanging in its ultimate intensity. For ever, for ever.

But Eustace is too spiritually immature to enjoy this state for very
long. As the brightness increases in radiance he feels oppressed by
the excess of light; and what is, in fact, Eustace's ego-consciousness starts, as if in self-defence, to impose itself between him and
the radiance. The process is described by Evans-Wentz: 'In the
realm of the Clear Light . . . the mentality of a person dying
momentarily enjoys a condition of balance, or perfect equilibrium,
and of oneness. Owing to unfamiliarity with such a state, which is
an ecstatic state of non-ego, of subliminal consciousness, the
consciousness-principle of the average human being lacks the
power to function in it; *karmic* propensities becloud the consciousness-principle with thoughts of personality, of individualized being, of dualism, and, losing equilibrium, the consciousness-
principle falls away from the Clear Light. It is ideation of ego, of
self, which prevents the realization of *Nirvāna* . . . and so the
Wheel of Life continues to turn.'[1]

What follows for Eustace is an agony of conflict in which the
ego seeks to reassert itself. This is analogous to the 'dark night of
the soul', the harrowing experience described by Christian mystics when the separate self is on the point of extinction; but,
whereas the mystic is striving for 'self-naughting', Eustace, of
course, is struggling to resume his former identity. At first the ego
is only an 'unhappy dust of nothingness, a poor little harmless clot
of mere privation, crushed from without, scattered from within,
but still resisting, still refusing, in spite of the anguish, to give up
its right to a separate existence'. Then there is a new participation
in the light with the accompanying knowledge that 'there was no
such right as a right to separate existence, that this clotted and

---

[1] op. cit., footnote to p. 97.

disintegrated absence was shameful and must be denied, must be annihilated'. But the unregenerate ego refuses to be annihilated and the struggle continues:

As though balanced, as though on a knife edge between an impossible intensity of beauty and an impossible intensity of pain and shame, between a hunger for opacity and separateness and absence and a hunger for a yet more total participation in the brightness.

Finally, the ego's hunger for separateness triumphs, the brightness begins to lose its intensity and the light is momentarily eclipsed. With the fading of the light, the separateness that is Eustace Barnack becomes aware of itself and memories begin to flood back: at first the inevitable cigar, a single phrase, 'Backwards and downwards' and the recollection of obscene laughter.

The return of the memory signifies that Eustace is now moving 'backwards and downwards' away from the supreme principle of spiritual reality to the *karmic* illusions of the Chönyid Bardo. In the words of Evans-Wentz: 'After the Fifth Day the *Bardo* visions become less and less divine; the deceased sinks deeper and deeper into the morass of *sangsāric* hallucinations; the radiances of the higher nature fade into the lights of the lower nature.'[1] In Christian terms the Chönyid and Sidpa Bardos might be compared to a kind of purgatory where the unregenerate are purged of their ego-enhancing sins, although in Buddhist theology this, for the great majority, is merely a prelude to rebirth. It is in no sense a hell, as many critics have suggested, nor is there any question of judgment. As Huxley says in *The Perennial Philosophy*: 'For oriental theologians there is no eternal damnation; there are only purgatories and then an indefinite series of second chances to go forward towards not only man's, but the whole creation's final end—total reunion with the Ground of all being' (ch. xiv). At this state the deceased is subjected to a kaleidoscopic newsreel of the consciousness-content of his personality or, more specifically, in Eustace's case, those events of his worldly life which have been significant to his spiritual advancement or regression.

[1] op. cit., p. 17.

This return to past experience begins in a typical Huxleyan manner with childhood recollections of suppressed pleasure and shame:

And here . . . was the image of an enormous, firm-fleshed presence, smelling of disinfectant soap. And when he failed to do *Töpfchen*, Fräulein Anna laid him deliberately across her knees, gave him two smacks, and left him lying face downwards on the cot, while she went to fetch the *Spritze*. Yes, the *Spritze*, the *Spritze*. . . And there were other names for it, English names; for sometimes it was his mother who inflicted the pleasure-anguish of the enema. . . And though, of course, he could have done *Töpfchen* if he had wanted to, he wouldn't—just for the sake of that agonizing pleasure. (ch. xv)

Poor Eustace, as Sebastian surmised, has never outlived the sensualities of childhood; the next scene of 'agonizing pleasure' is with Mimi:

The claret-coloured dressing-gown fell apart, and he discovered another fragment of his being—a memory of round breasts, wax-white, tipped with a pair of blind brown eyes. And in the thick flesh, deeply embedded, the navel, he recalled, had the absurd primness of a Victorian mouth. Prunes and prisms. *Adesso commincia la tortura.* (ch. xv)

Meanwhile the light persists and it is implicit that Eustace still has a choice between continued bondage and redemption. (The deceased can, in fact, be redeemed at any stage of the *Bardo* life.) He realizes that the recovered fragments of himself are 'nothingness' to be annihilated to make way for the supreme knowledge of the light.

Sebastian later insists that, since the life of the spirit is life out of time, the 'memory must be lived down and finally died to', but Eustace is totally unprepared for this kind of 'self-naughting' and when he realizes that he can identify himself with the images to the degree of being transubstantiated into them the temptation is too hard to resist. But grace has not yet deserted him, and the next series of images portray the odd glimpses of reality which Eustace enjoyed during his early life and chose to ignore: there is the church at Nice where the choir sang Mozart's *Ave Verum Corpus*, the half-holiday going back to his schooldays when something suddenly 'had broken through the crust of customary appearance' and, in a later chapter, 'a memory of the Vale of the White Horse as the July sunshine poured down with a kind of desperate intensity out of a blue gulf between mountainous continents of thunder-cloud'. These moments of revelation, which Sebastian refers to as 'country ecstasies', are merely the signposts, the invitations to seek for the greater reality beyond. They are the positive aspects of Eustace's largely negative *karma*, reminders that grace has always been close at hand and never totally withdrawn.

It is a further characteristic of life on the *bardo* plane that the dead person can be aided by those still alive. This is a common feature of all the great religions, and the *Bardo Thödol* asserts that the deceased can both see and hear those praying for his redemption. It is therefore in keeping with the source material that Eustace should be aware of Bruno's intercession on his behalf. The light which is associated with Bruno's intervention is 'tenderly blue'; this is no longer the Clear Light of the Dharma-Kāya, but what the *Thödol* calls the 'divine blue light' of the Dharma-Dhātu, the secondary light which is experienced in the Chönyid Bardo, and a further indication that Eustace is moving 'backwards and downwards' through the *bardo* plane. Eustace, like all the deceased in the *bardo* realm, is unaware that he is dead (an odd feature that Western spiritualism has in common with Eastern doctrine), and he interprets Bruno's pleading as an invitation to suicide:

The silence and the brightness were pregnant with the unequivocal answer: there was no way round, there was only the way through. And of course he knew all about it, he knew exactly where it led.

But if that way were followed, what would happen to Eustace Barnack? Eustace Barnack would be dead. Stone dead, extinct, annihilated. There'd be nothing but this damned light, this fiendish brightness in the silence. (ch. xvii)

Of course, Eustace is right in the sense that the ego-consciousness that is Eustace Barnack would be annihilated; however, he is saved from further torment by the sudden and unexpected acquisition of a corporeal frame, 'of something infinitely precious, something of which, as he now realized, he had been deprived throughout the whole duration of these horrible eternities—a set of bodily sensations'. This is, in fact, the body of Mrs Gamble's medium.

In *The World of Light*, a comedy written in 1931, Huxley had played, somewhat lightheartedly, with the ideas of spiritualism; in this novel he takes a more serious look at the phenomena of the séance, adhering closely to the 'psychic factor' theory of C. D. Broad. The psychic factor is not the mind but 'something which in combination with a suitable organism is capable of producing a mind'.[1] This, according to Broad's theory, survives after death and is capable of combining with the 'vacated' body of a medium to form a 'mindkin', a kind of temporary mind which exists for the duration of the séance. The mindkin then is an amalgam of the psychic factor of the deceased and the mind-body of the medium, which explains to some extent the garbled nature of the messages received at the séances, 'that idiotic squeak quoting Uncle Eustace's smallest jokes'. What Sebastian has actually heard is a pseudo-personality, composed of Eustace's psychic factor and Mrs Gamble's medium, an alien combination lacking any real sense of rapport. The translator of *The Tibetan Book of the Dead* writes: 'In the *Bardo Thödol*, the deceased is represented as retro-grading, step by step, into lower and lower states of consciousness. Each step downwards is preceded by a swooning into uncon-sciousness; and possibly that which constitutes his mentality on the lower levels of the *Bardo* is some mental element or com-pound of mental elements formerly a part of his earth-plane con-sciousness, separated, during the swooning, from higher or more spiritually enlightened elements of that consciousness. Such a mentality ought not to be regarded as on par with a human mentality; for it seems to be a mere faded and incoherent reflex of the human mentality of the deceased.'[2] Huxley has endorsed this view in other contexts: in *Music at Night* the dead survive 'only

[1] *The Mind and its Place in Nature* (1949), p. 541.   [2] op. cit., p. 44.

fragmentarily, feebly, as mere wisps of floating memories', and what remains of Pete Boone and Henry Maartens after death is hardly more substantial. Eustace, however, is a good deal more 'human' than the *Thödol's* 'faded and incoherent reflex' would suggest; and, in some respects, is more characteristic of Sir Oliver Lodge's Raymond, who also experiences difficulties in communication through the intractability of the medium. Huxley's ideas seem to have wavered somewhat on this point; his final view is one of typical compromise: '. . . that modern spiritualism and ancient tradition are both correct. There *is* a posthumous state of the kind described in Sir Oliver Lodge's book, *Raymond*; but there is also a heaven of blissful visionary experience; there is also a hell . . . and there is also an experience, beyond time, of union with the Divine Ground' (*Heaven and Hell*). This, perhaps, implies a more concrete form of survival than Huxley has hinted elsewhere, but it is in no way contradictory to the main statement of *Time Must Have a Stop*: as Bruno explains to Sebastian, 'Summerland and Lodge are perfectly compatible with Catherine of Genoa and . . . even the *Inferno*' (ch. xxvi).

By the end of the first séance it is evident that Eustace is already on the threshold of the Sidpa Bardo. At this state, assuming that the deceased has not obtained liberation in the Chönyid Bardo, the visions of the past begin to recede and are replaced by those of the future. This signifies that the dead person is being carried along towards a future existence in which, in a remote sense, he is already participating. He is further warned that he will see visions of copulation, a sign that his growing desire for a new worldly life will shortly be fulfilled. Meanwhile the nature of the images becomes more confused and degenerate as the deceased proceeds 'downwards and backwards' towards rebirth; in the words of the *Thödol*, the intellect is tossed like a feather 'by the ever-moving wind of *karma*'.[1] Eustace's visions of the future begin with Veronica Thwale cuckolding de Vries with a young naval officer; this is followed by the *lathi* charge in Calcutta and the hideous murder of Eustace's nephew, Jim Poulshot, by the

[1] op. cit., p. 161.

Japanese. As the images become more horrific they merge into one another, a phantasmagoria of cruelty and lust, exemplary of the world to which Eustace chooses to return:

The bleeding face, the horror of the bayonets, but all somehow mixed up with Mimi in her claret-coloured dressing-gown. *Adesso comincia la tortura*—and then the dandling, the fumbling, the fondling. And at the same time the stamping, the stabbing. . . *Ave Verum Corpus*, the true body, the prim Victorian mouth, the brown, blind, breast-eyes. And while the bayonets stabbed and stabbed, there was the shameful irrelevance of a pleasure that died at last into a cold reiterated friction, automatic and compulsory. And all the time the yelping and the bassoons, the iron teeth, combing and carding the very substance of his being. For ever and ever, excruciatingly. (ch. xxv)

Eustace is now all but committed to rebirth and in the second séance the body of the medium is correspondingly more inviting than on the previous occasion: '. . . what pleasure to listen to the waves of blood as they beat against the ear-drums, to feel them throbbing under the skin of the temples!' The arrival of the Weyls proves the turning point of Eustace's post-mortem existence; he immediately recognizes them as the future instruments of his deliverance:

There was a living uterine darkness awaiting him there, a vegetative heaven. Providence was ready for him, a providence of living flesh, hungry to engulf him into itself, yearning to hold and cradle him, to nourish with the very substance of its deliciously carnal and sanguine being. (ch. xxviii)

After all the breast surrogates this premonition of a return to the womb is not totally unexpected. There is yet another glimpse of the future: this time of the Weyls caught up in the stream of refugees fleeing before the German invaders. Weyl's young child stands by to witness the brutal death of his mother:

The little boy crouched there, his face in his hands, his body trembling and shaken by sobs. And suddenly it was no longer from outside that he was thought about. The agony of that grief and terror were known directly, by an identifying experience of them. . . Eustace Barnack's

175

awareness of the child had become one with the child's awareness of himself; it *was* that awareness. (ch. xxviii)

Eustace has been granted a pre-vision of his future life and with this doubtful assurance the *bardo* life ends.

The moral of *Time Must Have a Stop*, then, is essentially the same as that of *After Many a Summer*: that every enhancement of the separate self produces a corresponding diminution of the self's awareness of spiritual reality, with the corollary that there can be no participation in eternity after the death of the body unless there has been a previous participation in it in the world of time and matter. The choice that confronts Eustace on the *bardo* plane is basically no different from the choice confronting him during his earthly life, except that in the after-life the possibility of redemption is greatly reduced. To say, as one critic has done, that the 'adult reader is utterly unable to make the required connection between Uncle Eustace's trivial sensualities—his cheerful over-indulgence in wine, women and cigars,—and the bathetic solemni-ties of his post-mortem experiences'[1] is to beg the question. Eustace's over-indulgence, which is after all the immediate cause of his death, is relevant to his after-death experiences because, above all else, it typifies his evasion of reality and is the direct means of intensifying his selfhood. His brother, John Barnack, whose life is shaped to very different ends is equally at fault in this respect, although in his case it is liberalism and power politics rather than brandy and cigars which provide the means of bondage. It is not Eustace's 'trivial sensualities' but his insistence on being a separate self that provides the ultimate and most for-midable obstacle between himself and the unitive knowledge of the Ground. As Bruno puts it, 'There's only one effectively redemptive sacrifice . . . the sacrifice of self-will to make room for the knowledge of God' (ch. xxx).

The epilogue fills out the narrative and adds to the 'unifying philosophy' of the novel. The subsequent career of Sebastian, briefly summarized, follows the pattern of Anthony Beavis in

[1] D. S. Savage, op. cit., p. 155.

Eyeless in Gaza. There are the same betrayals; first of Bruno, and then of the 'despairing and embittered' Rachel, with the final acceptance of responsibility and the realization that nothing one does is unimportant and nothing wholly private. The return and death of Bruno offers a poignant contrast to the fate of Eustace. Bruno, like Helen in *The Genius and the Goddess*, is the theocentric saint who knows how to die because he has known how to live; he had, like Helen, 'been dying by daily instalments. When the final reckoning came, there was practically nothing to pay'. For Bruno there would be no *bardo* experience to record; he was already participating in the knowledge of the light.

The analysis of the epigraph, the two and a half lines spoken by the dying Hotspur:

> But thought's the slave of life, and life's time's fool,
> And time, that takes survey of all the world,
> Must have a stop.

presents a concise summary of the main tenets of Huxley's thought up to this time. First, scientific materialism:

Thought's enslavement to life is one of our favourite themes. Bergson and the Pragmatists, Adler and Freud, the Dialectical Materialism boys and the Behaviourists—all tootle their variations on it. Mind is nothing but a tool for making tools; controlled by unconscious forces, either sexual or aggressive; the product of social and economic pressures; a bundle of conditioned reflexes.

Huxley, of course, had 'tootled' his own variation on it. 'Thought's enslavement to life' became something of an obsessional neurosis in the novels of the twenties; the very existence of the body was considered a cynical comment on the soul, and it was not until *Eyeless in Gaza* that the chains of determinism finally slipped away. For Sebastian it is no longer possible to 'cherish the illusion that one was identical with a body that behaved in direct opposition to all one's wishes and resolutions'; and he safely concludes: 'Thought's the slave of life—undoubtedly. But if it weren't also something else, we couldn't make even this partially valid generalization'.

But if man is not quite the automaton that the 'nothing-but' philosophies would have us believe, there still remains the unpleasant fact of the second clause, 'life's time's fool'.

By merely elapsing time makes nonsense of all life's conscious planning and scheming. . . . And yet the only faith of a majority of twentieth-century Europeans and Americans is faith in the Future—the bigger and better Future, which they *know* that Progress is going to produce for them, like rabbits out of a hat. For the sake of what their faith tells them about a Future time, which their reason assures them to be completely unknowable, they are prepared to sacrifice their only tangible possession, the Present.

Science and progress—capitalist or Marxist; these are the great heresies of our time, the twentieth century's *hubris* that condemns man to the mechanistic nightmare of *Brave New World* or the post-nuclear holocaust of *Ape and Essence*. Fifty millions liquidated in wars and revolutions 'in order that a process of industrialization might be made a little more rapid and a great deal more ruthless than it otherwise would have been. . . Faraday and Clerk Maxwell working indefatigably that the ether might at last become a vehicle for lies and imbecility' (ch. xx). This is the great cosmic joke, the subject of the enormous hilarities that echo through Eustace's *bardo* hallucinations. As Carlo Malpighi insists, there is no way except Bruno's way:

'. . . there's only one corner of the universe you can be certain of improving, and that's your own self. . . So you have to begin there, not outside, not on other people. That comes afterwards, when you've worked on your own corner. You've got to *be* good before you can *do* good—or at any rate do good without doing harm at the same time. Helping with one hand and hurting with the other—that's what the ordinary reformer does.' (ch. vii)

Goodness, whatever its source, limited by ignorance of the end and purpose of existence is little more than a kind of perpetual suicide. As Hotspur's final clause suggests: 'It is only by taking the fact of eternity into account that we can deliver thought from its slavery to life. . . . Seek it first, and all the rest—everything from an adequate interpretation of life to a release from compulsory self-destruction—will be added.'

The social problem is the individual problem: reform can only be achieved when the individual takes himself in hand and turns from the affairs of man to the affairs of God. This is what Huxley had been asserting since *Eyeless in Gaza*. Now he sees that the only hope of a universal peace lies where 'there's a metaphysic which all accept and a few actually succeed in realizing'. The idea of a shared theology as an indispensable condition of world peace had appeared in Huxley's writings as early as 1937; the basis of a universal faith, however, presented itself in concrete form when he came under the influence of Swami Prabhavananda of the Vedanta Society in 1940. Vedanta is essentially the teachings of the *Upanishads*, the *Bhagavad-Gita*, and the works of Shankara and Patanjali, but its philosophy was sufficiently all-embracing to integrate the mystical element of all the higher religions. From the doctrines of Vedanta emerged the minimum working hypothesis:

That there is a Godhead or Ground, which is the unmanifested principle of all manifestations.

That the Ground is transcendent and immanent.

That it is possible for human beings to love, know and, from virtually, to become actually identified with the Ground.

That to achieve this unitive knowledge, to realize this supreme identity, is the final end and purpose of human existence.

That there is a Law or Dharma, which must be obeyed, a Tao or Way, which must be followed, if men are to achieve their final end.

That the more there is of I, me, mine, the less there is of the Ground; and that consequently the Tao is a Way of humility and compassion, the Dharma a Law of mortification and self-transcending awareness.[1]

This, Huxley believed, constituted the highest common factor present in all the major religions of the world, and in *The Perennial Philosophy*, published in the following year, he set out to show that

---

[1] This extract and other parts of Sebastian's notebook were originally printed in *Vedanta and the West*, the magazine of the Ramakrishna Vedanta Society of California, and later in book form in *Vedanta for the Western World*.

the minimum working hypothesis had been the metaphysical system of the prophets, saints and sages of all times.

There is little at first glance to connect the *bardo* existence of Eustace Barnack with the cause of world peace; but, since *Time Must Have a Stop* was written during the closing years of the war it was inevitable that Huxley should have been concerned with the peace that was to follow: Eustace's last visions on the *bardo* plane are centred on death and destruction; Sebastian's journal is written within the sound of the guns on Primrose Hill; and John Barnack gloomily envisages the decline of liberalism and a future dominated by tyranny. Huxley was convinced that world peace could never be maintained until most human beings accepted a common metaphysical system and its ethical corollaries; until the perennial philosophy was universally recognized as the highest factor common to all religions and there was a world-wide rejection of all the political pseudo-religions which placed man's supreme good in future time.

XI

Island (1962)

In the epilogue to *Time Must Have a Stop*, Sebastian reflects on the difficulties which the artist or intellectual must face if he is desirous of enlightenment. 'He has to remember, first, that what he does as an artist or intellectual won't bring him to knowledge of the divine Ground, even though his work may be directly concerned with this knowledge. On the contrary, in itself the work is a distraction.' In *Island* the incompatibility of art and spiritual life is stated in more specific terms: 'Dualism . . . Without it there can hardly be good literature. With it, there most certainly can be no good life'; and in the final summing up, literature is 'incompatible with individual sanity and a decent social system, incompatible with everything except dualism, criminal lunacy, impossible aspirations and unnecessary guilt' (ch. xi). It is tempting to sympathize with those critics who see in Huxley's mysticism the cause of his decline as a novelist. If the conflict which Sebastian portrays was a real one, then Huxley was confronted with a choice between a way of life and his career as an artist; on the evidence, it would seem that the novel was the loser. Whatever the reason the seventeen years which separate *Time Must Have a Stop* from *Island* were relatively unproductive in the way of fiction; there is only *Ape and Essence*, the brief satire on the aftermath of a nuclear war, and the *The Genius and the Goddess*, a novella exposing the shortcomings of cerebration and sensuality—neither of which can be seriously classified as major works of fiction. It could be argued that *Island* itself hardly merits the title of novel; it is, as Anthony Burgess noted, 'profoundly didactic, less concerned with telling a story than with presenting an attitude to life, weak on character but strong on talk, crammed with ideas, uncompromisingly intellectual'.[1] While the burden of this criticism is not new, it is

[1] *The Novel Today*, p. 14.

more appropriate to *Island* than to Huxley's previous novels; far too few of the ideas, for example, are really acted out in the sense that they are in *Brave New World*. And although the figures of Huxley's degenerates, Will Farnaby, Murugan and the Rani of Pali are lively enough, the utopian Palanese tend to be little more than the uniform voices of Huxley's didacticism with nothing to distinguish between them. There is no doubt that Huxley's final attempt to present a society living in accordance with 'all the facts of human experience' is not only drastically overburdened with unassimilated ideas, but that the interest centred on the customary features of the novel is minimal.

However, whatever weaknesses *Island* betrays as a novel, as a moral document it is worthy of the highest consideration. One reviewer pointed out that Huxley was 'far more concerned with helping the world forward than with writing a praiseworthy book',[1] and Huxley's own account of his intentions in writing *Island* is equally revealing:

Most of us mean well and would prefer, on the whole, to behave decently... The difficulties arise when we try to translate the ideal into practice. To achieve our noble ends, what are the means which must be employed? Precisely how do we intend to implement our high purposes? What must multiple amphibians do in order to make the best, for themselves and for other multiple amphibians, of all their strangely assorted worlds?

These are the questions to which ... I have been trying to find answers plausible enough to take their place in a kind of Utopian and yet realistic phantasy about a society (alas, hypothetical) whose collective purpose is to help its members to actualize as many as possible of their desirable potentialities. (Foreword to Laura Archera Huxley's *You Are Not the Target*)

As an answer to the problem of man's moral and physical welfare, *Island* represents the product of Huxley's eclecticism over a period of almost two decades, and must be considered as the final and most important chapter of the Huxleyan synthesis.

It was always conceivable that Huxley would write a successor

[1] Philip Toynbee, *The Observer*, 1 April 1962.

to *Brave New World*: unless the way of life championed by the men of good will could be integrated into the framework of a larger society, there was little hope that it would ever be more than an escape shaft for a few dedicated contemplatives. The basic problem was raised by the Kansas transients in *After Many a Summer*:

Many are called, but few are chosen—because few even know in what salvation consists. Consider again this man from Kansas. . . Everything was against the poor fellow—his fundamentalist orthodoxy, his wounded and inflamed egotism, his nervous irritability, his low intelligence. The first three disadvantages might perhaps be removed. But could anything be done about the fourth? The nature of things is implacable towards weakness. . . All the same, there must surely be something to be done for people like the man from Kansas. . . (Pt. i, ch. viii)

How could the ignorant and stupid be taught to share something of the world of the enlightened? Propter's self-help for the transients had merely scratched the surface of the problem. The old Raja, in *Island*, had written:

Science is not enough, religion is not enough, art is not enough, politics and economics are not enough, nor is love, nor is duty, nor is action however disinterested, nor, however sublime, is contemplation. Nothing short of everything, will really do. (ch. ix)

This was Huxley's conclusion: there was no simple answer to the problem; there were no panaceas. The reformers of the past had failed because they had always tackled the problem piecemeal. In his introduction to J. D. Unwin's *Hopousia*, he asserts that 'the battle will never be won until we learn to make a simultaneous and perfectly co-ordinated assault on all the more important fronts'. To achieve this end will require not only much goodwill and intelligent co-operation, but also 'an enormous amount of detailed knowledge, synthesized in terms of a general philosophy'. This 'perfectly co-ordinated assault' could only be realized within the framework of a utopian society. Pala is Huxley's model, an example of what could be done, here and now (as the Mynah birds insist), if all our knowledge were synthesized into a philosophy of universal reform.

On a thematic level *Island* is fittingly a work of reconciliation: the forbidden island is itself a symbol of the resolution of opposites; inhabited by a kind of ideal Eurasian race who speak both Sanskrit and English, it was conceived in its modern guise by that strangely assorted pair, the Scottish doctor and the Palanese king, whose joint ambition 'To make the best of *all* the worlds' has turned Pala into a *summum bonum* of all cultures, Oriental and European, ancient and modern. Pala, which owes its geographical features to the Indonesian island of Bali, has remained Buddhist by an historical freak so that when Dr Andrew MacPhail arrived in the middle of the nineteenth century he found a tropical paradise ruled by a Tantrik Buddhist. In a symbolic meeting of the two cultures, Dr Andrew, the scientific humanist, discovers the value of pure and applied Mayahana, while the Palanese Raja, the oriental mystic, discovers the value of pure and applied science. Thus, with the ideal of experimental science at one end of the spectrum and experimental mysticism at the other, the way is cleared for the resolution of the conflicting themes of the earlier novels. It is illustrative of Huxley's new eclecticism that the once negative features of *Brave New World*—eugenics, Pavlovian conditioning, sexual licence and soma—are now absorbed into the higher aims of Buddhism and applied metaphysics. 'Wisdom', as Huxley puts it, 'takes Science in its stride and goes a stage further' (ch. xii).

Modern Pala is described as a democracy, 'a federation of self-governing units', but while it is clear that there is no central government, the political organization of the island is characteristically vague. Huxley is not interested in applied politics; providing the fundamentals of education, population and natural resources are taken care of, the technicalities of government can safely be left to themselves. Pala, in fact, owes its economic welfare not to socialism, communism, or any other theory of political well-being, but to plentiful food and birth-control. This is in accord with the ideas expressed in 'The Double Crisis' where

Huxley argues that underlying the political crisis of the post-war years is a demographic and ecological crisis of equal importance; that the problems of power politics and atomic warfare can only be solved by reference to those of population and world resources. Overpopulation invariably creates an economic situation which is so precarious that some form of government control of production and consumption becomes inevitable. The twentieth century is the century of highly centralized governments and totalitarian dictatorships for the simple reason that it is the century of planetary overcrowding. Further, as the population goes up, the fertility of the soil declines. (It will be remembered that the man from Kansas was a victim of the great dust bowl of the Mid West.) The two great evils of our time are the atomic bomb and soil erosion: 'atomic war may destroy one particular civilization—the Western-Industrial variety, for example; soil-erosion, if unchecked, can put an end to the possibility of any civilization whatsoever.' Rendang, Pala's militant neighbour, provides an example of the double crisis; here overpopulation—an increase nine times that of Pala, although in fact no greater than that of Ceylon's—has brought all the consequent evils of totalitarianism and mass-starvation:

After the glare of the cocktail party, after the laughter and the luscious smells of canapés and the Chanel-sprayed women, those alleys behind the brand new Palace of Justice had seemed doubly dark and noisome, those poor wretches camping out under the palm trees of Independence Avenue more totally abandoned by God and man than even the home-less, hopeless thousands he had seen sleeping like corpses in the streets of Calcutta. And now he thought of that little boy, that tiny pot-bellied skeleton, whom he had picked up, bruised and shaken by a fall from the back of the little girl, scarcely larger than himself, who was carrying him—had picked up and, led by the other child, had carried back, carried down, to the windowless cellar that, for nine of them . . . was home. (ch. vi)

In contrast, for over a hundred years, the Palanese have never allowed themselves to produce more children than they could adequately feed, clothe, house and educate. The result has been a working democracy and plenty for all. While Palanese birth-control has its origin in the esoteric rites of Tantra, plentiful food is the result of one of Dr Andrew's scientific ventures—the experimental agricultural station, Rothamstead-in-the-Tropics, founded in the 1850's. Experimental agriculture has given the Palanese new strains of rice, millet and breadfruit, better breeds of cattle and chickens and better ways of cultivating and composting. The principles of Palanese economics can be summed up in a sentence: 'Electricity minus heavy industry plus birth control equals democracy and plenty' (ch. ix).

The demographic and ecological factors which provide the staple of Palanese civilization are, not surprisingly, incorporated into the educational syllabus; children are taught a form of birth-control at the same time as trigonometry and advanced biology, while science teaching begins with elementary ecology. Discussing the exploding population and its effect on land fertility, Julian Huxley suggests that 'In the educational systems of under-developed territories, children should be introduced to science by the biological way of ecology and physiology and their applications in conservation and health, not by way of physics and chemistry and their applications in technology and industry.'[1] Just as Rendang provides a warning, so Pala, in many respects, provides a model for the underdeveloped territories. The Pala-nese, in Huxley's words, have chosen 'the road of applied biology, the road of fertility control and the limited production and selective industrialization which fertility control make possible' (ch. xiii). Consequently they have no need for the large-scale research required to support heavy industries mass-producing consumer goods and armaments. Physics and chemistry have neither interest nor value to them, and in their formal education all the emphasis is placed firmly on the sciences of life and mind; children are introduced to science 'by the biological way of ecology' through examples of soil erosion and conservation, which are then placed in the context of a universal morality:

Treat Nature well, and Nature will treat you well. Hurt or destroy

[1] *Essays of a Humanist* (1964), p. 128.

Nature, and Nature will soon destroy you. . . The morality to which a child goes on from the facts of ecology and the parables of erosion is a universal ethic. There are no Chosen People in nature, no Holy Lands, no Unique Historical Revelations. Conservation-morality gives nobody an excuse for feeling superior, or claiming special privileges. 'Do as you would be done by' applies to our dealings with all kinds of life in every part of the world. We shall be permitted to live on this planet only for as long as we treat all nature with compassion and intelligence. (ch. xiii)

If the immediate answer to 'the man from Kansas' is education, the ultimate answer must lie with eugenics and early conditioning. In *Brave New World* the controllers had ruthlessly employed the techniques of advanced eugenics and Pavlovian conditioning for the creation of a uniformly servile race. The rulers of *Island*, it would seem, have employed strikingly similar means, although for rather different ends. The Brave New Worlders had ecto-genesis; the Palanese have Deep Freeze and Artificial Insemination. In Pala almost every third child is the product of A.I., so that slowly a race of superior beings is evolving which after a century will possess an average I.Q. of up to a hundred and fifteen. Among the Brave New Worlders Pavlovian conditioning was the tech-nique whereby they were able to be content with their servitude; in Pala, conditioning is seen as an approach to the ethical problem, 'How can I get myself to do what I really want to do, and how refrain from doing what I really don't want to do?' In answer to the problem Huxley elsewhere concludes:

The only kind of universal conditioning that might be an unqualified blessing to all concerned is that which Arapesh mothers give their infants. While suckling and fondling the child, the mother brings it into physical contact with other members of the family, with visiting friends and with the domestic animals of the household and, as she does so, repeats the words 'Good, good, good. . .' The blissful experience of being held, caressed, and nursed comes to be associated in the child's mind with affectionate contacts between itself and other human or sub-human creatures. This association is then associated with the sound of the word 'good'—a sound to which, in due course, the child will learn to attach a meaning, so that a first-order experience will come to be interpreted in terms of a positive value-judgement. ('Human Potentialities', *The Humanist Frame*[1])

This is the technique which Dr Andrew discovered while serving as a naturalist on the *Melampus* and which Will finds himself a party to at the Vijaya household—'Pavlov purely for a good purpose. Pavlov for friendliness and trust and compassion'. As well as being conditioned to feel more affectionate towards their fellow beings, Palanese infants are also conditioned against fear. Death conditioning was, of course, a feature of *Brave New World* education: there were regular visits to the Hospital for the Dying where all the best toys were kept and chocolate cream served on death days. The Palanese approach is psychologically more profound and acknowledges the child to be more than a bundle of reflexes; here is Mary Sarojini explaining how she overcame her fear of death:

'I did what they teach you to do—tried to find out which of me was frightened and why she was frightened.'

'And which of you was it?'

'This one.' Mary Sarojini pointed a forefinger into her open mouth. 'The one that does all the talking. Little Miss Gibber—that's what Vijaya calls her. She's always talking about all the nasty things I remember, all the huge, wonderful impossible things I imagine I can do. She's the one that gets frightened.'

'Why is she so frightened?'

'I suppose it's because she gets talking about all the awful things that might happen to her, talking out loud or talking to herself. But there's another one who doesn't get frightened.'

'Which one is that?'

'The one that doesn't talk—just looks and listens and feels what's going on inside. And sometimes . . . she suddenly sees how beautiful everything is. No, that's wrong. *She* sees it all the time, but *I* don't—not unless she makes me notice it. That's when it suddenly happens. Beautiful, beautiful, beautiful! Even dog's messes.' She pointed at a formidable specimen almost at their feet. (ch. xiv)

[1] Edited Julian Huxley (1961).

The Brave New Worlders, it will be recalled, had a popular song which began, 'Bottle of mine, it's you I've always wanted!' Nevertheless ectogenesis had outmoded the mother fixation. In Pala the Freudian bogey has likewise been dispelled by less drastic means. The term Oedipus remains only to name a character in a marionette show, a puppet, moreover, as Mary Sarojini explains, who never had a MAC. MAC, the Mutual Adoption Club, is the salient feature of Palanese family life, a group of fifteen to twenty-five couples in which everyone adopts everyone else. This gives every Palanese child about twenty different homes: 'Mother', which in *Brave New World* was a term of obscenity, is now simply the name of a function, and once the function has been fulfilled the title lapses. Murugan and the clutching, devouring Rani serve to show what happens when there is no MAC and, should the reader still be in any doubt, there is Susila to contrast the Western and Palanese recipes for family life:

'Take one sexually inept wage-slave . . . one dissatisfied female, two or (if preferred) three small television-addicts; marinate in a mixture of Freudism and dilute Christianity; then bottle up tightly in a four-room flat and stew for fifteen years in their own juice.' *Our* recipe is rather different. 'Take twenty sexually satisfied couples and their offspring; add science, intuition and humour in equal quantities; steep in Tantrik Buddhism and simmer indefinitely in an open pan in the open air over a brisk flame of affection.' (ch. vii)

The Palanese freedom of movement in their family life is extended to their working hours. The controllers of Huxley's earlier utopia tailor-made their citizens for their individual tasks; the Palanese have preferred to sacrifice mechanical efficiency for human satisfaction. In Pala Fordism is non-existent; the result is that everyone does their share of the available work: professors and government officials put in their two hours of digging and delving a day. 'Sampling all kinds of work—it's part of everybody's education. One learns an enormous amount that way—about things and skills and organizations, about all kinds of people and their ways of thinking' (ch. ix).

In his contributory essay to *The Humanist Frame* Huxley draws attention to what he calls 'the two gravest weaknesses . . . in the current systems of formal education—the failure to give children an understanding of the nature and limitations of language, and the failure to take account of the all-important fact of human variability'. The detection of variability is not only one of the premises of the Palanese system of education, it is also a safeguard of democracy. The Hitlers and Stalins belong to two distinct and dissimilar groups—the Peter Pans and the Muscle People (In *Island* Colonel Dipa is a typical representative of the wayward somatotonic, whereas Murugan shows all the characteristics of a 'Peter Pan'.) At the age of four and a half, Palanese children are subjected to somato-typing and X-rays of the wrist, so that the physiologically immature and the vigorous-bodied somatotonics can be identified whilst still harmless. The physiologically immature are easily cured while the extreme somatotonics are trained to be aware and sensitive, and are given difficult and strenuous tasks to satisfy their craving for domination. In *The Perennial Philosophy* Huxley had defined civilization as 'a complex of religious, legal and educational devices for preventing extreme somatotonics from doing too much mischief, and for directing their irrepressible energies into socially desirable channels' (ch. viii). For the Palanese, educational devices alone are sufficient: among these climbing has an important role, a little for everyone with advanced rock-work for the full-blown Muscle People. Susila's husband, Dugald, was one of those who practised rock-climbing and had been killed in an accident shortly before Will's arrival; but as Dr Robert points out it is far better to risk one's own life than risk the lives of others, harming them because one is either too cautious or too ignorant to work off one's aggressions on a rock-face. The children themselves are taught what to expect of people whose physique and temperament differ from their own. W. H. Sheldon, who recommends differential education, describes the nursery school in which there are often 'a few vigorous-bodied somatotonics who take the lead in all enterprises, a few round, healthy-looking viscerotonics who join in with excellent fellowship, and a few little pinch-faced cerebrotonics who constitute a watchful and unsociable periphery.'[1] In Pala the little cerebrotonics are given every opportunity to adjust themselves to their fellow boys and girls. The shyest, most over-responsive and introverted children are brought together and introduced by degrees to small numbers of 'children with tendencies towards indiscriminate sociability'; only then are one or two of the 'children with tendencies towards aggressiveness and love of power' allowed to mix with the group. After a month or two of this controlled mixing, the three polar extremes are found to understand and tolerate one another.

The outstanding feature of Palanese education, however, is its all-embracing character; its simultaneous 'assault on all the more important fronts'. Every Palanese citizen is trained to be a 'guardian' of Huxley's ideal republic, and the education of a Palanese citizen, like that of Plato's 'ideal rulers', serves as an exposition of the author's total philosophy. What is perhaps the most original feature of this training, one which penetrates to the centre of Huxley's view of man, lies in the field of non-intellectual or non-verbal education. In 'The Education of an Amphibian', an essay in *Adonis and the Alphabet*, Huxley likens man to an amphibian inhabiting different and incommensurable universes; below the threshold of the consciousness every human being has a not-self, or more accurately 'five or six merging but clearly distinguishable not-selves'. There is the personal not-self, the region of the subconscious drives and repressions to which Freud paid so much attention; the not-self in charge of the body, the vegetative soul or the entelechy; the not-self from which 'we derive our insights and inspirations'; the not-self of the shared symbols which stand for man's deepest tendencies, the Jungian archetypes; the not-self of visionary experience which provides the various religions with their 'notions of the Other World, of Heaven and Hell'; and

[1] *The Varieties of Human Physique* (1940), p. 260. Julian Huxley comments 'After Sheldon's work, not even the most aprioristic theorist could expect that a skinny ectomorph would react to the educational process in the same way as a comfortable endomorph with perhaps double the ratio of guts to muscle and a radically different pattern of hormones being squirted into his bloodstream.' *Essays of a Humanist*, p. 133.

finally, 'beyond all the rest, but immanent in every mental or material event . . . that universal Not-Self, which men have called the Holy Spirit, the Atman-Brahman, the Clear Light, Suchness'. The true function of education, therefore, is to find out how human beings can be taught to make the best of all worlds, from 'the world of self-conscious, verbalized intelligence' at one end of the mind's spectrum to the 'world of the unconscious intelligences immanent in the mind-body' at the other. This calls for a system of education that is more than a device for passing on correct knowledge. In terms of the two cultures controversy, the answer to too much specialization is not a few more courses in the humanities:

'By themselves, the humanities don't humanize. They're simply another form of specialization on the symbolic level. Reading Plato or listening to a lecture on T. S. Eliot doesn't educate the whole human being; like courses in physics or chemistry, it merely educates the symbol-manipulator and leaves the rest of the living mind-body in its pristine state of ignorance and ineptitude.' (ch. xiii)

The only cure for specialization is an extensive course in non-verbal learning. For the Palanese child there is a systematic training of the whole mind-body in all its aspects from practical instruction in Maithuna to an introduction to mystical experience with Moksha medicine.

The curriculum of a hypothetical course in 'what may be called the non-verbal humanities' is briefly outlined in 'The Education of an Amphibian'. This includes a training of the kinesthetic sense; a training of the perception and the memory; a training in the control of the autonomic nervous system and finally a training for spiritual insight. In one way or another all these ideas have been incorporated into the education of Huxley's utopians. First the kinesthetic sense: Huxley had championed F. M. Alexander's method for training the conditioned reflexes ever since Anthony Beavis re-learnt to sit on a chair in *Eyeless in Gaza*, and not surprisingly this has found its way into Pala. Everyone is taught psycho-physical co-ordination from an early age:

From the first moment they start doing for themselves. For example, what's the proper way of handling yourself while you're buttoning your clothes? . . . We answer the question by actually putting their heads and bodies into the physiologically best position. And we encourage them at the same time to notice how it feels to be in the physiologically best position, to be aware of what the process of doing up buttons consists of in terms of touches and pressures and muscular sensations. By the time they're fourteen they've learned how to get the most and the best—objectively and subjectively—out of any activity they may undertake. (ch. ix)

Next, under the heading of non-verbal education, are a whole range of exercises designed to transform the energy built up from negative emotions into specific kinds of muscular action. These exercises take 'the power generated by fear or envy or too much noradrenalin' and instead of repressing it direct it along channels where it can be useful or at least harmless. Rock-climbing and wood-chopping, of course, belong to this category, but for the children there are other simpler techniques for the re-direction of power. Deep-breathing games free suppressed emotions—'Which of two antagonists can inhale most deeply and say "OM" on the out-going breath for the longest time?' and the Rakshasi Hornpipe helps to let off 'those dangerous heads of steam raised by anger and frustration' (ch. xiii). Then there are exercises in visual imagination which help to liberate the mind from painful memories and anxieties about the future.[1] An example of this kind of technique is illustrated early in the novel, when young Mary Sarojini makes the injured Will repeat the story of his climb up the snake-infested ridge until the memory of his fear is finally purged.

To harbour unpleasant memories is to invite neurosis as Mary Sarojini knew only too well; on the other hand positively charged memories, used correctly, can be made to have a definite therapeutic value. That memory 'charged with pleasant emotions is a soporific or, more accurately, an inducer of trance' was discovered empirically by an American hypnotist, Dr Fahnestock

[1] For a detailed description of these techniques see Laura Archera Huxley's *You Are Not the Target*.

(*Adonis and the Alphabet*). Hypnotism, as a means for gaining some kind of control over the autonomic nervous system, was one of the original contributions of Dr Andrew MacPhail; a century later, Susila MacPhail, in the best family tradition, puts Will's conscious self to sleep by evoking memories of a pleasant April week-end in the Mendips. Dr Fahnestock's method provides a technique whereby the troublesome 'children' of the mind-body, the conscious ego and the personal subconscious, can be persuaded to let the body take care of itself. Susila explains to Will:

'In your part of the world doctors get rid of the children by poisoning them with barbiturates. We do it by talking to them about cathedrals and jackdaws.' Her voice had modulated into a chant. 'About white clouds floating in the sky, white swans floating on the dark, smooth, irresistible river of life. . .' (ch. vii)

Meanwhile the children of Pala learn to shut off pain with their own brand of auto-hypnosis or Self-Determination. Finally, to complete this curriculum in the 'non-verbal humanities', there is an introduction to the twin arts of sexual perfection and spiritual insight, which serve to lay the foundation for a full and satisfying adult life. Pala is an island where, as Will reflects, the Fall is an exploded doctrine: sexual freedom is taken for granted as in *Brave New World*. The boy and girl in 'Oedipus in Pala'

> Are bound for rosier gardens and the absurd
> Apocalyptic rite that in the mind
> Calls forth from the touched skin and melting flesh
> The immanent Infinite. (ch. xiv)

Maithuna is a recognized part of the school syllabus, while the sad fate of Murugan, playing Antinous to the black moustached Hadrian, serves as a warning of what happens to Palanese who are educated outside the confines of sanity.

Sex had always been an unfailing source of pessimism in Huxley's novels, and this sudden change of attitude was almost totally without warning. In fairness it can be argued that his 'puritanism' was aimed at sexual abuse rather than at sex itself. But the fact remains that after Rampion all Huxley's men of good will are, without exception, unqualified celibates. The first hint of a change is expressed in an important essay published as an appendix to *The Devils of Loudun*. There Huxley describes what he calls 'the three most popular avenues of downward self-transcendence', drugs, elementary sexuality and herd-intoxication. 'Downward self-transcendence' is defined as the escape beyond the limits of the insulated ego, not to liberation but to enslavement. This leads him to consider the difficult question as to what extent and in what circumstances it is possible to make use of the descending road as a way to spiritual enlightenment: 'At first sight it would seem obvious that the way down is not and can never be the way up. But in the realm of existence matters are not quite so simple as they are in our beautifully tidy world of words. In actual life a downward movement may sometimes be made the beginning of an ascent. When the shell of the ego has been cracked and there begins to be a consciousness of the subliminal and physiological otherness underlying personality, it sometimes happens that we catch a glimpse, fleeting but apocalyptic, of that other Otherness, which is the Ground of all being. . . Any escape, even by a descending road, out of insulated selfhood makes possible at least a momentary awareness of the not-self on every level, including the highest.' If elementary sexuality is considered from this point of view, then the road invariably runs downhill, but there had been notable exceptions. In India, the exponents of Tantric yoga had evolved a psycho-physiological technique for transforming elementary sexuality into a means of self-enlightenment. And in the West, the sexual disciplines practised by the Oneida community had been made compatible with a form of Protestant Christianity. These were the twin origins of Palanese Maithuna.

Buddhism, Huxley tells us, came to Pala about 800 A.D.; not from Ceylon but from Bengal so that the Palanese were not only Mahayanists but also Tantrics. Pala, in fact, owes its name to that of a Bengal dynasty, dating back to the eighth century, under whose patronage Tantric doctrines flourished and developed.[1]

---

[1] See Edward Conze, *Buddhism*, pp. 178–9. An interesting confirmation of Huxley's historical accuracy.

What distinguishes Tantra from all other schools of Hinduism and Buddhism is the way it employs the functions normally regarded as impediments to spiritual progress as a direct means of enlightenment. In Tantra 'the natural functions of eating, drinking and sexual union may be used as Upachāra of worship. . . . Worship and prayer are not merely the going aside at a particular time or place to utter set formulae or to perform particular ritual acts. The whole of life, in all its rightful particulars, without any single exception, may be an act of worship if man but makes it so'.[1] Or, as Ranga puts the matter to Will, a Tantric doesn't renounce the world or deny its value; rather he accepts the world and makes use of it, makes use of everything that happens to him as so many means to liberation. By making the old Raja a Tantric initiate, who had learned the art of Maithuna, Huxley was able to credit his utopians with an acceptable form of sexuality that is both a method of birth-control and a technique for enlightenment. The sexual problem in a contemplative society had finally been solved.

Huxley's main evidence for the excellence of Maithuna or Karezza, as it is more commonly called, comes not from the east, but from the experience of the Oneida community, where the 'reconciliation between sex, religion and society was an accomplished fact':

Sex is 'the lion of the tribe of human passions'; to tame the lion, John Humphrey Noyes devised, and for thirty years his community at Oneida put into effect, a system of 'Complex Marriage', based upon 'Male Continence'. Separated, by means of a carefully inculcated technique, from propagation, the 'amative function' was refined, taught good manners, reconciled with Protestant Christianity and made to serve the purpose of religious self-transcendence. ('Ozymandias', *Adonis and the Alphabet*)

The accounts of life at Oneida lend support to Radha's enthusiastic declamation that 'For women—*all* women . . . the yoga of love means perfection, means being transformed and taken out of

[1] Sir John Woodroffe, *Shakti and Shakta* (Madras, 1951), p. 602.

themselves and completed'. Or, as Ranga explains in more Freudian terms:

'What we're born with, what we experience all through infancy and childhood, is a sexuality that isn't concentrated on the genitals; it's a sexuality diffused throughout the whole organism. That's the paradise we inherit. But the paradise gets lost as the child grows up. *Maithuna* is the organized attempt to regain that paradise.' (ch. vi)

While admitting that Maithuna was not for everyone, Huxley felt that here was a natural method of birth-control which, for the woman at least, was free from all the bad psychological consequences normally associated with a controlled birth rate.

What of Maithuna as a yoga or technique for self-enlightenment? Downward self-transcendence, the 'yoga of anti-love . . . of lust and the self-loathing that reinforces the self and makes it yet more loathsome' (ch. xiv), is the usual result of love-making in Huxley's novels. This is typified in *Island* by the sexual frenzies of Will and Babs. Maithuna, in contrast, offers a technique that lends itself to contemplation: 'The Kulārnava Tantra says that man must be taught to rise by the means of those very things which are the cause of his fall. . . Man falls through the natural functions of drinking, eating, and sexual intercourse. If these are done with the feeling (Bhāva) and under the conditions prescribed, then they become . . . the instruments of his uplift to a point at which such ritual is no longer necessary and is surpassed.'[1] In other words, as Ranga insists, it is not the special technique that turns Maithuna into a yoga; it is rather the kind of feeling or awareness that the technique permits. To the Palanese trained from an early age in the art of awareness, Maithuna is indeed a means of liberation; otherwise it would be, as Will suggests, merely another means of birth control without contraceptives. To sum up in the words of Alan Watts, whose excellent essay on the relationship between sex and spirituality seems more than relevant to Huxley's solution to this age-old problem: '. . . the problems of sexuality cannot be solved at their own level. The full splendour of sexual experience

[1] Woodroffe, op. cit., p. 634.

does not reveal itself without a new mode of attention to the world in general. On the other hand, the sexual relationship is a setting in which the full opening of attention may rather easily be realized because it is so immediately rewarding. . . But to serve as a means of initiation to the "one body" of the universe, it requires what we have called a contemplative approach. This is not love "without desire" in the sense of love without delight, but love which is not contrived or "wilfully" provoked as an escape from the habitual empty feeling of an isolated ego.'[1] This is the secret Huxley has bestowed on the Palanese: they have solved the problem of sex, not by a technique, but through a new mode of awareness—'the Future Buddha won't have to leave home and sit under the Bodhi Tree. He'll have his Enlightenment while he's in bed with the princess' (ch. xiv).

That the Fall is an exploded doctrine, that a future Buddha should seek liberation, not under the Bodhi tree, but with his princess—these reflect more than a new attitude to sexuality; they suggest a whole new approach to religious experience. It would be untrue to say that *Island* expounds a doctrine which contradicts Huxley's earlier teaching. The Palanese are, if nothing else, a society of contemplatives, whose way of life remains firmly anchored to the basic tenet of *The Perennial Philosophy*, *Tat tvam asi*, 'thou art That'. The underlying dogmatism, however, has been transformed. The hostility to organized religion which Huxley expressed in *Do What You Will* had relaxed over the years following his conversion—if the theology of the West still came under critical fire, that of the East remained largely beyond reproach. Now, this uneasy truce is broken. Organized religion, of whatever origin, is seen as the harbinger of universal discord:

Enter the Gods of Light, enter the Prophets, enter Pythagoras and Zoroaster, enter the Jains and the early Buddhists. Between them they usher in the Age of the Cosmic Cockfight—Ormuzd versus Ahriman, Jehovah versus Satan and the Baalim, Nirvana as opposed to Samsara, appearance over against Plato's Ideal Reality. And except in the minds

[1] *Nature, Man and Woman* (1958), pp. 173-4.

of a few Tantriks and Mahayanists and Taoists and heretical Christians, the cockfight went on for the best part of two thousand years. (ch. xii)

On a philosophical and psychological level theology has encouraged the pointless conflicts between Man and Nature, Nature and God, and the Flesh and the Spirit. 'Self-division's cause' is in the end the result of looking at humanity through the distorting lens of religions which have dichotomized the fundamental relationships which shape mankind. The new wisdom, which doesn't make these insane separations, is of the kind 'prophetically glimpsed in Zen and Taoism and Tantra'. What is striking about this is that Huxley was, at last, seeing a way through to resolving the antitheses which had so burdened his early thought. In the process there is a conscious narrowing of the doctrinal field. All the mainstream religions are, in fact, excluded; excluded, because they have taught dogma which has lent itself to the error of dualism. What remains is a narrow segment of the perennial philosophy ranging from the Tantric schools of Hinduism and Buddhism at one end to Taoism and Zen at the other. The essence of religious experience, according to 'the new Wisdom', is non-verbal and non-dualistic—what Huxley defines as 'the blessed experience of Not-Two'. Religious belief by 'the systematic taking of unanalysed words . . . too seriously' has opened the doors to dualism and in consequence sown the seeds of suffering and discontent. As the old Raja puts it, 'in religion all words are dirty words. Anybody who gets eloquent about Buddha, or God, or Christ, ought to have his mouth washed out with carbolic soap'[1] (ch. v).

In the original formulation of the perennial philosophy, Huxley postulated a godhead that was both transcendent and immanent. For the Palanese only the concept of immanence remains; transcendence has invariably led to the idea of a personal God, and the acceptance of a supreme authority over man and nature has been

[1] Adapted from Chao-Chou's 'When you pronounce the word Buddha clean your mouth for three years'. Quoted by D. T. Suzuki, *The Zen Doctrine of No-Mind* (1949), p. 113.

one of the prime sources of dualistic thought—of Man as opposed to Nature, of Nature as opposed to God. Huxley's 'new Wisdom' with its blend of humanism and Mahayana sees the godhead as integral to the cosmic whole, of which the primary symbol is the open sky, 'the Buddha Nature in all our perpetual perishing'. Palanese children are given scarecrow duty—jerking the strings of life-sized marionettes shaped like future Buddhas and East Indian versions of God the Father—to remind them that the Gods are home-made; that, 'it's we who pull their strings and so give them the power to pull ours' (ch. xiii). In the puppet play, 'Oedipus in Pala', they are reminded that Oedipus had been taught 'all that horrible stuff about God getting furious with people every time they made a mistake' (ch. xiv), and finally, there is Dr Andrew MacPhail's contribution, the theory that child-beating is the origin of original sin and Jehovah. The ideal is to think of God as immanent and of man as potentially self-transcendent.

Religious symbolism is, of course, tolerated in Pala. There was the old Raja who buttered the family lingam; and at the initiation ceremony, the climbers offer their accomplishment to Shiva, 'their own Suchness visualized as God'. But it is always clear that these representations of a personal deity are nothing more than symbols. The little girl who lays a spray of white orchids on the upturned palm of the huge golden Bodhisattva is already old enough to know that Amitabha is not a person. She is also aware, in spite of her desire to think otherwise, that the temple is not the house of the Buddha; that it is just 'a diagram of her own unconscious mind—a dark little cubby-hole with lizards crawling upside down on the ceiling, and cockroaches in all the crevices' (ch. xi). The results of taking a transcendental deity too seriously are seen in Colonel Dipa's use of God as his alibi for his campaign against Palanese independence, and the Rani of Pala's Crusade of the Spirit. Huxley has never spared false religiosity. In *Island*, theosophy and Moral Rearmament are the targets. The Rani of Pala, the 'female tycoon who had cornered the market . . . in Pure Spirituality and the Ascended Masters' with her World-Movement to save humanity and her favours from Koot Hoomi, is directly descended from Priscilla Wimbush, the Madame Sosostris of *Crome Yellow*, who had 'the Infinite to keep in tune with'.

The main approach to non-dualism, that level of consciousness 'in which the distinction between the *ego* and the external world, and the distinction between the subject and the object, fall away',[1] lies through awareness, or, as it is sometimes called, mindfulness. This is the function of the talking Mynah birds with their incessant cries of 'Attention', to remind the Palanese of the here and the now. 'Understanding comes when we liberate ourselves from the old and so make possible a direct, unmediated contact with the new, the mystery, moment by moment, of our existence' (*Adonis and the Alphabet*). This unmediated contact with the mystery of existence is what the Mahayana Buddhists have named 'Suchness' or *Tathata*: 'What is Suchness? It is to see things as they are in themselves, to understand them in their state of self-nature, to accept them as themselves. This seems easy for when we see a flower before us we know it is a flower and not an inkstand or a lamp, but our knowledge is always coloured with all kinds of feelings, desires and imaginations, and no such knowledge is pure and free from subjective "defilements". . . . To the Buddha's mind the flower is the inkstand and the inkstand is the lamp.'[2] Or, as Huxley puts it:

. . . Good Being is in the knowledge of who in fact one is in relation to *all* experiences; so be aware—aware in every context, at all times and whatever, creditable or discreditable, pleasant or unpleasant, you may be doing or suffering. This is the only genuine yoga, the only spiritual exercise worth practising. (ch. v)

This is the last and most important aspect of non-verbal education: training in the art of spiritual insight. Under ordinary conditions we are never able to experience 'suchness', for without constant and intense self-awareness, free from all preconceptions and comparisons, it is our nature to discriminate, to divide and to dwell on dualities. Suchness, which is essentially non-verbal and non-conceptual, can be approached through a state of pure receptivity

[1] Edward Carpenter, quoted by Kenneth Walker, *The Conscious Mind* (1962), p. 45.

[2] Beatrice Lane Suzuki, *Mahayana Buddhism* (1959), pp. 24–5.

of which the first step is a systematic training in perceptual awareness. In his *Lectures on Zen Buddhism*, Suzuki draws a distinction
between the scientific and the Zen approaches to reality. The
scientific approach typifies the Western analytical and schematic
mind; the Zen approach, the Eastern integrative, intuitive mind:

The scientific method in the study of reality is to view an object from
the so-called objective point of view. For instance, suppose a flower
here on the table is the object of scientific study. Scientists will subject
it to all kinds of analyses, botanical, chemical, physical, etc., and tell us
all that they have found out about the flower from their respective
angles of study, and say that the study of the flower is exhausted and
that there is nothing more to state about it unless something new is
discovered accidentally in the course of other studies. . .

The Zen approach is to enter right into the object itself and see it, as
it were, from the inside. To know the flower is to become the flower,
to be the flower, to bloom as the flower, and to enjoy the sunlight as
well as the rainfall. When this is done, the flower speaks to me and I
know all its secrets, all its joys, all its sufferings; that is, all its life
vibrating within itself. Not only that: along with my 'knowledge' of
the flower I know all the secrets of the universe, which includes all the
secrets of my own Self, which has been eluding my pursuit all my life
so far, because I divided myself into a duality. . .

Now, however, by knowing the flower I know my Self. That is,
by losing myself in the flower I know my Self as well as the flower.

I call this kind of approach to reality the Zen way, the ante-scientific
. . . or even antiscientific way.[1]

In his description of Palanese elementary education, Huxley makes
a similar distinction between botany and self-knowledge, using
the story of Mahakasyapa and Buddha's Flower Sermon. Each
child is given a common flower which is described in scientific
terms: its petals, stamen, pistil, ovary and the rest. The children
then write a detailed analysis, illustrated by an accurate drawing.
After this the Mahakasyapa story is read to them. (This is an
account of the Buddha's Flower Sermon: instead of preaching as
usual, he merely picked a flower and held it up for his disciples to

[1] D. T. Suzuki, *Zen Buddhism and Psychoanalysis* (1960), pp. 11–12.

look at. No one understood the meaning of the 'sermon' except Mahakasyapa, who simply smiled). The question is then asked whether the Buddha was giving a lesson in botany or teaching something else, and if so, what.

'And of course, as the story makes clear, there's no answer that can be put into words. So we tell the boys and girls to stop thinking and just look. "But don't look analytically. . . Don't look as scientists, even as gardeners. Liberate yourselves from everything you know and look with complete innocence at this infinitely improbable thing before you. Look at it as though you'd never seen anything of the kind before, as though it had no name and belonged to no recognizable class. Look at it alertly but passively, receptively, without labelling or judging or comparing. And as you look at it, inhale its mystery, breathe in the spirit of sense, the smell of the wisdom of the other shore." ' (ch. xiii)

Reduced to their simplest terms, the scientific and contemplative approaches are merely complementary ways of examining the same object, although in the hierarchy of values, the contemplative approach is greatly superior. In Suzuki's words, 'The sciences deal with abstractions and there is no activity in them. Zen plunges itself into the source of creativity and drinks from it all the life there is in it'.[1] This distinction between the scientific and the contemplative, the verbal and the non-verbal is Huxley's final answer to the moral dilemma which first darkened the pages of *Antic Hay*: God as exultation as opposed to God as $2 + 2 = 4$. Gumbril had asked whether there was any chance of their being the same; 'were there bridges to join the two worlds?' In Pala the problem has been solved: bridge-building sessions (which Gumbril might have envied) join the two worlds as a regular feature of every study:

Everything from dissected frogs to the spiral nebulae, it all gets looked at receptively as well as conceptually, as a fact of aesthetic or spiritual experience as well as in terms of science or history or economics. Training in receptivity is the complement and antidote to training in analysis

[1] op. cit., p. 12.

and symbol-manipulation. Both kinds of training are absolutely indispensable. If you neglect either of them you'll never grow into a
fully human being. (ch. xiii)

Training in pure receptivity is an everyday affair in Pala. Grace
at meals consists of chewing the first mouthful of each course
until nothing is left; attention is paid to the flavour, consistency
and temperature of the food, to the pressure on the teeth and the
feel of the jaw muscles. Attention, Huxley explains, is the whole
point: attention to the experience of something given, a momentary escape from the memories and anticipations, from all the
symptoms of the conscious 'I'. In a similar way work and love-
making, through constant awareness, are transfigured into the
yoga of work and the yoga of love-making. This is the kind of
preparation for enlightenment, here and now, in the everyday
world envisaged by the exponents of Tantra:

'What is this life beyond form pervading forms?' the goddess enquires
of her consort, Shiva. 'How may we enter into it fully, above space and
time, beyond names and descriptions?' Shiva answers her in the most
practical and scientific way, with a list of 112 exercises in awareness—
awareness of first-order experiences, visual and auditory, tactile and
visceral, imaginative and imageless. 'Radiant one, this consciousness
may dawn between two breaths. After breath comes in and just before
it goes out—*the beneficence.*' 'See as if for the first time a beauteous person or some ordinary object.' 'Intone a sound audibly, then less and less
audibly, as feeling deepens into *this silent harmony.*' 'When eating or
drinking, become the taste of the food or drink and *be filled.*'
'While being caressed, sweet princess, enter the caressing *as everlasting
life.*' 'Wherever your attention lights, at that very point *experience.*'[1]
('Human Potentialities', *The Humanist Frame*)

After the yogas of living, there is the yoga of dying—in spite of
their utopian aspirations, the Palanese have not been spared the
ravages of disease and death: Susila has lost a husband, Robert

---

[1] Adapted from 'the Vigyan Bhairava and Sochanda Tantra, both written
about four thousand years ago, and from Malini Vijaya Tantra, probably another
thousand years older yet'. See Paul Reps, *Zen Flesh, Zen Bones* (New York, 1961),
pp. 159–74.

MacPhail a son, while his wife, Lakshmi, is dying of cancer. What Huxley has called the 'art of dying' is something of a recurring theme in his last novels. There is Helen, in *The Genius and the Goddess*, who had been 'dying by daily instalments' so that when 'the final reckoning came, there was practically nothing to pay'; and, in contrast, Henry Maartens who faced his death-bed 'frantically alive and unprepared, by any preliminary dying, totally unprepared for the decisive moment'. And in *Time Must Have a Stop* there is Eustace Barnack unhappily shrinking from an encounter with the Clear Light of the Void, while in *Island*, Lakshmi, more prepared for 'the decisive moment' meets the same Clear Light without fear or alarm. The technique for dying is, in essentials, the same as that for living. Helen, we recall, 'managed to make the best of life while she was dying. . . [She] knew how to die because she knew how to live—to live now and here and for the greater glory of God'. In *Island*, Susila explains how the dying are taught to go on being aware:

We help them to go on practising the art of living even while they're dying. Knowing who in fact one is, being conscious of the universal and impersonal life that lives itself through each of us—that's the art of living, and that's what one can help the dying to go on practising. To the very end. Maybe beyond the end. (ch. xiv)

Lakshmi is kept fully awake and conscious during her last hours—the very opposite treatment to that given to Linda in the Hospital of the Dying in *Brave New World*—so that she can be kept constantly aware of who she is, not as an ego, as a separate 'conscious I', but as a Not-Self, as the underlying reality or suchness that 'lives itself through each of us'. This is done by reminding her of her own experiences of the Clear Light:

'When you were eight years old', said Susila, 'that was the first time. An orange butterfly on a leaf, opening and shutting its wings in the sunshine—and suddenly there was the Clear Light of pure Suchness blazing through it, like another sun.'
  'Much brighter than the sun', Lakshmi whispered.
  'But much gentler. You can look into the Clear Light and not be

blinded. And now remember it. A butterfly on a green leaf, opening and shutting its wings—and it's the Buddha Nature totally present, it's the Clear Light outshining the sun.' (ch. xiv)

As in *Time Must Have a Stop*, Huxley follows the *Bardo Thödol*: Lakshmi sees the same Clear Light of the Dharmakāya, which so terrified Eustace Barnack; but Lakshmi, freed from the encumbrances of the unregenerate ego, can go forward 'into the living peace of the Clear Light', without fear or anxiety. The Clear Light is the Godhead from which the soul emanates and to which, freed from the meshes of the clinging self, it will eventually return. Or put another way, the soul or Not-Self *is* the Clear Light—'thou art that', as Susila tells Lakshmi:

'Your own consciousness shining, void, inseparable from the great Body of Radiance, is subject neither to birth nor death, but is the same as the immutable Light, Buddha Amitabha.' (ch. xiv)

Education in spiritual insight will not, of course, as Huxley admits, give everyone the kind of visionary experience Lakshmi enjoyed at an early age. This is the function of *moksha*-medicine, the island's brand of psilocybin, the hallucinogen derived from the psilocybe mushroom. In an article written shortly before his death, Huxley tells us that in his utopian fantasy he speculated 'in fictional terms about the ways in which a substance akin to psilocybin could be used to potentiate the non-verbal education of adolescents. . .' ('A Philosopher's Visionary Prediction'). One result is that Palanese children are introduced to *moksha*-medicine as the climax of their initiation out of childhood into adolescence. The symbolism of Nataraja and Muyalaka—Muyalaka, the embodiment of greedy, possessive selfhood is being stamped underfoot by the dancing Nataraja, whose other foot, dancing in defiance of the law of gravity, stands for liberation—which is closely bound up with the ceremony, suggests that *moksha*-medicine brings, at least, temporary respite from the bondage to the self. This is the first phase of mystical experience, the breaking down of the subject-object relationship, the dissolving of duality, the 'One joined in marriage to the many, the relative made absolute by its union with the One' (ch. x).

Since this is probably the most controversial issue raised by *Island*, it is perhaps worth considering Huxley's claims for the psychedelics in some detail before continuing further. R. C. Zaehner, in *Mysticism, Sacred and Profane*, accuses Huxley of 'equating his experience under the influence of mescalin both with the Beatific Vision and with the *Sac-cid-ānanda* or "Being-Aware-ness-Bliss" of the Hindus' and therefore 'denying any specific religious basis to either Hinduism or Christianity'; further since mescalin has been used clinically to produce a state akin to schizo-phrenia, it follows, from Huxley's premises, that 'both mescalin and mania are capable of producing the Beatific Vision'. This, Zaehner concludes, 'is to reduce all meditative and contemplative religion to pure lunacy'.[1] It would not be necessary to take this view too seriously except for the fact that Zaehner bases his exegesis on a quotation from *The Doors of Perception*: 'The Beatific Vision, *Sat Chit Ananda*, Being-Awareness-Bliss—for the first time I understood, not on the verbal level, not by inchoate hints or at a distance, but precisely and completely what those pro-digious syllables referred to.' This, according to Zaehner, is what Huxley claims for mescalin; his argument would have been a little less damaging, one feels, if the evidence had been examined more closely in its original context. The preceding sentence to the offending passage reads, 'My eyes travelled from the rose to the carnation, and from that feathery incandescence to the smooth scrolls of sentient amethyst which were the iris'. Huxley is ob-viously recording his feelings verbatim while still under the influence of the drug. Some forty pages further on, reflecting on his experiences, he concludes more soberly: 'I am not so foolish as to equate what happens under the influence of mescalin or of any other drug, prepared or in the future preparable, with the realization of the end and ultimate purpose of human life: En-lightenment, the Beatific Vision. All I am suggesting is that the

[1] 1961, p. 84. See also Introduction and Chapters I and II, 'Mescalin' and 'Mes-calin Interpreted.'

mescalin experience is what Catholic theologians call "a gratuitous grace", not necessary to salvation but potentially helpful and to be accepted thankfully, if made available.' This passage Zaehner chooses to dismiss with the brief comment, that 'on a later page Huxley's claims for his experience are less outrageous'.[1]

In *Island*, the old Raja states that a 'century of research on the *moksha*-medicine has clearly shown that quite ordinary people are perfectly capable of having visionary or even fully liberating experiences'; and Vijaya claims that 'with four hundred milli-grammes of *moksha*-medicine in their bloodstreams, even begin-ners . . . can catch a glimpse of the world as its looks to someone who has been liberated from his bondage to the ego'. It is clear, however, that Huxley does not envisage consciousness-expanding drugs as an end in themselves, but rather as a kind of supplement-ary aid to the normal practice of meditation:

. . . all that *moksha*-medicine can do is to give you a succession of beatific glimpses, an hour or two, every now and then, of enlightening and liberating grace. It remains for you to decide whether you'll co-operate with the grace and take those opportunities. (ch. x)

. . . *moksha*-medicine prepares one for the reception of gratuitous graces—pre-mystical visions or the full-blown mystical experiences. Meditation is one of the ways in which one co-operates with those gratuitous graces. (ch. xi)

This seems to be the general conclusion of those who have used the hallucinogenic drugs as a means of elevating the conscious-ness. Gerald Heard, experimenting with lysergic acid, states 'that when taken under the right conditions, L.S.D. helps the meditator to stop the constant flow of associative thinking which prevents him from reaching the serene and silent region of his mind to which he is seeking admission'.[2]

Nevertheless, the recommendation of the hallucinogens as a sort of universal panacea has met some harsh criticism. Huxley con-cedes that 'mescalin is not yet the ideal drug. Along with the

[1] op. cit., p. 9.   [2] See Kenneth Walker, *The Conscious Mind*, p. 137.

happily transfigured majority of mescalin takers there is a minority that finds in the drug only hell or purgatory' (*The Doors of Perception*); and the Palanese claim only eighty-five per cent effectiveness. Experimental research has not appeared to have justified even this optimism; although it seems that what Leary calls the 'set and suggestive context' is highly critical: if both the environmental factors and the state of the subject are favourable, then 'a shatteringly sacred experience results'—if both are negative then the result can only be the same.[1] In *Island*, Susila sounds a cautionary note: 'The *moksha*-medicine can take you to heaven; but it can also take you to hell. Or else to both, together or alternately. Or else (if you're lucky, or if you've made yourself ready) beyond either of them' (ch. xiv). This is an adequate description of Will's experience, but the key phrase would appear to be 'if you've made yourself ready'; to sum up in the words of Kenneth Walker, 'It would seem therefore that what one gets from an experiment with mescalin or lysergic acid is, to a great extent, determined by the mental and emotional equipment with which one embarks on it'.[2] On the evidence, given the training in spiritual insight and the environment of a contemplative society, there seems no reason to question Huxley's enthusiasm for the use of these drugs. In the hands of the uninitiated it is rather a different matter.

Island ends with Will's vision of 'heaven and hell' under the influence of *moksha*-medicine. This is perhaps too all-revealing for a beginner, even under the expert guidance of a Susila MacPhail; however, as this is the climax of the novel, the experience had necessarily to be of a highly significant nature. After taking the drug, the ego is completely eclipsed and Will is plunged straight into the 'luminous bliss' of the Clear Light:

Its presence was his absence. William Asquith Farnaby—ultimately and essentially there was no such person. Ultimately and essentially there

---

[1] Timothy Leary, 'How to Change Behaviour', reprint from *Clinical Psychology*. Proceedings of the XIV International Congress of Applied Psychology, vol. 4. (Copenhagen: Munksgaard, 1962), pp. 63-4.

[2] op. cit., p. 134.

was only a luminous bliss, only a knowledgeless understanding, only union with unity in a limitless, undifferentiated awareness.

The oneness is marred only by the slowly emerging excrescences, fragments of lingering selfhood, which disturb the otherwise blissful union with the Light:

In the firmament of bliss and understanding, like bats against the sunset, there was a wild criss-crossing of remembered notions and the hangovers of past feelings. . . And then bat-feelings of anger and disgust as the thickening horrors became specific memories of what the essentially non-existent William Asquith Farnaby had seen and done, inflicted and suffered.

But behind and around and somehow even within those flickering memories was the firmament of bliss and peace and understanding. There might be a few bats in the sunset sky; but the fact remained that the dreadful miracle of creation had been reversed. From a praeternaturally wretched and delinquent self he had been unmade into pure mind, mind in its natural state, limitless, undifferentiated, luminously blissful, knowledgelessly understanding.

Later the Light recedes, heaven gives way to hell, and Will is exposed to the full flood of the Essential Horror as the fragments of selfhood become unified into a phantasmagoria of his own past. There is the mirror image of the 'two pale bodies, his and Babs', frantically coupling to the accompaniment of his memories of Molly's funeral', powerfully symbolized by the *gongylus gongyloides*, the 'two little working models of a nightmare . . . shaken spasmodically by the simultaneous agonies of death and copulation.' The insects multiply and dissolve into a diabolic vision of lust and power on a cosmic scale; all of Will's life as professional execution watcher is epitomized in a single scene of mindless horror:

The endless columns of insects had turned abruptly into an endless column of soldiers. Marching as he had seen the Brown Shirts marching through Berlin, a year before the War. Thousands upon thousands of them, their banners fluttering, their uniforms glowing in the infernal brightness like floodlit excrement. Numberless as insects, and each of them moving with the precision of a machine. . . And the faces, the faces! . . . Huge idiot faces, blankly receptive. Faces of wide-eyed sleepwalkers. Faces of young Nordic angels rapt in the Beatific Vision. Faces of Baroque saints going into ecstasy. Faces of lovers on the brink of orgasm. . . Knowledgeless understanding of nonsense and diabolism.

This is Huxley's man-created hell, the downward self-transcendence of mindless sexuality and the mechanical horror of a machine universe, glimpsed in *Brave New World*. The vision ends with the marching columns reaching their destination: the thousands of corpses in the Korean mud, the 'innumerable packets of garbage littering the African desert', the fly-blown bodies in the courtyard of an Algerian farm; and the final hideous certitude that suffering is not only cumulative but self-perpetuating.

It is no coincidence that the pattern of Will's visionary experience bears a striking resemblance to that of Eustace Barnack in the *Bardo* world of *Time Must Have a Stop*: first, the Clear Light, pure and undifferentiated; then, the clots of selfhood partially eclipsing the brightness and lastly, the resurgence of past memories, coming to a climax in a feverish nightmare of copulation and death. The visionary experience and the after-death states are, according to Huxley, analogous. What the mystic sees is a foretaste of the *Bardo* existence, in which the various 'not-selves' flood the conscious mind. The negative nature of Will's experience, at this stage, like that of Eustace Barnack, is a mirror image of his own negation. What Will lacks is *Karuna* or compassion, the other half of the Mynah birds' message: 'the Void won't do you much good unless you can see its light in *Gongylus gongyloides. And* in people.' Without compassion duality cannot be permanently transcended. Huxley seems to suggest that the ecstasy and the Essential Horror are in themselves both manifestations of the world of duality, which the true mystic seeks to transcend. In *Heaven and Hell* he insists that visionary experience and mystical experience are not the same: 'Mystical experience is beyond the realm of opposites. Visionary experience is still within that realm. Heaven entails hell, and "going to heaven" is no more liberation than is the descent into horror. Heaven is merely a vantage point from which the divine Ground can be more clearly seen than on the level of ordinary individualized existence.' Will is still imprisoned in the 'realm of opposites', so that after his preliminary foretaste of the Clear Light, he is plunged into the horror of his own selfhood. However, under Susila's guidance, he is weaned from the visionary world—suffering is not perpetual, for ever. 'Nothing is for ever, nothing is to infinity. Except, maybe, the Buddha Nature.' Gradually lifted beyond the polarity of heaven and hell, he is granted a glimpse of what lies beyond; and with it comes the final knowledge of the 'manifest nonsense' that 'God is Love'. He sees 'the Suchness of the world and his own being blazing away with the clear light that was also (how obviously now!) compassion— the clear light that, like everyone else, he had always chosen to be blind to, the compassion to which he had always preferred his tortures, endured or inflicted . . .'; he grasps the mystic's intuitive knowledge 'that there was this capacity even in a paranoiac for intelligence, even in a devil-worshipper for love; the fact that the ground of all being could be totally manifest in a flowering shrub, a human face; the fact that there was a light and that this light was also compassion.' The novel ends with the same reassurance that closes the *Four Quartets*: 'All manner of thing shall be well.' The forces of reaction move into Pala; the armies of Rendang-Lobo begin their work of terror and destruction: 'The work of a hundred years destroyed in a single night. And yet the fact remained—the fact of the ending of sorrow as well as the fact of sorrow.'

XII

The Moralist and the Artist

Huxley's achievement as a novelist lay in his ability to make moral concepts exciting; perhaps no English novelist since Peacock has possessed such a ready facility for animating ideas, for clothing them with a life and vitality of their own. Our interest is held in his novels by the verbal clashes, the liveliness of the dialectic, the exuberance of the erudition. Without these qualities Huxley would have undoubtedly shared the fate of that other novelist of ideas, H. G. Wells. While it is profitable to compare, say, *Brave New World* with *Men Like Gods* and *The Shape of Things to Come*, it is worth noting that none of Huxley's novels have yet fallen into the ranks of literary curiosities. His novels have always been something more than mere vehicles for the popularization of ideas; and, although the polemical element is never totally absent from his work, it is almost invariably subordinated to the wider demands of his art. That his interest in the novel declined towards the end of his career is indisputable, but this is no reason for our dismissing him as an inferior talent. Indeed it is a point of discussion and, in this final chapter, I shall consider something of the nature of his art and in particular those aspects which have a close bearing on his development as a moralist.

The single unifying feature in Huxley's work is irony. The moral dilemma is sustained in novel after novel by the irony inherent in the dilemma itself: man as a product of his genes and glands; man as a creature of sensitivity and suffering. The mechanomorphic nightmare of *Brave New World* or the island paradise of Pala: this is the antithesis Huxley continually sets before us as the central dilemma of our time. The ironic mode gives his novels their unmistakable character, the cold touch of the consulting room which filled Lawrence with such despair when he first read *Point Counter Point*. The scientific modulations of the latter novel are not only obvious parodies of the scientific attitude; they are the *reductio ad absurdum* of Huxley's own method, the method of Philip Quarles, the zoologist of fiction. To explore the human heart through the abstractions of scientific jargon is for Huxley the supreme irony. Huxley's early critics, those who praised his short stories at the expense of the novels, undoubtedly failed to recognize the ironic mode as the organizing principle of his work. If we accuse Huxley of a lack of warmth, a lack of sympathy towards humanity, then we fail to discern the essential difference between the satirist and the objects of his satire. Huxley's style, his clinical detachment—at times as subtle and stark as that of that other master of irony, Swift himself—is in itself a manifestation of the attitude he is satirizing.

All of Huxley's major novels, with the exception of *Island*, are conceived as ironic structures. The death of Grace Elver in *Those Barren Leaves*; the isolation and suicide of the Savage in *Brave New World*; the discovery of the senescent Fifth Earl in *After Many a Summer*, all provide the final twist of the screw, the ironic reversal which is the characteristic of Huxley's art. Even in *Island*, the least ironic of Huxley's novels, the forces of reason are crushed at the very moment of Will Farnaby's conversion, a piece of super-added irony that caused at least one critic to lose his bearings. What, however, distinguishes Huxley's art is the breadth of his ironic vision, the intensity of the viewpoint which it provides. Nothing is spared, nothing assumed or taken for granted. No one since Swift—certainly not Peacock, to whom Huxley's satire owes a great deal—has viewed the totality of human activity with such complete scepticism. There is a comment in one of Anthony Beavis's diaries on the conditioned reflex, the feeling of satisfaction he once had from reading Pavlov: 'The ultimate debunking of all human pretensions. We were all dogs and bitches together. Bow-wow, sniff the lamp-post, lift the leg, bury the bone. No nonsense about free will, goodness, truth and all the rest.' There can be no doubt that the ironist in Huxley shared more than a little of Beavis's enthusiasm. 'The ultimate debunking of all human pretensions': this was Huxley's self-appointed task; and, above all, it was the irony inherent in the human situation which claimed his attention—'We were all dogs and bitches together'. That there was a Manichean streak in Huxley's make-up, one which provided his critics with the cutting comment about him not liking human beings, is evident; but when irony reaches a Swiftian intensity it is probably always born of a mixture of love and hate. That Huxley recoiled with horror from what he saw around him is unquestionable; but neither can it be denied that he also felt an intense pity and compassion for human suffering. His irony was always a safety-valve, an outlet for the intolerable burden of events. *The Farcical History of Richard Greenow*, Huxley's first venture into fiction, while far from being one of his outstanding works, illustrates perfectly the artist turning to irony as an escape from the insupportable horror of the time. In spite of his disgust, his concern for humanity finally triumphed, as his moral development clearly reveals; the other way lay that of Swift as Lawrence so rightly surmised.[1] But, whatever its original impulse, the ironic outlook provides the mainspring for Huxley's art. It is at work as Gumbril meditates on 'the nature and existence of God' in the opening pages of *Antic Hay*:

Standing in front of the spread brass eagle and fortified in his convictions by the sixth chapter of Deuteronomy . . . the Reverend Pelvey could speak of these things with an enviable certainty. 'Hear, O Israel', he was booming over the top of the portentous Book: 'The Lord our God is one Lord.'

One Lord; Mr Pelvey knew; he had studied theology. But if theology and theosophy, then why not theography and theometry, why not theognomy, theotrophy, theotomy, theogamy? Why not theophysics and theo-chemistry? Why not that ingenious toy, the theotrope or wheel of gods? Why not a monumental theodrome?

'One Lord; Mr Pelvey knew; he had studied theology.' Gumbril

[1] Lawrence thought that Huxley, at the time of writing *Point Counter Point*, was endangering his sanity. See *The Letters of D. H. Lawrence*, edited Aldous Huxley, p. 758.

who has not studied theology is not so sure; then, reminding himself of the gravity of the problem, he plunges straight into the heart of the dilemma, the antithesis between scientific truth and human truth: God as exultation as opposed to God as $2 + 2 = 4$. The voice booming 'over the top of the portentous Book' offers no solution and, led on by the promptings of Deuteronomy, Gumbril's thoughts take a new turn; he recalls his childhood and his mother's 'goodness':

. . . her diligence had not been dogmatic. She had been diligently good, that was all. It was a word people only used nowadays with a kind of deprecating humorousness. Good. Beyond good and evil? We are all that nowadays. Or merely below them like earwigs? . . . But good in any case, there was no getting out of that, good she had been. . . You felt the active radiance of her goodness when you were near her. . . And that feeling, was that less real and valid than two plus two? . . .

She had been good and she had died when he was still a boy; died—but he hadn't been told that till much later—of creeping and devouring pain. Malignant disease—oh, *caro nome!*

'Thou shalt fear the Lord thy God', said Mr Pelvey.

Even when the ulcers are benign; thou shalt fear. He had travelled up from school to see her, just before she died. . . All the fortitude, the laughter even, had been hers. And she had spoken to him. A few words only; but they had contained all the wisdom he needed to live by. She had told him what he was, and what he should try to be, and how to be it. And crying, still crying, he had promised that he would try.

'And the Lord commanded us to do all these statutes', said Mr Pelvey, 'for our good always, that he might preserve us alive, as it is at this day.'

And had he kept his promise, Gumbril wondered, had he preserved himself alive?

Here the problem of 'goodness' is stated in a few lines of typical Huxleyan juxtapositions: the empty dogmatism of Mr Pelvey contrasted with the radiant diligence of the fated Mrs Gumbril; the inherent irony of the human situation, 'She had been good and she had died . . . of creeping and devouring pain', to which Mr Pelvey has no discernible answer. Mr Pelvey, in spite of his

conviction is a hollow vessel; Mrs Gumbril, in spite of the teachings of science and the certitude of pain, is still unmitigated goodness, that is, until we remember the 'deprecating humorousness'
of the age. On the next page, Gumbril's thoughts—this time
prompted by the hardness of the chapel seats—take a sudden and
unexpected turn: pneumatic seats for sedentary people. The
element of the absurd is introduced and as Mr Pelvey chants the
Lord's Prayer the antithetical elements are woven together in a
close ironic texture.

For prayer Gumbril reflected, there would be Dunlop knees. Still, in
the days when he had made a habit of praying, they hadn't been
necessary. 'Our Father . . .' The words were the same as they were in
the old days; but Mr Pelvey's method of reciting them made them
sound different. Her dresses, when he had leaned his forehead against
her knee to say those words—those words, good Lord! that Mr Pelvey
was oboeing out of existence—were always black in the evenings, and
of silk, and smelt of orris root. And when she was dying, she said to
him: 'Remember the Parable of the Sower, and the seeds that fell in
shallow ground.' No, no. Amen, decidedly. 'O Lord, show thy mercy
upon us', chanted oboe Pelvey, and Gumbril trombone responded,
profoundly and grotesquely: 'And grant us thy salvation.' No, the
knees were obviously less important, except for people like revivalists
and housemaids, than the seat. Sedentary are commoner than genu-
flectory professions. One would introduce little flat rubber bladders
between two layers of cloth . . . and there would be perfect comfort
even for the boniest, even on rock.

The human situation is intolerable; it can only be supported when
it is translated into the absurd (one of the objects of irony, here, is
to destroy sentiment before it has time to take root). So Gumbril's
ultimate role is not the 'Rabelaisian complete man' but the clown,
and it is not without significance that the mask of comic despair
becomes the favourite persona of all Huxley's heroes from Gumbril to Farnaby. The yoking together of discordant elements, the
sudden reversal of values, the unexpected plunge from the serious
to the absurd: these are the familiar features of Huxley's art. But,
in spite of the descent into bathos, the moral remains clearly

stated: 'Remember the Parable of the Sower and the seed that fell in shallow ground.' It is the 'deprecating humorousness' of the age, not the hardness of the chapel seats, which demands Dunlop knees and pneumatic seats, as Gumbril's career subsequently shows.

The opening pages of *Antic Hay* reflect the major ironies in Huxley's work. Twenty chapters later, Gumbril is still meditating on the nature of 'goodness': symbols of childhood innocence, natural beauty and romantic love build up a pattern of positive affirmation, only to be destroyed in a single line of harsh obscenity. The technique is essentially the same but the basic incongruity is more clearly underlined:

Beyond good and evil? Below good and evil? The name of earwig . . . The tubby pony trotted. The wild columbines suspended, among the shadows of the hazel copse, hooked spurs, helmets of aerial purple. The Twelfth Sonata of Mozart was insecticide; no earwigs could crawl through that music. Emily's breasts were firm and pointed and she had slept at last without a tremor. In the starlight, good, true and beautiful, became one. Write the discovery in books—in books *quos*, in the morning, *legimus cacantes.* (ch. xxi)

A juxtaposition which needless to say would not have perturbed Joyce; but which for Huxley remained an inescapable reminder of the dual capacity of man (Sir Ferdinando, we recall, in *Crome Yellow* placed his privies in an exalted position and lined them with the 'ripest products of human wisdom' to 'testify to the nobility of the human soul'). Huxley's novels are rich in effects of this kind: sometimes the irony is Swiftian in its savagery, illustrating Huxley's supposed lack of warmth and sympathy towards his characters; sometimes it is merely playful, pointing gently at human weakness. His favourite antithesis expressed in a lighter mood occurs, for example, in *Those Barren Leaves*. The character is Irene Aldwinkle, who under pressure from her aunt has devoted herself to the fine arts of water-colour and lyric writing. Irene's true inclinations, however, lie elsewhere; she wonders whether her chain-stitch isn't superior to her painting, her button-holing

superior to her verse. The natural woman in Irene eventually
triumphs and we find her engaged in her favourite pastime,
stitching away at an unfinished garment in the privacy of her bed-
chamber at the Cybo Malaspina:

Round her, on the walls of the enormous room . . . fluttered an army
of gesticulating shapes. . . At a *prie-Dieu* in the far corner knelt Cardinal Malaspina, middle-aged, stout, with a *barbiche* and moustache. . .
The Archangel Michael, at the head of his troop of Principalities and
Powers, was hovering in the air above him, and with an expression
on his face of mingled condescension and respect . . . was poising above
him the red symbolic hat that was to make him a Prince of the Church.
On the opposite wall the Cardinal was represented doing battle with
the powers of darkness. Dressed in scarlet robes he stood undaunted
on the brink of the bottomless pit. . . From the pit came up legions of
hideous devils who filled the air with the flapping of their wings. But
the Cardinal was more than a match for them. Raising his crucifix
above his head, he conjured them to return to the flames. And the foiled
devils, gnashing their teeth and trembling with terror, were hurled
back towards the pit. . . In the wall space over the windows the Cardinal's cultured leisures were allegorically celebrated. Nine Muses and
three Graces, attended by a troop of the Hours, reclined or stood, or
danced in studied postures; while the Cardinal himself, enthroned in
the midst, listened to their conversation and proffered his own opinions
without appearing to notice the fact that all the ladies were stark
naked. . .
In the midst of the Cardinal's apotheosis and entirely oblivious of it,
Irene stitched away at her pink chemise. . . It was going to be one of
her masterpieces when it was done. She held it out in her two hands, at
arms length, lovingly and critically. It was simply too lovely. (Pt. III,
ch. xi)

Here the irony is at its least hurtful and the satire, of course, is not
all at Irene's expense. Her superb indifference and homely simplicity are in themselves a delightful comment on the pretensions
of her hostess, and the spiritual aspirations of mankind.

Perhaps no writer has ever been so fascinated by the inconsis-
tencies in human nature: 'Born under one law, to another bound',
Huxley's most oft-quoted line from Fulke Greville, might serve

as an epigraph to all his novels. Gumbril, in *Antic Hay*, forsakes the role of Emily's lover on the strength of a momentary whim and the more ephemeral attractions of Mrs Viveash; Calamy, in *Those Barren Leaves*, makes love to Mary Thriplow knowing that he is doing the one thing that bars him from the knowledge that he seeks; Anthony Beavis, in *Eyeless in Gaza*, seduces Joan Thursley, deliberately pursuing a course he knows to be both dangerous and wrong. There is no road to Damascus for Huxley's tortured heroes. *Video meliora proboque: deteriora sequor* are the five words which sum up the biographies of Gumbril, Calamy, and Anthony Beavis, The path to salvation is strewn with good intentions and wasted opportunities.

'God as a sense of warmth about the heart . . . that was all right. But God as truth, $2 + 2 = 4$—that wasn't so clearly all right.' Science has by its very nature always served to emphasize the dual nature of man. The higher religions, while recognizing man's duality have, ostensibly at least, identified themselves with the moral forces in nature; science, on the other hand, from its earliest interpretation of a mechanical universe, has always tended to identify itself with the amoral, the non-human aspects of humanity. The conflict between the abstractions of science and the claims of the human spirit, while presenting a crux to the moralist, have always provided the ironist with one of his richest veins of satire. Dr Ernest Jones's explanation of the inner meaning of the phrase, 'Art is the handmaid of Religion', for instance, drew forth a scathing commentary on this example of the '*Realpolitik* of psychology and philosophy'. Jones writes, 'Religion has always used art in one form or another, and must do so, for the reason that incestuous desires invariably construct their fantasies out of the material provided by the unconscious memory of infantile coprophilic interests.'[1] Such surely must be the origins of the frescoes of Fra Filippo Lippi at Spoleto, in *Those Barren Leaves*:

The shadowy apse was melodious with pious and elegant shapes and clear, pure colours. Anal-erotism was still the handmaid of incestuous

[1] Quoted by Huxley, *Along the Road*, Pt. III.

homosexuality, but not exclusively. There was more than a hint in these bright forms of anal-erotism for anal-erotism's sake. But the designer of that more than Roman *cinquecento* narthex at the west end of the church, he surely was a pure and unmixed coprophilite. How charming is divine philosophy. Astrology, alchemy, phrenology and animal magnetism, the N-rays, ectoplasm and the calculating horses of Elberfield—these have had their turn and passed. We need not regret them; for we can boast of a science as richly popular, as easy and as all explanatory as ever were phrenology or magic. Gall and Mesmer have given place to Freud. Filippo Lippi once had a bump of art. He is now an incestuous homosexualist with a bent towards anal-erotism. Can we doubt that human intelligence progresses and grows greater? Fifty years hence, what will be the current explanation of Filippo Lippi? Something profounder, something more fundamental even than faeces and infantile incestuousness; of that we may be certain. But what, precisely what, God alone knows. How charming is divine philosophy.

'I like vese paintings.' Lord Hovenden whispered to Irene. (Pt. IV, ch. ii)

The juxtaposition of scientific truth and human truth in *Point Counter Point* provides Huxley with some of his most characteristic and telling effects. The technique is one that he borrowed from Peacock,[1] but in Huxley's hands it becomes a weapon of devastating force. The scientific account of the Bach concert is harmless enough; but the biological description of Marjorie Carling's pregnancy on the second page of the novel strikes a more sinister chord. Marjorie is sick and ill; she is three months pregnant and on the point of being deserted by her lover. Our attention is drawn to her tiredness and ugliness; then without transition, the commentator intervenes. In six months time her baby will be born and the scientific data follows: 'Something that had been a single cell, a cluster of cells, a little sac of tissue, a kind of worm, a potential fish with gills, stirred in her womb and would one day become a man . . .' A month later, free of her lover, and under the influence of the religious Mrs Quarles, Marjorie is experiencing something akin to the peace of God. Once again the scientific commentator intervenes, this time in the person of Dr Fisher: her new-found

[1] See Chapter I, pp. 16–17.

state of happiness is attributed, not to the consolations of faith, but to the body settling down in the fourth month of pregnancy, to changes in the circulation and the beating of the foetal heart. There is nothing particularly wrong in itself in expressing human hopes and fears in biological terms: this is what the scientist is doing every day, although it is an unusual occupation for the novelist. But to the person involved the scientific account of an event must inevitably seem irrelevant and beside the point. To the detached observer the effect is precisely the opposite: it is human hopes and fears that are rendered irrelevant and void. This is the crux of Huxley's case against the scientist. The latter assumes a privileged viewpoint that deprives human feeling of whatever intrinsic validity it might otherwise possess; and it is perhaps worthy of note that Huxley's scientists, in the early novels at least, are either doctors, singularly ineffective in their curative powers, or biologists, like Shearwater, Lord Edward and Obispo, whose activities are largely restricted to vivisection—none of them particularly remarkable for their humanity. However, in *Point Counter Point*, Huxley places his reader momentarily in the privileged position of the scientist, having given him the human facts first. The effect is extremely disquieting. The point is heavily underlined in Chapter xxiv when the young radiographer studying the X-ray plate, which reveals the fatal nature of John Bidlake's illness, observes with unintentional irony that it was a 'remarkably successful exposure'. In the next scene, the once ebullient Bidlake, the great eater and taker of virginities, is seen entertaining his former mistress. His evasions of the critical question have a distinctly unpleasant undertone. Once again it is the reader who occupies the uncomfortably privileged situation of knowing all the facts.

Huxley's irony is, of course, at its best double-edged. Neither Marjorie Carling nor John Bidlake is a pleasant character; to render their intimate feelings in the language of scientific cause and effect is part of the deflatory technique. They are placed well beyond the reach of the reader's sympathy. The fate of Everard Webley perhaps deserves mentioning again. The invasion of

Webley's corpse by the 'invisible hosts of saprophytics' is described with the fervour of a mediaeval sermon on mortality; the moral is heavily pointed:

They would live among the dead cells, they would grow, and pro-digiously multiply and in their growing and procreation all the chemi-cal building of the body would be undone, all the intricacies and complications of its matter would be resolved, till by the time their work was finished a few pounds of carbon, a few quarts of water, some lime, a little phosphorus and sulphur, a pinch of iron and silicon, a handful of mixed salts—all scattered and recombined with the sur-rounding world—would be all that remained of Everard Webley's ambition to rule and his love for Elinor, of his thoughts about politics and his recollections of childhood. . . (ch. xxxiii)

This is the 'ultimate debunking of all human pretensions' with a vengeance, and no nonsense about free-will, goodness and truth at that.

'She had been good and she had died . . . of creeping and devouring pain.' To the humanist the death of 'goodness' like the suffering of innocence must always remain a point of conflict; it is the supreme irony from which there is no escape. In *Island*, the death of Lakshmi introduces a note of reconciliation but death, in Huxley, is rarely tragic; it is a gratuitous intervention over which man has no control, a symbol of human inadequacy in a world without moral order. It is invariably treated ironically, 'a disgust-ing stupidity' or 'a hideous farce' as two of Huxley's characters put it. When Cardan tries to save Grace Elver from her murderous brother, she is snatched away from him at the very moment when her freedom seems assured. The innocent Pete Boone is shot by the enraged Stoyte at the moment of his conversion; Propter is left to point the moral: 'To a being who is in fact the slave of circumstance there's nothing specially irrelevant about premature death.' The multiple deaths which mark the close of *Point Counter Point* point to the same conclusion. Philip Quarles has intimations of the necessity and significance of suffering; a few hours later Little Phil dies before his eyes, while Elinor is deprived of her son and her lover at a single stroke. (It seems absurd to protest, as one critic has done, that the death of Little Phil is a piece of deliberate masochism.[1] The same could be said of the death of Othon's son in *The Plague*; and while the suffering of innocence in Huxley is an essential part of the ironic structure of the novel, the point is basically the same: 'I shall refuse to love a scheme of things in which children are put to torture.') Everard Webley's hopes and ambitions, as we have seen are reduced to 'a few pounds of carbon, a few quarts of water . . . and a handful of mixed salts.' Even Spandrell's death which has the potentialities of tragedy—it is at least self-chosen and coincides with his momentary glimpse of the Beatitude—is robbed of its dignity. The Lydian harmonies of the *heilige Dankegesang* bring their 'ineffable peace' as he is cut down by the bullets of Webley's assassins. There immediately follows one of those sudden plunges into bathos, which are the quint-essence of Huxley's technique. A few lines further on, in a superb ironic coda, the fake Messiah, Burlap, and his Beatrice enjoy their own glimpse of the Beatitude:

That night he and Beatrice pretended to be two little children and had their baths together. Two little children sitting at the opposite ends of a big old-fashioned bath. And what a romp they had. The bathroom was drenched with their splashings. Of such is the Kingdom of Heaven. (ch. xxxvii)

In the ironic form the principle of nemesis is almost totally gratuitous: the innocent usually suffer, the Emilys and the Little Phils, while the Mercaptans, the Burlaps and the Obispos slip through the net of retribution. This, however, is only a part of the cosmic order: there are also those exemplars of wrong be-haviour, the morality figures of Cardan, Mrs Aldwinkle, John Bidlake and Jo Stoyte, on whom nemesis operates in the form of age and disease. 'Life's time's fool' is one of Huxley's favourite moral cruces and in fact his morality figures are almost always the victims of time. Old age, disease and death, like the abstractions of science are at one and the same time a source of inescapable

[1] See Arnold Kettle, *An Introduction to the English Novel* (2nd ed., 1967), vol. II, p. 168.

irony and an incisive weapon in the hands of the moralist. Huxley's 'Struldbruggs', the senescent Fifth Earl and his housekeeper, at the end of *After Many a Summer* illustrate with a devastating finality the moralist's comment on the conquest of old age and death. In Obispo's words, 'It was the finest joke he had ever known'.

In *Those Barren Leaves*, Chelifer asks the question, 'What did the Buddha consider the most deadly of the deadly sins?' The answer was 'Unawareness'. The purpose of Huxley's irony is to point consistently the moralist's function of 'forcing humans to be fully, *verbally* conscious of', not as Staithes puts it, 'their own and other people's disgustingness', although this is certainly a part of it, but to be fully conscious in Buddhist terminology, of who and what they are. As Herbert Davis says of Swift: '. . . it was his peculiar satisfaction as a moralist and a satirist, in all his various disguises, and employing all the tricks of his trade, to make us see what a world we live in, to make us feel its brutality and degradation, to disturb all our complacencies and to leave us unreconciled to the "unestimable sum of human pain".'[1] Huxley tried to make us see the 'brutality and degradation' of our world and in this he was eminently successful. In the end, unlike Swift, he tried to reconcile us, perhaps less successfully, to 'the sum of human pain'. To the nature of this failure we must now turn.

The weaknesses in Huxley's novels can almost always be traced back to his failure to find an adequate correlative for the presentation of 'goodness'. It is perhaps debatable whether a writer who is primarily an ironist and a satirist should in fact try to explore the more positive aspects of human nature. His appointed task is to tear away the mask of human pretensions, to shock us into awareness; if he momentarily drops the cloak of irony, he takes the risk of either lapsing into sentimentality or becoming merely a propagandist. It must be admitted that Huxley's attempts at moralizing bring him dangerously close to failure on both counts. In the early novels, whenever irony is absent, he is betrayed into sentimentality. The Emily episode in *Antic Hay*, with its recurrent

[1] *The Satire of Jonathan Swift* (New York, 1947), pp. 105-6.

references to wild flowers, 'barrel-bellied ponies' and the 'twiddly lanes of Robertsbridge', is at its best an unhappy interlude. What must be considered the most ineffective chapter in *Point Counter Point*—one which must have caused Lawrence considerable embarrassment—is that describing the early life of Mary and Mark Rampion, an impossibly idealized version of Lawrence's meeting and courtship of Frieda. These lapses into sentimentality disappear in the later novels although the brand of 'goodness' exhibited by Brian and Mrs Foxe in *Eyeless in Gaza* might give some readers a moment of uneasiness. However, it is clear from the nature of their relationship that 'sound, honest, better-than-average goodness' is no longer enough, and the redemptive characters of the later novels, Propter, Bruno Rontini and the utopian Palanese do not repeat the faults of their predecessors. Contemplative mysticism, whatever its weaknesses in other respects, does not lend itself to the kind of excesses which mar Huxley's earlier approaches to the problem of 'goodness'.

Furthermore, Huxley never really solved the problem of placing 'goodness' within a novel of this kind. It is indicative of his failure that the redemptive characters, the exemplary figures of Gumbril Senior, Rampion, Dr Miller, Propter and Bruno Rontini, all stand outside the ironic structure of the novel. Unlike the redemptive characters of E. M. Forster, they are largely powerless to influence events and share no significant part in the action of the novel. Gumbril Senior, the first of Huxley's redemptive figures, is, in fact, cast in more of a Forsterian role than any of his successors; he does exert a mildly benevolent influence but the effect is marginal. This perhaps would not be so important in a 'novel of ideas' where the action is minimal; but apart from the house-party novels, *Crome Yellow* and *Those Barren Leaves*, Huxley's novels are always something more than mere novels of ideas using the term in its narrowest sense. They are also moral fables demanding an active demonstration of 'goodness'. The weakness is particularly evident in *Point Counter Point* where Rampion stands idly by while Spandrell enjoys his momentary glimpse of the Beatitude and is subsequently killed. Rampion's role is reduced to that of a commentator and not a very effective one at that. (In fairness it should be pointed out that Rampion's commentary is not always so ineffective; his castigation of Burlap as a 'toddling wide-eyed little St. Hugh' in Chapter xvi is Huxley's dialogue at its best.) Propter shares a similar fate when his sole disciple, Pete Boone, is snatched away at the moment of his conversion. It is perhaps inevitable that the exemplary characters should have no significant part in an action that is predominantly ironic; their place is essentially to supply a higher moral norm, and provide an explicit commentary on human folly, but it does mean that as characters they can never be more than outlines and it is a weakness in an author who placed such weight on 'literary example' that he never, for instance, created a redemptive figure of the sustained depth of Forster's Mrs Moore.

When we think of Huxley's characters it is not the men of good will, the exemplary figures of Propter or Bruno Rontini, who readily come to mind, but the Mercaptans, the Burlaps and the Obispos, the Lucy Tantamounts and the Mary Amberleys. It was the egotistical scientists, the sham Messiahs, the seedy men of letters, and those products of female emancipation and post-war disillusionment, whom Huxley made his own. He had above all a genius for pin-pointing a particular kind of nastiness, a genius that failed him when it came to portraying their opposite numbers. It is in a sense ironical that the particular malice of an Obispo rather than the patent goodness of a Propter should hold our attention, but perhaps this is the fate of all reforming satirists: the portrayal of absolute goodness does not lend itself readily to the satirist's art. No one would claim that the last book of *Gulliver's Travels* or for that matter the last act of *Back to Methuselah* is among its author's happiest creations. Once Huxley got away from the portrayal of 'ideal characters' he was on firmer ground: Wren's London of *Antic Hay*, the Bach Suite and the *heilige Dankegesang* of *Point Counter Point* and Anthony Beavis's meditation in *Eyeless in Gaza*, all provide correlatives for the 'fine and noble' which bring us closer to the nature of 'goodness' than all the words of Huxley's prophets.

The theme of moral regeneration which plays an important part in Huxley's novels also demands an active demonstration of 'goodness' and once again we find Huxley involved in problems of a formal nature. In the early novels the mood of disenchantment predominates and, except for Calamy's precipitant conversion in the final chapters of *Those Barren Leaves*, the moral and satirical elements are for the greater part in harmony. In the later novels the theme of moral regeneration appears and this becomes a secondary principle of organization. As we have seen the theme of conversion is largely autobiographical; it begins in *Antic Hay* and reaches a climax in *Eyeless in Gaza*. As the theme develops so the problem of form becomes critical, the 'conversion episodes' trying to impose themselves, as it were, on the ironic structure of the novel. The formal weaknesses in Huxley's novels belong almost entirely to his failure to reconcile the two opposing elements. In *Antic Hay*, Gumbril's conversion is treated in only a tentative way: Gumbril foresees that one day he may become an 'unsuccessful flickering sort of saint', but this lies in the distant future; and apart from the odd discordant note of sentimentality (the night-club scene in Chapter xvi reads like a piece of self-parody) the conflicting demands of form are held in check. Gumbril's 'adventures' fall largely within the ironic pattern of the novel. *Point Counter Point* is unusual in that the conversion theme is itself treated satirically (Huxley's own conversion was temporarily suspended at this time when he was under the influence of Lawrence); it is the sham Messiah Burlap and the satanist Spandrell, not the autobiographical Philip Quarles, who seek the 'Kingdom of God'. As a novel in which everything is subordinated to the principle of irony, *Point Counter Point* represents the height of Huxley's formal achievement. The 'musicalization of fiction'—the parallel plots which reduplicate characters and situations—weaves a pattern in which 'birth, copulation and death' are juxtaposed in scenes of startling incongruity. Thus, in Chapter xxx, an episode from John Bidlake's fatal illness is followed by the later stages of Marjorie Carling's pregnancy; Burlap's seduction of Beatrice, in Chapter xxxiv, by the death agonies of Little

Phil, and so on. Further, by the device of repetition every situation is mirrored by its ironic counterpart: Elinor receives a telegram urging her to Gattenden where Little Phil lies stricken; a few pages later Philip is summoned to Chamford where his father imagines himself to be dying—the grotesque scene at Sidney Quarles's bedside being, itself, almost a burlesque of an earlier chapter, where John Bidlake, now certain of his approaching end, sees Lady Tantamount for the last time. By the twin devices of contrast and repetition, Huxley evolved a form that was artistically satisfying and, at the same time, served the purpose of his ironic vision.

The real difficulties appear in *Those Barren Leaves* and *Time Must Have a Stop* where the 'conversion episode' is superimposed on the ironic structure of the novel, either in the closing chapter or in the form of an epilogue. The fault lies in the fact that neither Calamy nor Sebastian Barnack can be conceived as a serious candidate for conversion within the body of the novel, and their change of heart placed at the end is presented in an unconvincing and peremptory manner. Here there is a clear failure to resolve the conflicting demands of form. Further, it is evident that while Huxley excelled as a satirist and a novelist of ideas he was ill-equipped to explore the intricacies and complexities of character demanded by the conversion novel; and his formal difficulties suggest a shying away from the problem. In fairness, it is probably wrong to read *Time Must Have a Stop* as a novel of this type; the epilogue which contains the substance of Sebastian's conversion can be dispensed with, but its presence suggests the type of problem Huxley faced when he stepped outside his natural orbit.

Eyeless in Gaza is another novel which must have promised a long and unsatisfactory epilogue and, although Anthony Beavis is Huxley's strongest candidate for conversion, the structure of the work betrays a certain uneasiness in facing the issue. Huxley's solution to counterpoint the several narratives, so providing an ironic contrast between Anthony's unregenerate youth and his conversion in middle-age, can hardly be considered ideal. It makes heavy demands on the reader's attention and the novel must be read twice before the several episodes fall into place. Yet to a certain extent it can be said to work: the clumsy device of the epilogue is avoided and the unity of the novel is preserved, while at the same time a degree of vitality is gained from the tension between the counterpointed narratives. Formally, it must be considered a less satisfactory novel than *Point Counter Point*; nevertheless it remains Huxley's most interesting work. It has the quality of felt experience from beginning to end; the novel is imprinted with the author's own search for a metaphysic and the excitement proves infectious, so that even the familiar notebook extracts have an air of drama about them. Beavis, as a candidate for conversion, is no more sympathetic than Quarles, but the sincerity of his moral struggle is such that the reader becomes involved. Calamy's spiritual divagations were an added luxury, something imposed on the surface of life; Beavis's struggle comes from within and a sense of urgency permeates the narrative. As D. H. Lawrence once said, 'Most books that live, live in spite of the author's laying it on thick'. The same might be said of *Eyeless in Gaza*: it succeeds in spite of one of the most unprepossessing formal devices in fiction. Huxley was never so successful again: once his personal problem was solved the imaginative tension lapsed, the struggle is never so immediate and the reader is never involved in quite the same way.

The mainspring of Huxley's genius is his gift of irony; and this provides us with a means for making value-judgements on his art. Certainly, *Island*, the least ironic of the major novels, is the least typical, the least Huxleyan. As a synthesis of ideas it is impressive by any standard, nevertheless it remains the one work which clearly approaches failure. Huxley's art depends above all on a dialectic of ideas, a dialectic engendered by the major ironies inherent in the human condition. This dialectic is absent in *Island* and in consequence, the sense of urgency present in the earlier novels, is lacking. Here the utopian theme could not be treated ironically; thus the situation presents basically the same problem Huxley faced earlier, the portrayal of goodness, only this time on a larger scale. It is significant that the utopian Palanese are the least effective of Huxley's redemptive figures; they fail to emerge as individuals and their virtues are expounded rather than lived. The failure to provide an adequate core of dialectic can be attributed to a great extent to the sketchy characterization of Farnaby. Will Farnaby, whose antecedents lie in Chelifer and Anthony Beavis, is an ineffective foil to the Palanese; as a world-weary Gulliver among the Houyhnhnms, he is too quickly charmed by the superior virtues of his hosts; as a result whatever conflict might have centred on his conversion is immediately lost and with it the dialectic which might have provided a backbone to the novel. The only centre of dramatic interest lies in the Mescalin experience where, in the closing chapter, the inner struggle within Farnaby is brought to life. Here Farnaby's attachment to the ego, his fears and disgust, his lacerations of remorse and self-loathing, are revealed in a cluster of powerful images: the mechanical coupling of the cannibalistic *gongylus gongyloides*, the tin-bright insects eating and being eaten for ever; the brown insect-like hordes of the storm troopers, their uniforms 'glowing in the infernal brightness like floodlit excrement'; the fly-blown corpses, like packets of garbage, in the Korean mud; and with them the certitude of his own death, his own suffering, immortal in its pointlessness:

. . . the routine of successive agonies in the bargain basement and the final crucifixion in a blaze of tin and plastic vulgarity—reverberating, continuously amplified, they would always be there. And the pains were incommunicable, the isolation complete. The awareness that one existed was an awareness that one was always alone. Just as much alone in Babs' musky alcove . . . as one would be alone with one's final cancer, alone, when one thought it was all over, with the immortality of suffering.

And against this vision of universal pointlessness, the luminous bliss which is mind in its natural state—the 'felicity so ravishing, so inconceivably intense that no one can describe it'—the knowledgeless understanding of the Light, which Eckhart had called

231

God, giving rise to the eternal problem: 'By what sinister miracle had the mind's natural state been transformed into all these Devil's Islands of wretchedness and delinquency?' This is perhaps the most powerful evocation of good and evil in the whole of Huxley; it has the same quality of felt experience which we have noted in *Eyeless in Gaza*, but it is a brief interlude only. Huxley's inability to animate the ideas in *Island*, to provide a central point of conflict lies not so much in the fact of his conversion, but in the nature of the conversion itself. Mahayana Buddhism, as Huxley insists, is a way of looking at life which reconciles opposites: 'the blessed experience of Not-Two'. In brief, it dissolves the opposing elements which lie at the heart of the ironist's vision: man as a product of his genes and his glands; man as a creature of sensitivity and suffering. To the Mahayanist, 'Born under one law, to another bound' is not a theme for ironic commentary, but merely a distorted vision of reality. It is impossible to be an ironist without being a dualist at the same time; irony depends for its strength on the co-existence of two irreconcilable sets of ideas and this is inimical to the whole concept of Buddhist thought. The point is worth emphasizing because this kind of reconciliation is rare in Western thought; dualism is in fact the basis of Western culture, and it was within the framework of a dualist philosophy that Huxley created his major work. In the end it was the peculiar nature of Huxley's final beliefs rather than the beliefs themselves which undermined his position as a novelist. As he puts it himself, without dualism 'there can hardly be good literature. With it, there most certainly can be no good life'. The harmony which Huxley achieves as a moralist in *Island*, then, was gained at the expense of his ironic vision. Farnaby, of course, remains attached to the old way of life as his Mescalin experience illustrates; but his cynical asides, the puppet figures of the Rani and Colonel Dipa— these are little more than left-overs from the earlier novels. The ideas remain, ideas which I have said provide an important closing chapter to Huxley's development as a moralist, but the unifying factor has gone; what is left is certainly a novel with ideas but one which rightly belongs to the province of the essayist rather than the novelist. The history of Huxley's decline as a novelist is in effect the history of his decline as an ironist and his failure to find an alternative form.

Huxley was as well aware of this as his critics, and perhaps the final word may be left to one of his admirers: 'His last novel, *Island*, was written when he already knew that he was doomed. In this he deliberately abandoned the satirical approach whose pungency and biting wit his public had always appreciated, in favour of a positive and constructive declaration of faith, though he knew that this would be considered by many as tedious and rather unbelievable didactic stuff. . . This was a small sacrifice for him, who was in the first place a modern saint, and only in the second place a great literary artist.'[1]

[1] Dennis Gabor, *Aldous Huxley, A Memorial Volume*, ed. Julian Huxley (1965), p. 72.

Conclusion

It would be true to say that Huxley failed to write the great religious novel which his 'conversion' at one time promised. What he did write, however, was one of the most comprehensive blueprints for utopia in the history of fiction. This was Huxley's final attempt to restore the meaning, to frame a philosophy that would measure up to all the facts of human experience. Time was short and there is an inevitable air of compromise about some of his solutions, but as he said himself: 'Even the fragmentary outline of a synthesis is better than no synthesis at all' (*Ends and Means*, ch. xv). But whatever the final view of the Huxleyan synthesis, its importance lies in its attempt to reconcile the two great opposing forces of our time, science and religion. Huxley, in his role as the moral conscience of a scientific age, had constantly pointed out the dangers inherent in the scientific concept of unlimited progress. 'Science is one thing, and wisdom is another' is the unspoken thought underlying everything he wrote. The great vice of the intellect, Huxley insisted following Lawrence, is cerebration. Science is one aspect of cerebration. The preoccupation with scientific truth leads to a 'one-sidedness', a distortion of human aspirations which has resulted in a decline in moral values —the elevation of the material at the expense of the spiritual. The danger of science is that it gives a partial picture of events, an abstraction, a truth of a special kind. What is wrong is that this truth has been elevated to the position of the only truth. Moreover the facts of the laboratory, along with the products of technology, can be turned out like 'those laborious webs of learning' of the schoolmen, 'admirable for the fineness of thread and work, but of no substance or profit'. In the end, neither the knowledge of science nor the fruits of technology in themselves necessarily add to human happiness, and whether we call scientific advancement 'progress' or not depends entirely on the meaning we attribute to the term. 'Wisdom', on the other hand, 'is the fruit of a balanced development.' It demands attention to all the facts of human experience, not merely some of them—the facts of eternity as well as the facts of the laboratory. And, as Huxley never tired of pointing out, it belongs to all times and all creeds. It was to the neglected wisdom of the past that Huxley directed his energies: to 'advise the constant reiteration of the truths' of the past three thousand years. The knowledge had always been there: in the wisdom of the East, in Tantra, Zen and the teachings of Lao-Tsze, Huxley's quest for a metaphysical principle was finally brought to a close. In *Ape and Essence*, the Arch-Vicar, contemplating the vast sum of human folly, points the moral: 'Eastern mysticism making sure that Western science should be properly used: the Eastern art of living refining Western energy. . . Why, it would have been the kingdom of heaven.' The wisdom of the East was the necessary corrective to scientific 'one-sidedness'. Science, properly controlled, could take care of man's physical and mental needs; only the contemplative life could nurture the human psyche.

At the root of Huxley's beliefs were the basic tenets of the perennial philosophy: that there is a Godhead or divine Ground immanent in all things; that it is possible for all human beings to become identified with the Ground; and that to achieve this unitive knowledge is the final end and purpose of human existence. To achieve a unitive knowledge of the Ground necessitates a dying to the self: for the less there is of 'I', the more there is of God. All the spiritual techniques described in the novels, from meditation to self-awareness, are directed towards this common end—freedom from bondage to the ego. Science is morally neutral: the truths of the abstracting scientist neither assist nor retard this process of 'self-naughting'. They are potentially dangerous, however, because they encourage an attitude to life which restricts truth to the level of cerebration and, by so doing, deny the possibility of those other kinds of awareness so necessary to human salvation. To Huxley it was an empirical fact that the absence of 'goodness' on any level, physiological or psychological, increases the bondage to the ego. All his ameliorative measures, whether psychophysical co-ordination, syndicalism or *satyagraha*, are designed to promote 'goodness' on the final-end principle. The good life is that which carries man forward towards his final goal; evil that which retards him. After *Eyeless in Gaza*, the development of the moralist and the mystic are irrevocably bound.

Huxley has often been accused of thinking of religion 'too exclusively in terms of the highest sanctity and mystical experience, strangely forgetful of the fact that the vast millions of mankind . . . can only approach God through the humanistic channels of everyday life with its multiplicity and fullness.'[1] The charge that mystical theocentrism is for the few is one which Huxley took seriously. It was desirable that enlightenment should be for all. The difficulties were insuperable. For this reason Huxley believed that only everything was enough. Human freedom, political, social and economic, was a first necessary step. After that it was a matter of attacking the problem of human nature on all its fronts: even Maithuna and psilocybin, perhaps the most bizarre features of Huxley's final utopian vision, were only the means, amongst others, of bringing enlightenment within the grasp of the unregenerate many. *Island* is essentially an attempt to portray a society in which 'God' can be approached 'through the humanistic channels of everyday life with its multiplicity and fullness'. Huxley was never prepared to accept the 'popular way' to religion through faith—not that he would have denied that faith has its own intrinsic merit. Ultimately, he believed, man can only be redeemed through his own efforts: salvation is not a matter of faith or 'good works' but of direct insight into the great religious truths.

There is no tradition in Western thought to describe Huxley's final standpoint. In the East Buddhism, with its emphasis on enlightenment through self-knowledge, is the nearest equivalent. But Huxley refuses to be pinned down by any labels. As Eliot

[1] Robert Hamilton, 'The Challenge of Aldous Huxley', *Horizon*, XVII (June 1948), p. 455.

said of Irving Babbitt, he knew 'too many religions and philosophies', had 'assimilated their spirit too thoroughly . . . to be able to give himself to any'. For Babbitt the result was humanism. Perhaps one might say that for Huxley, too, the final result was humanism. In spite of his opposition to all that passed under the name of 'progress' he never gave himself entirely to any religious creed. As he advanced in years he became increasingly pragmatic: breaking free from the bonds of scientific determinism on one side and anti-Pelagianism on the other, he finally arrived at a humanistic world-view—a belief that man can and will improve himself if he so desires. The vision of *Island* is not something placed in a remote future: it is an ideal to be realized here and now; but it demands a ready acceptance of the wisdom of all ages, of the best of the rational and the intuitive, a humanistic belief

about creatures, in whose minds, far more deeply interfused than any scientific hypothesis or even any archetypal myth, is the Something whose dwelling is everywhere, the essential Suchness of the world, which is at once immanent and transcendent—'in here' as the profoundest and most ineffable of private experiences and at the same time 'out there', as the mental aspect of the material universe, as the emergence into cosmic mind of the organization of an infinity of organizations, perpetually perishing and perpetually renewed. (*Literature and Science*)

INDEX

(Italic references are used to indicate mention of the person or subject named by Huxley himself)

239

DATE DUE

APR 09 '01			
	DISCARDED		
GAYLORD			PRINTED IN U.S.A.